D0217105

ANATOMY
OF A
MERGER

THE CAUSES AND EFFECTS
OF MERGERS AND ACQUISITIONS

Alexandra Post
Post Associates
Austin / London

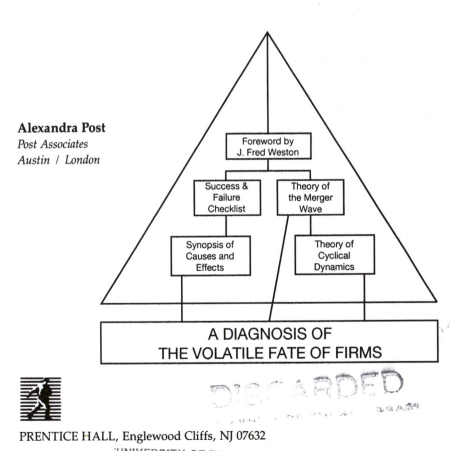

Foreword by
J. Fred Weston

Success &
Failure
Checklist

Theory of
the Merger
Wave

Synopsis of
Causes and
Effects

Theory of
Cyclical
Dynamics

A DIAGNOSIS OF
THE VOLATILE FATE OF FIRMS

PRENTICE HALL, Englewood Cliffs, NJ 07632

DISCARDED

UNIVERSITY OF TULSA–McFARLIN LIBRARY

Library of Congress Cataloging-in-Publication Data

Post, Alexandra.
  Anatomy of a merger : the causes and effects of mergers and
acquisitions / Alexandra Post.
    p.   cm.
  Includes bibliographical references and index.
  ISBN 0-13-179243-1. -- ISBN 0-13-179235-0 (pbk.)
  1. Consolidation and merger of corporations.   I. Title.
HD2746.5.P67   1994
338.8'3--dc20
                                                    93-16695
                                                    CIP

To
Harry Goff
and Neil Salmon

for their example of diligence, persistence,
and calm application
in the pursuit of ambitious objectives.

Acquisition Editor *Leah Jewell*
Cover Designer *Violet Lake Studios*
Prepress Buyer *Trudy Pisciotti*
Manufacturing Buyer *Patrice Fraccio*
Editorial Assistant *Eileen Deguzman*

© 1994 by Prentice-Hall, Inc.
A Simon & Schuster Company
Englewood Cliffs, New Jersey 07632

Contemporary Issues in Finance Series
John McConnell, SERIES EDITOR

All rights reserved. No part of this book may be
reproduced, in any form or by any means,
without permission in writing from the publisher.

Printed in the United States of America
10 9 8 7 6 5 4 3 2 1

ISBN 0-13-179235-0

Prentice-Hall International (UK) Limited, *London*
Prentice-Hall of Australia Pty. Limited, *Sydney*
Prentice-Hall Canada Inc., *Toronto*
Prentice-Hall Hispanoamericana, S.A., *Mexico*
Prentice-Hall of India Private Limited, *New Delhi*
Prentice-Hall of Japan, Inc., *Tokyo*
Simon & Schuster Asia Pte. Ltd., *Singapore*
Editora Prentice-Hall do Brasil, Ltda., *Rio de Janeiro*

HD 2746
.5
.P67
1994

CONTENTS

PART ONE: WHY FIRMS MERGE

PART TWO: CHECKLIST REVIEW OF THE LITERATURE

LIST OF TABLES AND ILLUSTRATIONS

ABOUT THE AUTHOR

After previous experience with Bankers Trust of Thailand, Kanematsu-Gosho, the State Trading Corporation of India, and the U.S. State Department, Alexandra Merle Post manages a corporate advisory service based in the USA and UK—with clients and associates located in Europe, North America and Asia.

Dr. Post was also a Faculty Member at the University of Sussex, the University of British Columbia and University of Maryland. She studied at Cornell University (BA), the University of Paris, the University of California at Berkeley (MA), the Swiss Institute of Management Development (IMD), and the University of Munich (PhD).

Based on several years in the international finance of energy and mining in North America, Europe and Asia, Dr. Post has written a standard reference book and other publications on offshore mining and the law of the sea. Her current research interests include analysis of the characteristics of cyclical (nonlinear) models with three areas of application: merger waves; interest rate and exchange rate forecasting; and multi-sided Betas and "risk waves". The author speaks English, German, French and Spanish fluently, and some Thai.

FOREWORD

This book provides an insightful journey through the literature and ideas of a major force in international financial economics—mergers, takeovers, and corporate control. A comprehensive coverage of the literature is achieved. New perspectives are developed in the broad perspectives of economic long waves in an international setting.

The dominant cause of the burst of merger and acquisition activity that began in the early 1980s was the full emergence of global competition. The increased intensity of international rivalries caused business firms throughout the world to rethink their long-term prospects and to reformulate their strategies for survival and growth. This book is especially strong in its international orientation, reflecting the background, experience, and interests of the author.

This book is different from a purely academic approach or an applied business consulting orientation. It combines the best of both. Many new perspectives are developed. It does not espouse one theory or a particular school of thought. It review many concepts and approaches.

After a comprehensive survey of the literature and innovative ideas of the author in part one of the book, the author develops action guidelines in part two. Checklists are provided on the reasons why firms merge. Post-acquisition outcomes are reviewed. Finally, checklists of success and failure factors are developed. The reader will be stimulated, challenged, and informed by this innovative treatment of mergers, takeovers and corporate control.

> J. Fred Weston
> Cordner Professor Emeritus
> of Money and Financial Markets
> Anderson Graduate School of Management
> University of California, Los Angeles

ACKNOWLEDGMENTS

For his continuous consultation and support I am indebted to Professor Kenneth White of the Economics Department of the University of British Columbia. For their exemplary work and guidance I must also thank J Fred Weston and his former research assistants Tim Opler and Dan Asquith at the UCLA Business School as well as Julian Franks of the London Business School. Professor Espen Eckbo and others of the Department of Finance at the University of British Columbia have been generous with their advice. Geoff Harcourt, A Sen and Alan Hughes were kind enough to delineate current lines of thought regarding corporate finance in Applied Economics at University of Cambridge. Charles Johnson and Alan Clarke of the University of Hawaii's East-West Center as well as David Allan of the Harvard Law Faculty have provided valuable insights into the role of acquisitions during sectoral shifts in the mining sector.

Much thanks also to Philip Healey for providing information from *Acquisitions Monthly,* a premier M&A publication in the UK which has developed AMDATA with Computusoft, an extensive archive on global mergers and acquisitions; and to Graham Hatton and David Mitchell of Business International who have put together excellent publications on mergers and acquisitions oriented towards the working requirements of the corporate world.

Useful perspectives were also provided by Christopher Hanke of CMOS-Logic Motorola, Inc., and his colleagues Sue Leveritt of Hoskyns PLC, Anthony de Guingand of the London Stock Exchange (taken over on 1 February 1992), J.R. Simplot of Simplot, Jerry Hobbs who sits on many Canadian boards of directors, Harry Goff of Scientific Pacific, George Schneider of the Shell Group, Linda Iversen, private consultant to the airlines industry, David Kass, Senior Economist to the Office of the Chief Economist US General Accounting Office, as well as Anthony Stoddard and Clive Ward of Shandwick PLC.

Friends and colleagues working in mergers and acquisitions have given me many insights and observations: Marlene Groen of Chartered WestLB ; Andrew Jordan and Sherry Speakman of Coopers&Lybrand; Hiroshi Nonomiya of MCF International (Mitsubishi); John Harley of Price Waterhouse; Kevin Jach of Touche Ross; Tom Angear of M&A International; Roland Whitehead of Crédit National; Joylon Moss, Peter Dean and Steve Wilton and especially K. Courtenay Hawkins of Security Pacific Bank; Karl Michael Krüger and Alessandro Parenti of Bayerische Vereinsbank; Tony

Caplin of First City Great Britain; George Montgomery, Bruce Dorhmann, Richard Kulp and Benny Varon of Hambrecht & Quist; John McCruden, Mike Cope, Cliff Sweeney, Doug Wade and David Ross of Toronto Dominion Bank; Tim Pendry of Bas•Pendrya; Dr Günther F. Moeser of Siemens; Barry Giddings of Antares Group; Neil Salmon, previous member of the UK Mergers and Monopolies Commission; Dr Wolfgang Vehse of the Treuhand; Ferdinand Graf von Spiegel and Volker Diesenberg of Mandatus; Selman Selvi of SPGF, George Adams and Joe Montana, Sr., of Montana and Adams Financial Resources, Steve Marsh of KPMG Peat Marwick, and many others. This presentation is aimed in part at providing them with a panorama of the full impact of their current M&A work.

Many thanks to friends in economics and other fields working in the areas of technological change and also nonlinear modelling for their patience and guidance: Christopher Freeman, Giovanni Dosi, Daniele Archibuchi, and Eric Arnold who work **inter alia** at SPRU at the University of Sussex, as well as Maynard Smith of the Biology Department there who has been kind enough to almost tolerate my deviations from pure empiricism; Fabio Archangeli of the Economics Department at the University of Venice; Jerry Silverberg of the MERIT Institute in Maastricht; and Willi Semmler of the New School of Social Research in New York. Although I only discovered him in the last phases of preparing this script, Barkley Rosser must be acknowledged for lending at least some respectability at least to applying nonlinear approaches—a trend we feel will prevail in the future.

Exceedingly patient over the years in putting forth the applicable premises of theoretical physics have been Andrew Norris of AMEX and U of Sussex, Kelly Stelle of the Physics Department at Imperial College, Vytanis Vasyliunas (who shall be proud to see his name spelled properly in print), Head, Max Planck Institute for Aeronomi, Martin Walker, Monica Beltrametti, and Martin Sohnius, previously of the Max Planck Institute in Munich, Bernard Carr of the Physics and Mathematics Deparment Queen Mary's College, Judith Perry at Cambridge University's Astrophysics Dept, and Leo Mestel, head of Astrophysics at the University of Sussex. Finally, much appreciation is due to Guenter Haag and Wolfgang Weidlich of Theoretical Physics at the University of Stuttgart for their example of creative interdisciplinary approaches to economics. Special thanks is also due to research assistant John Kilpatrick for his assistance in compiling the checklists and to Peggy Lai, an engineering student at the University of British Columbia for her help with the Literature Synopsis. Final thanks to the perplexed but always supportive staffs of the Northwest Airlines World Clubs and the crew of the Ocean Princess in Antarctica who queried but never questioned this traveling manuscript.

PART ONE: WHY FIRMS MERGE

CHAPTER 1
INTRODUCTION

"They sell the pasture now to buy the horse."

SHAKESPEARE, HENRY V, 2.II.CHORUS I

The 1980s was the mergers decade. New ways of forming companies and financing them enabled vast changes in company ownership and the dispersing of risks and rewards. The eighties opened with a "big bang" of consolidation and "de-regulation" in the financial services and closed with a whimper of bankruptcies and forced company sales. As the recession continues, the winners of this world—Norstar, Bank of America, United Airlines, News Corp.Ltd, the Hanson Group—scramble for the pickings of the losers—Bank of New England, Pan Am and Eastern Airlines, and many others.

Is "M&A" "good" or "bad"? Do its victories outweigh its losses? For whom in particular? The complex answers to these questions evade common sense. Empirical research continues to address the issues. Fragmentary conclusions are based on limited data, individual perceptions, and different motives for undertaking M&A detective work in the first place. Besides that the merger curve is not especially smooth. The jaggedness of merger waves depends on outside factors—overall economic growth, the business cycle, technology and sector changes, the availability of money, and many other interrelated factors.

This book was undertaken in order to address the forces that jarred the foundations of finance in the 1980s. Actually it is two books in one. The second part was written first for my M&A colleagues and clients—people who want to know but don't have much time to read. Its purpose was to provide business people as well academicians specialized in certain areas of M&A research with a grand overview of the causes and effects of M&A. In undertaking this effort I hoped to discover what was going on myself. One year ago I was ready to set off for the publishers when Harry Goff, a founder of venture capital in San Francisco, a CEO many times over and President of the Book Club of California pointed out to me that there are still those who prefer to read. Thus was born *the more verbal interpretation in Part One. Included is perhaps the first theory of the merger wave and an underlying theory of cyclical dynamics in Chapter 7 and its Appendix.*

Another byproduct of this sequential reversal is two sets of references. There is a lengthy Literature Synopsis which encompasses the comprehensive M&A literature survey and deals mostly but not exclusively with Part Two. Recent work and sources that provide journalistic flavor as well as literature from other fields such as foreign investment and product cycle analysis are included as footnotes in the text. Information which is *not* footnoted, for example in Chapter Three, is easily sourced in the financial press.

1. THE DATA

Before trying out a new volatility approach, data on mergers and acquisitions was examined with Kenneth White, Professor of Econometrics. The M&A data was found to be discontinuous and incomplete with significant breaks[1]. The decision was thus taken to avoid a purely empirical approach. Since this book was started existing data chasms have been spanned by Margaret Blair, Martha Schary and Sarah Lane[2] in their formidable integration of M&A statistics. Their US efforts would be well compared to the more European-oriented AMDATA[3]

1.1.1 M&A AND FIRM SIZE

A research bias exists—probably because of data problems—towards large public deals which bypass the M&A majority of small, privately owned firms. Quantifiable data is most at hand for large transactions. Noted in 1955 by

---

[1]   Similar observations by Golbe and White (D22). Multiple regression analysis of merger activity against selected variables have been criticized by Steiner *et al* because proxies vary with truly causal factors over time, and specific variables may activate merger activity intertemporally in different ways (I35). Blair *et al* (A6a) of Brookings Institution have made a notable contribution in aggregating data. Also Margaret Blair, *The Deal Decade,* Brookings, Wash. DC, 1993.

[2] See Chapter 1, Footnote 7 as well as A6a in the Literature Synopsis.

[3] AMDATA is perhaps the most global data base created by *Acquisitions Monthly* (UK), a premier European M&A Journal, and Computasoft Ltd., London.

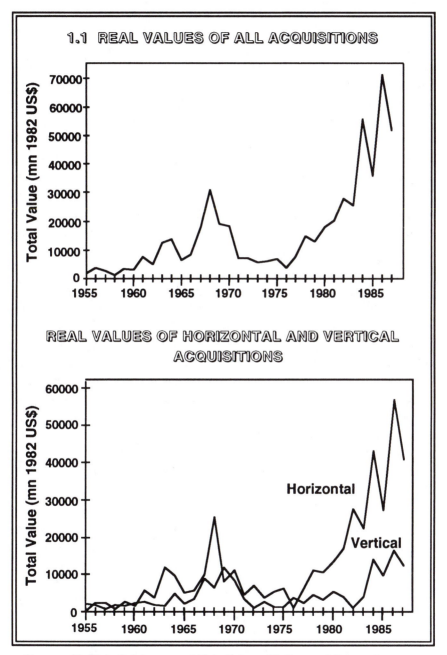

Source: M. Blair, S.J. Lane, and M.A. Schary, "Patterns of Corporate Restructuring, 1955-1987", Brookings Discussion Papers in Economics, No. 9H, The Brookings Institution, 1991.

Markham (I24) and more recently by Weston (B32), M&A analysis is dominated by large mergers with scale economics and monopoly arguments. To make matters worse, firm and transaction details for private, smaller firms are notoriously confidential and inaccessible, especially in countries like Germany where free circulation of data may have tax consequences and loss of prestige. Moreover, it is easier to quantify the effects of M&A as opposed to the qualitative motivations of their instigators. Smaller mergers—including the bulk of management buyouts (MBOs) and management buy-ins (MBIs) are driven by distinctive objectives. Some writers write off smaller transactions pointing out that the bulk of national GNP is contributed by large, Fortune 200 firms. However, by concentrating on large takeovers, much of the motivational fiber of M&A is lost. The research proclivity towards large deals may change due to the current vogue towards smaller transactions.

1.1.2 M&A AND THE STOCK MARKET

Another popular approach is to observe stock price performance or "stock events" that happen before, during and after a takeover of selected sample firms. We do not follow this well worn path because the results represent **only** some of the motives for undertaking corporate buying and selling, and then only for large, public companies. Hughes reconfirms that studies to date have been "focused ....excessively on the monopoly power-efficiency trade-off and upon an analysis by proxy using stock market returns as a guide to welfare" (C46). Kass also points out that because merging firms do not integrate their joint operations instantly, changes in stock market values serve merely as *predictions* and not evidence of any actual increase in the overall value of the firm[4].

Data is also relatively more available for stock-event studies. Kaplan and Weisbach (B21) assert that managers also make acquisitions for *non-value* maximizing reasons with negative acquirer returns, say, in order to turn around companies and divest of them once again[5]. Furthermore, rigorous efforts to measure shifts in stockholder wealth as reflected by changes in stock prices at announcement date and other specified events conclude that there

---

[4] David I. Kass, "State and Federal Regulation in the Market for Corporate Control: a Comment," *The Antitrust Bulletin* XXXII/3, Fall 1987.

[5] Further divestment of target firms acquired from 1971 to 1982 occurred to 44% of the 271 firms studied by Kaplan and Weisbach by the end of 1989.

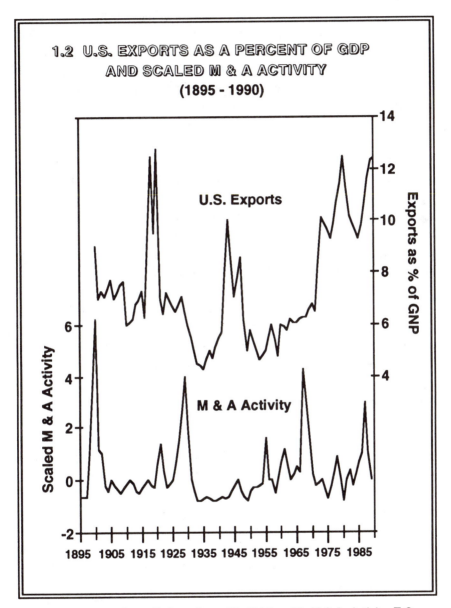

1.2 U.S. EXPORTS AS A PERCENT OF GDP AND SCALED M & A ACTIVITY (1895 - 1990)

Sources: Export Data: Forbes, Sept. 19, 1992, p. 53; M & A Activity: T.C. Opler, "Studies on Leveraged Buyouts, Finance, and Corporate Mergers", Dissertation, 1990, UCLA.

may be a long-run, post-merger stock price gain for the firm buyer, but usually not a short-term gain. Moreover, negative buyer returns are associated with stock financing, but not with cash financing. Other interesting results have emerged from the event-study analyses as cited in Chapter Eight. However, a wide range of less measurable motivations and post-acquisition effects are not fully exposed by stock-event studies.

1.2 THE ISSUES

After decades of M&A research several issues have been resolved. Besides the stock performance of large acquirers and targets, the first great wave of M&A literature also dealt with how to buy a company and the valuation techniques required. In addition, it is now fairly clear why the selling price of a firm is high or low (sold at a premium or a discount). In the last half of the 1980s a large amount of work emerged on leveraged finance and leveraged buyouts. The effects of new legislation and taxation on M&A have also been examined. Antitakeover measures—acquire or be acquired—have also been investigated, although they are not included here. More recently, attention has been devoted to post-acquisition outcomes—why some firms succeed where others fail, for example the relationship of firm size to merger success.

Surprisingly, four areas have not been addressed in a conclusive manner:

1.2.1 CAUSES

Why do companies merge? What benefits accrue to acquiring companies, and what compels companies to surrender corporate identity and corporate control by selling out? Why do buyers take over rather than invest directly in a subsidiary, branch or joint venture, or forming a strategic alliance with other companies? What market forces encourage or inhibit M&A? The chain of causalities in the financial markets also remains unclear: How does the availability of finance and the relative costs of capital affect the volume and types of merger activity?

1.2.2 EFFECTS

How do mergers affect corporate performance and the economy at large, for example, sectoral shifts in productivity? Who are the net benefactors in the short- and longer-term?

1.3. TYPES OF TRANSACTIONS
(1st - 3rd Quarter 1992)

NUMBER OF BIDS

TRANSACTION TYPE	No Value	0 - 1 Mn $	1 - 5 Mn $	5 - 10 Mn $	10 - 50 Mn $	50+ Mn $
TOTAL PUBLIC BIDS **Total Value = $71,828 mn**	28	4	7	21	52	121
MANAGEMENT BUYOUTS **Total Value = $5,113 mn**	184	19	44	29	22	21
REVERSE TAKEOVERS **Total Value = $0 mn**	1	0	0	0	0	0
PRIVATE ACQUISITIONS **Total Value = $65,566 mn**	1916	83	193	169	208	220
STAKE **Total Value = $13,628 mn**	110	4	15	15	56	55
DIVESTMENTS **Total Value = $7,949 mn**	74	17	55	54	49	38
TOTAL NO. OF BIDS	2313	127	314	288	387	455
TOTAL VALUE=164,084 mn	0	71	842	2,573	11,160	149,437

Source: AMDATA Database by *Computasoft Co.* (London), *Acquisitions Monthly Jl*, Tunbridge Wells, UK, 1992.

1.2.3 FLUCTUATIONS

If mergers occur significantly more in some periods than others, how do mergers relate to:

- Corporate restructuring and ownership changes
- Sectoral shifts and product cycles
- Business and GNP cycles?

1.2.4 M&A PERSONAE

Who are the key players in merger deals? The motivations and methods of M&A prime movers were driving forces in the 1980s acquisitions boom. The effects on employees are just beginning to be understood.

1.3 THE BOOK

In the search for the M&A "engine", a full range of M&A literature has been encompassed— business, technical, and academic. The causes and effects of M&A are presented in Part Two in three main categories: financial, strategic, legal. The data is interpreted with particular attention to financial and economic variables. Over one hundred causes and one hundred effects are listed from 300 publications on mergers and acquisitions through 1991. More recent studies are incorporated in the text. The number of references in any one category in Part Two indicates how much attention that subject has already received. For example, until most recently, employee and staff issues have been largely overlooked. The results are incorporated in a theory of merger behavior.

1.3.1 OBJECTIVES

This comprehensive review of the M&A literature and interpretation includes:

1. An overview of reasons for successful mergers and failures.

2. Wealth distribution effects—the gains and losses—of mergers and acquisitions.

3. The role of M&A waves in the economy and shifts that they provoke.

4. Discernment of the fundamental forces of M&A. Sound negotiations and due diligence have not lowered the high rate of post-acquisition failures.

5. An understanding of the ambivalent financial developments during the 1980s. "Goodness and badness" criteria for acquisitions are established, and a foundation laid for the development of proper regulatory law.

3.2 OUTLINE OF THE BOOK

Mergers and acquisitions are first approached historically to determine how specific sectors and technologies have been swayed by M&A, and to begin the arduous exploration of how M&A interacts and macroeconomic events. The geographic migration of mergers as well as the changing nature of corporate consolidation is discussed in Chapters Two and Five.

After the motivational fiber of mergers and acquisitions is dissected (see the Checklists in Part Two), it is reconstituted in Chapter Three in order to identify the master keys to merger events which are divided into three categories: financial, strategic and legal. The major carvers of the M&A financial pie are then brought forth because of their tremendous influence during the early emergence of trusts and holding companies, the rise of the corporate raiders the 1960s and 1970s, and their presence on center court in the eighties along with the investment banker equipped with a new bag of financial instruments. Included is the evaded corporate employee. Special attention is given to motives to gain and control merger returns.

The cyclical nature of M&A is explored for the first time in depth in Chapter Four. Leveraged buyouts (LBOs) are reviewed as a major phenomenon in the financial environment. The new techniques of creative financing are evaluated, particularly with regard to the costs of capital and the interest rate; the increase in debt financing and bank pressure, and stock market price effects. Vehicles created to couple institutional investors cruising for enhanced returns with fastlane entrepreneurs are also described. A financial cycle is proposed.

Chapter Five focuses on strategic reasons for acquisition and divestment within the context of corporate control and expansion via M&A. The notable distinction between *why* firms merge and *how* is illustrated. Chapter Six explores the critical influence of government on cyclical behavior. By probing the inter-relatedness of product or technological cycles as well as business cycles with M&A waves, the foundation is laid in Chapter Seven for the integration of preceding chapters into an interpretation of the general merger wave based on a theory of cyclical dynamics.

Findings are classified in Part Two in checklist form for easy reference. Gaps indicate where knowledge is limited. Chapter Ten summarizes postacquisition success and failure factors.

————— .***. —————

CHAPTER 2
THE RECENT HISTORY OF M&A WAVES

"Some of the cycles companies ride in the process of becoming successful are getting shorter: Product cycles, changes in technologies or industrial structures, performance cycles."

DAVID MITCHELL, MAKING ACQUISITIONS WORK
LONDON: BUSINESS INTERNATIONAL, 1988

2.1 INTRODUCTION

Up until recently, the literature on the "violent fluctuation in merger activity" (B32) has largely focused on large, public takeovers in the USA, followed to a lesser degree by the UK, Canada and Australia. The reason is that M&A simply has not been a major phenomenon in most countries until the 1980s. To complicate matters, merger-related company data (especially for private European firms) is not readily available because of confidential accounting practices outside the Anglo-Saxon regions.

In 1990 there was a surge of acquisitions in Ireland, Spain, Italy, and Switzerland, and even in more distant newcomers to the M&A scene such as Brazil and New Zealand. Buyouts and restructuring are also a growing source of deal flow in Asia. It has been estimated that the premium for investing in more volatile Asia is 8—12 percent.[6]

---

[6] Assuming a yield on US funds in the low 20s, US investors, for example, would require a 30-35 percent return in Asia, estimates Hancock Venture General Partner Kevin Delbridge (A26).

Of the four or sometimes five waves cited in American history since 1898, it is commonly maintained that the current wave and the super-giant wave at the turn of the century were dominated by horizontal mergers, whilst that of the roaring twenties was dominated by vertical mergers, and of the 1960s by a disproportionate number of conglomerate mergers (B32). However, no support has been found for six major theories tested about why waves occur. Indeed, some claim that each wave has its own unique causes (I36).

Opler and Brealey and many others state that as yet there is no explanation for the merger wave, except with the possible exception of Bittlingmayer's investment analysis. Based on the most comprehensive and consistent transaction-level merger data base on US mergers in existence, Blair, Lane and Schary analyze the broad characteristics of merger waves since 1955, although they refer to earlier waves such as the "great Monopolies wave" from 1887 to 1904. This team sponsored by Brookings Institution define two great waves: 1967-1971 and 1983-1987. Peak years were 1967 and 1987. One salient finding is that the merger cycle is one of the most volatile of all the time series[7]. A major concern of their study was defining those industries most effected by mergers and acquisitions, which are categorized in Chapter Seven.

A major discovery of the Brookings study is that *in any one year overall M&A activity may be driven by a few lead sectors*. Furthermore, in the United States *merger waves are driven by a few large serial acquirers*. We expect the same would hold true in Britain and Canada and elsewhere where acquisitions have been frequent.

The study by Blair, Lane and Schary and work by Bittlingmayer demonstrate that there are no surprises. Analysis of over 15,000 US transactions from 1955 to 1987 reveals merger patterns as expected, with the possible exception many break-ups in the 1980s and high conglomerization in the 1960s. Most of the big public acquisitions have been conglomerates, closely followed by an ever increasing number of horizontal acquisitions. As explored in Chapters Three

---

[7] In 35 years, eight year-to-year periods occurred in which real transaction values increased by more than two-thirds, and four year-to-year periods in which the value of transactions fell by a third or more. See Margaret Blair, Sarah J. Lane and Martha A. Schary, "Patterns of Corporate Restructuring, 1955-87", Brookings Discussion Papers in Economics No. 91-1, The Brookings Institution, 1991 (A6a).

and Four, many if not most of the large financial conglomerate acquirers have crashed: Maxwell, Campeau, Trump (although leveraging may be to blame, not acquisitions). Members of the Australian Big League have been particularly hard hit. Holmes à Court died last year at 52 of a heart attack, Skase has back problems so that he is unable to fly from his home in Majorca, Spain, to angry creditors back in Australia. Alan Bond has just come out of jail. Focussed serial acquirers have often fared well (international public relations specialist Shandwick PLC was an example until fairly recently), although not necessarily. Advertising and p.r. companies like WPP and Saatchi remain in the acquisition doldrums due to excessive leveraging and post-acquisition pitfalls. To provide the whole picture, below is an overview of twentieth century merger waves.

2.2 THE FIVE GREAT AMERICAN MERGER WAVES

2.2.1 HORIZONTAL CONSOLIDATION: 1898—1902/4

The first "great merger wave" peaked at the turn of the century in 1899. The trend was constituted primarily by **horizontal consolidations** in the heavy manufacturing industries (B38). Turn-of-the-century mergers were led by primary metals, food, non-electrical machinery, transportation equipment, tobacco, chemicals and metal products[8]. The movement accompanied **major changes in economic infrastructure and production technologies** (I24) allowing *inter alia* for economies of scale and specialization. The wave in the US followed the completion of the transcontinental railway system, the advent of *electricity,* and the increased use of *coal* (B38). Its demise was due to the introduction of the Sherman Act, anti-trust legislation in responding to the decision of firms to control by external acquisition in the march towards industrial consolidation (D44), rather than fix prices, a practice which was also subject to government prosecution (D17). According to empirical results concerning antitrust case filings presented by George Bittlingmayer to the American Economic Association Conference in January, 1992, trust-busting by Teddy Roosevelt and later by Harding was particularly active in 1895, 1907, 1908—1909, and 1911—1912. Thereafter, antitrust activity dropped off during the twenties, then peaked again from 1937-1942. Bittlingmayer's results lead him to conclude that the expectation of sustained trustbusting leads

---

[8] See George Bittlingmayer, "Merger as a Form of Investment," Wissenschaftszentrum Berlin für Sozialforschung, Berlin, May 1987, Discussion Paper IIM/IP 87-13.

consistently to a drop in the Dow Jones Industrial Average. A trend in trustbusting would seem to lead not only to merger waves but also to stock market cycles. In sum, from the onset the US Government played an important role in modulating corporate strategy for expansion. The first American wave also can be attributed to the influence of speculative promoters (I24, I33).

2.2.2 CAPTURING RENTS VERTICALLY: 1919/22—1929

During a second American merger wave in the roaring 1920s **public utilities** and **banking industries** were among the most active. About 60 percent of M&A occurred in the still fragmented **food processing** and **retailing, chemicals,** and **mining sectors** which lent themselves to vertical integration (I34). Other important sectors were petroleum, stone, clay and glass (typically cement mergers as is currently common in Spain). Causes cited are **developments in transportation** (automobile); **home radio and advertising; mass distribution** and **lower profit margins.** Integration also ensured the benefits of production efficiencies that shortened processes and elimination of waste motion, as well as the securing of inputs and product outlets: (I37). Other reasons cited are market refinement, and the creation of national sales and marketing teams (B27, D44).

2.2.3 REGULATORY IMPETUS: 1940—1947

A third wave is related to war and **post-war growth;** however, with less technological and environmental developments, the movement was smaller than earlier ones (B38). Electrical equipment also emerged as a merger-intensive industry. Efforts to circumvent government wartime price controls and other regulations—as well as high income and estate taxes compared to relatively low capital gains taxes—were primary impetuses for the third merger wave.

2.2.4 CAPTURING PROFITS THROUGH PRODUCT DIVERSIFICATION: The 1960s

A fourth wave occurred during the 1960s, peaking in 1968 at the height of a boom in the US economy. **Antitrust legislation** was expanded to cover acquisition of assets as well as stock, therefore increasing conglomerate takeovers (as compared to vertical and horizontal), and especially product extension, as opposed to market extension. During this wave, almost half of the firms regarded as conglomerates were based in the **defense and aerospace** industries. These sectors regularly experienced wide fluctuations in demand and supply, and were dependent upon the defense budget, which was substantially reduced during this period before the VietNam buildup. Firms therefore diversified into other sectors. Furthermore, **diversification** was undertaken into more promising industries by small- or medium-sized firms facing diminished prospects for growth and profits (B38). Acquisitions in the durable good sectors peaked in the late 1960s. Other active sectors in the 1960s wave were petroleum and coal products, paper products, and industrial chemicals.

Leading sectors in the 1960s as well as the next 1980s wave were engines, turbines and general industrial machinery as well as radio, television and communication equipment. Following in both periods were iron ore mining, crude petroleum and natural gas, aircraft, guided missiles and parts, drugs, food products, tobacco, household appliances, holding companies radio and television broadcasting.

2.2.5 CORE CONSOLIDATION: 1975—1989

The latest wave took place for strategic reasons (D44, D19) in the USA starting in the second half of the 1970s and the 1980s (D24,D44). An analogous wave occurred in the United Kingdom from 1985—1987 (C71). In the US, there was exceptional merger activity in **oil and gas extraction, electronic equipment, industrial machinery** and **transportation equipment** (B32), and more recently, in **foods, cement, banking, airlines,** and **chemicals.** The leading trend was horizontal, for example, the integration of a variety of financial services (retail and investment banking with discounting, currency trade and the brokerage of stocks, bonds and other financial services under one roof). Towards the end of the period as specialty companies (boutiques, niches) became prevalent, mergers and acquisitions tended to focus on core activity. Even as late as September 1992, the emphasis remained on core or horizontal acquiring. As can be observed en the following table, the highest number of deals in the same sector occurred in the paper manufacture and products sector. Of 209 paper completions, 156 were in the same SIC industry code sector manufacturing. Of 213 transactions in wholesale distribution, 139 were in the same sector. In the highly visible food industry, of 135 deals 105 were in the same broad sector. Of the 134 chemical deals, 101 were in the minerals and chemical sector. It is interesting to note that in sectors where there have been fewer transactions during the first three quarters of 1992, there is a tendency to have less core focus and more diversification, perhaps because cash flows and asset values do not support the level of debt required to support successful M&A. This in turn suggests that *M&A occurs in those sectors where the coverage ratio allows it.*

M&A was particularly influenced by financial events during this time. In the 1970s, buyouts gave slow returns—in about three to five years—compared to the "fast money" that could be made in the trading room (B24). Then, on October 6, 1979, Paul Volcker of the US Federal Reserve announced that the money supply would cease to fluctuate with the business cycle. Instead, previously fixed interest rates would be allowed to float. Once set free, interest rates began to swing wildly. So did bond prices, but in the opposite direction—transforming bonds from conservative vehicles for capital preservation to highly speculative instruments—a means of creating wealth as opposed to merely storing it. Short-term interest rates skyrocketed. The prime rate peaked at a high of 21.5 percent and the bill rate at 17.5 percent in the early 1980s.

Homeowners, primarily financed by savings and thrift societies who were heavy purchasers of new instruments called mortgage bonds, faltered on their payments. By mid-1981, the entire structure of home lending was said to be on the verge of collapse. The US Congress provided massive relief by allowing the thrifts to turn over their mortgage loan portfolios for huge fees on Wall Street, and to have tax subsidies. The peak of longterm interests rates was reached in October 1981, when long government bonds reached 15.25 percent. By late 1982, short-term interest rates had fallen below longterm interest rates. Thrifts made new mortgage loans at 14 percent while taking in money at 12 percent, a 2 percent spread that was a loss!

Then in 1982, former US Treasury Secretary William Simon privatized Cincinnati-based Gibson Greetings, using only one million dollars of the company's money for an $80 million takeover. Simon sold Gibson eighteen months later for $290 million, turning Simon's personal investment of $330,000 into $66 million in cash and securities. The financial community was alerted to a new path towards high reward. Between 1979 and 1983 the number of LBOs increased ten times over (B24). In August 1982, the stock market realized the biggest gain in history.

2.1 GLOBAL AQUISITIONS BY SECTOR (SIC CODE)						
(1st - 3rd Quarter 1992)						
			NUMBER OF BIDS			
CATEGORY	AGRI	ENERGY WATER	MINS/ CHEMS	MANUF	DISTRIB/ HOTELS	OTHER
AGRICULTURE Total Value = $61 mn	8	0	0	3	0	1
ENERGY & WATER	2	61	11	3	29	61
Coal mining & solid fuels	0	3	0	0	8	7
Mineral oil & natural gas	0	31	7	0	10	12
Mineral oil processing	1	3	3	2	3	2
Neclear fuel production	0	0	0	0	1	0
Electricity/gas	1	23	1	1	7	28
Water supply industry	0	1	0	0	0	12
Total Value = $11,992 mn						
MINERALS/CHEMICALS	2	4	186	11	29	34
Metalliferous ores	0	2	7	1	1	0
Metal Manufacturing	0	0	30	1	11	13
Other mineral extraction	0	0	2	0	0	0
Non-metal min. products	1	0	44	3	5	9
Chemical industry	1	2	101	6	12	12
Prod. of man-made fibers	0	0	2	0	0	0
Total Value = $11,465 mn						
MANUFACTURING	4	0	16	476	60	55
Food industry	3	0	7	105	11	9
Sugar & sugar by-products	1	0	0	78	21	3
Textile industry	0	0	3	42	2	4
Footwear & clothing indus.	0	0	0	29	6	0
Timber & wooden furniture	0	0	1	35	0	1
Paper manuf. & products	0	0	1	156	16	36
Rubber & plastics processing	0	0	2	14	3	1
Other manufacturing indus.	0	0	2	17	1	1
Total Value = $15,899 mn						
DISTRIBUTION/HOTELS	7	4	12	32	302	38
Distribution - wholesale	7	3	10	24	139	30
Commission agents	0	0	0	1	1	1
Distribution - retail (domestic)	0	0	1	5	81	5
Distribution - retail (other)	0	0	1	1	48	2
Hotels and catering	0	0	0	1	32	0
Repair of goods & vehicles	0	0	0	0	1	0
Total Value = $7,693 mn						
OTHERS Total Value = $116,973 mn	7	28	108	246	243	1801
TOTAL NO. OF BIDS	30	97	333	771	663	1990
TOTAL VALUE= $164,084 mn	382	14,346	15,897	22,295	12,045	99,117

Source: AMDATA Database by *Computasoft Co.* (London). *Acquisitions Monthly Jl*, Tunbridge Wells, UK, 1992.

2.2 TARGETS AND BIDDERS BY COUNTRY AND REGION
(1st - 3rd Quarter 1992)
NUMBER OF BIDS

COUNTRY/REGION	US $ mn	UK	USA & Canada	EEC	Eastern Europe	Austral. & N.Z.	Rest of Europe
UNITED KINGDOM	26,850	585	34	67	0	2	16
USA & CANADA	62,109	55	377	53	0	3	18
Canada	2,743	4	30	6	0	1	3
United States	57,961	51	346	44	0	2	14
Rest of N. Am.	1,384	0	1	1	0	0	1
EEC	37,401	87	95	1521	1	5	146
Belgium	511	3	2	46	0	1	5
Denmark	1,026	1	1	81	0	0	8
Ireland	185	4	3	15	0	1	0
France	13,828	21	19	354	0	1	17
Germany	5,020	25	45	602	1	0	78
Greece	734	0	0	5	0	0	2
Italy	4,528	9	13	194	0	0	8
Luxemburg	94	1	0	1	0	0	0
Netherlands	5,121	14	3	95	0	2	9
Portugal	1579	2	2	6	0	0	3
Spain	4,774	7	7	122	0	0	16
EASTERN EUROPE	841	6	12	33	3	0	12
Czechoslovakia	528	1	6	14	0	0	1
Hungary	122	3	4	13	1	0	2
Poland	143	1	2	4	1	0	2
Russia	0	0	0	1	1	0	0
Estonia	46	1	0	0	0	0	6
Latvia	2	0	0	0	0	0	1
Lithuania	0	0	0	1	0	0	0
AUSTRALIA / NZ	8,544	5	3	0	0	21	2
REST OF EUROPE	13,887	20	18	2	2	1	361
Austria	424	1	1	0	0	0	3
Finland	411	1	4	1	1	0	167
Norway	762	8	4	0	0	1	69
Sweden	12,049	7	7	1	1	0	111
Switzerland	174	1	2	0	0	0	9
Turkey	72	2	0	0	0	0	2
OTHERS	12,495	8	22	2	2	2	3
TOTAL NO. OF BIDS	3884	778	562	1761	6	34	564
TOTAL VALUE	164,085	27,954	57,111	30,773	0	8,437	19,901.38

Source: AMDATA Database by *Computasoft Co.* (London), *Acquisitions Monthly Jl,*
Tunbridge Wells, UK, 1992.

During the early 1980s, bids tended to be financed through equity, usually accompanied by a cash alternative produced by underwriting that equity. Sellers of assets received exceptionally high prices throughout the 1980s due to relaxed antitrust laws, financial innovations, and other reasons (B21, and in Chapter Four).

The bond departments of the major banks experienced a heyday during the first part of the 1980s. Major buyers of bonds were governments, consumers and corporations. The combined indebtedness of these three groups in America in 1977 was $323 billion, much of it consisting of loans by commercial banks. By 1985 the three groups had borrowed $ 7 trillion, a much greater percentage as bonds. In 1977 bonds were newly issued below investment grade for the first time in significant quantities. Although Lehman Brothers is attributed with having underwritten the first issue, Drexel Burnham Lambert quickly became the market leader in the new "junk bonds" (D53). Born of interest rate volatility and inflation, overcompetition in the financial services, and industrial growth and restructuring, junk bond financing quickly became a major means of mobilizing large amounts of capital quickly[9] for a booming acquisition trend triggered in part by inflation. As put forth by Peter F Drucker,[10] the current merger movement in the United States paralleled the tremendous wave of acquisitions in Germany in 1920—1922, a period of chronic inflation when fixed assets were purchased by buying companies at market prices well below book value and even further below replacement costs.

Mortgage bonds and junk bonds share one attribute in common: investors could now loan directly to homeowners and infirm companies previously viewed as less worthy of receiving funds. During the 1980s two sorts of companies were sought by banks that previously had encountered serious borrowing obstacles: small new companies, and the "fallen angels", or large, mature companies with problems (B7).

---

[9]New sources of funds sought by corporations also included the Eurodollar bond **markets** which increased for U.S. corporations alone from $300 million in 1975 to *$20 billion* in 1984; and direct borrowing from investors via the **commercial paper market** in which the outstanding paper of nonfinancial corporations *quadrupled* to more than $80 billion between 1978 and 1985 (D53).

[10] "The Five Rules of Successful Acquisition," *The Wall Street Journal*, October 15, 1981.

This sharp explosion in debt—the leveraging of America and then of Europe—was due to factors old and new. Firstly, the easing of regulation and traditional lending guidelines allowed brisk market-making by highly competitive bankers and traders. Innovation was also facilitated, as described earlier, by new financial products and allocative structures of risk and reward that "stripped" both and designated their holding to investors depending on the risk-reward requirements of each "individual", typically a large financial institution such as a pension or insurance fund, or a savings and loan institution. Secondly, a new wave of financial entrepreneurship entered the traditionally conservative financial community: aggressive senior managers who groomed their entrepreneurial dark horses in the business community while minding to their young teams of traders and "sales forces" who aggressively sought to place the new financial packages in the institutional and corporate markets. Rather than traditional lender of the first resort, the Wall Street or City banker is now a matchmaker between the businessman seeking operating capital and growth finance, and large-scale mutual, pension, mortgage and insurance funds seeking portfolio growth while preserving safety through diversification. The enormous impact of entrepreneurial dark horses sponsored by aggressive bankers on the drive towards M&A restructuring explains in part the constraints of a purely quantitative approach to understanding merger waves and merger behavior.

In summary, the 1980s were characterized by the deregulation of financial institutions, increasing competition in the financial services and a subsequent downward pressure on fees and earnings. Bankers eager to hold onto their clients (and to their jobs) aggressively sought raiders, tycoons or just plain entrepreneurs with sufficient weight to borrow funds to takeover firms. The bank not only received interest on acquisition funds borrowed, but also fees for underwriting and issuance. Under auspicious circumstances, fees for acquisition advisory services were also forthcoming.

In general, during the 1980s due to new technologies and products as well as market globalization and to the increase in numbers of variety-seeking consumers, suppliers' markets took off. **New medium-sized competitors** with **more flexible production technologies** needed financing, yet only 6% of 11,000 US public corporations qualified for investment grade ratings (F11). External financing via new financial innovations such as the junk bond hence increased.

These trends eventually culminated in leveraged buyouts (LBOs) by management (Management Buyouts, or MBOs) and third parties (Management Buy-ins, or MBIs). Debt capacity also increased, at least in the short-term. The major primary investors were financial institutions: savings and loan associations, high-yield bond mutual funds, pension funds, insurance companies, commercial banks and investment banking firms.

A new enthusiasm for gearing contributed to the explosive emergence of leveraged buyouts in October 1987. Financial institutions became involved in funding buyouts through LBOs. Banks capturing enhanced fees syndicated LBO deals and resorted to mezzanine finance, or "high yield" junk bond financing, at the middle level between senior debt and equity financing.

In 1985—86, even smaller companies began to acquire larger and less actively managed companies, which influenced bid financing right up until the 1987 crash. The crash resulted in the inability or unwillingness of more vulnerable companies to issue equity. The equity market initially dropped by some 26 per cent. Major investing institutions became much more discriminating in their underwriting activity (C5).

As late as the spring of 1988, the stock markets were still suffering from the impact of the October market crash. Stock prices remained low and volume flagging. The flotation of new stock offerings held little appeal. Fueled by bargains available because of lower stock prices, there was an unprecedented flare of takeover activity starting in January, 1988. More takeovers were attempted during the first half of 1988 than during all of 1985, itself a very good year (B24). LBOs increased from $11 billion during the period 1976—1982 to $181.9 billion during 1983—1988 (B7).

By the mid-1980s the large merchant banks were not only advising on takeovers, but participating more actively in deals, sometimes owning a substantial percent of the acquisition vehicle. Money was lent through interim financing arrangements known as "bridge loans" . These loans were typically refinanced, or bridged, by the later sale of junk bonds (B24). As the number of competitors for "done deals" increased, the only remaining path for expansion was up in terms of deal size (B24). And as banks became more active in the acquisition phase, their presence became more evident in post-takeover boardrooms.

Financial packages put together in the 1980s were based on cash flow and interest rate assumptions that seemed reasonable in the 1980s, but proved catastrophic in 1989 and 1990: high interest rates in the UK and USA fatally cut into the debt-carrying capacity of the newly merged firms (C5).

Taggart has made the startling observation that during the takeover wave of the 1980s *junk bond financing constituted only a small part of overall corporate borrowings,* and an even smaller percent of merger financing.[11] Auerbach and Reishus were also startled to confirm that merging firms do not borrow more but less: The debt-equity ratio for large acquirers actually declines (D6). Most junk bonds are actually used—not to buy other companies, but to undertake the much more mundane matter of financing ongoing business operations. Public issues of straight junk bonds as a percentage of total corporate public bond issues ranged from 4.6% in 1977 to a high of 21.4% in 1984 (D53). Even though Taggart's figures do not cover the period from 1987 to the present, junk financing was certainly curtailed by market conditions starting in late 1989. Even if junk bonds did not play a major role in the 1980s merger deals, the dramatic increase in corporate leveraging during the 1980s served to deteriorate the quality of debt worldwide—especially when coupled with high interest rates supported by governments contending with inflation caused by increased liquidity—itself due in part to more lending and easier consumer credit. This has led to the highest levels of foreclosure and bankruptcies since the Great Depression in the 1930s.

According to one source, in 1990, Toronto Dominion Bank was the only bank left in North America with an AAA rating. TD Bank has subsequently been downgraded to AA. Whether junk or not, the capitalization of management buyouts in the early 1980s was associated with debt-equity ratios typically

---

[11] The figures vary. Drexel Burnham estimated that in 1984 about 11%, or $1.7 billion, of total public junk bond issues were associated with acquisitions and leveraged buyouts, of which 4 % of the total were associated with hostile takeovers. Morgan Stanley estimated that junk bond financing of acquisitions and leveraged buyout came to about $3.3 billion, or 21 % of total 1984 junk bond issues. The Federal Reserve Board estimated that 41 %, or $6.5 billion, of 1984's total junk bond issues were related to mergers or acquisitions in some way. The contribution of junk throughout the decade remains to be assessed. In any case, Taggart considers the junk segment in mergers financing to be "significant, but not predominant"-in any case hardly threatening enough to overwhelm the market (D53).

ranging from 6:1 to 12:1. This has allowed among other things 50 percent premiums to new manager shareowners. Sponsoring investment bankers have been able to levy high fees and realize, say, 50 percent annual returns over five to seven years on their equity investment in the new firm (D49).

In 1990, the most significant sign of the financial squeeze was the number of large deals that failed due to a lack of funding (A5).[12] The seeds of restructuring were sown in the buoyant world economy of the mid to late 1980s by a corporate sector hungry for debt eagerly fed by fierce competitors in the banker's market. As a consequence, lending margins sank along with the quality of client relationships. With increased interest rates and recession, companies found no loyalty or feeling of commitment on the part of their previously enthusiastic bankers. As stated by one observer "the lending bank umbrella has collapsed with the first drops of rain". The demand on internal resources created by financial fire fighting with bankers hastened rather than curtailed corporate collapse (A15).

In 1990 sellers (stand-alone businesses and corporate divestors) surprisingly remained reluctant to accept reduced prices for their properties. The deal failure rate, however, remained about even, with one transaction failing for every 14 completed (A5).

Massive takeovers declined as the debt load on corporate America and elsewhere became severe. In the first eight months of 1989 alone there were $4 billion dollars of junk-bond defaults and debt moratoriums. Henry Kaufman estimates that debt servicing consumed twenty-six percent of America's cash flow. However, the debt load has not caused takeovers to cease altogether. To the contrary, heavy debt burdens sustain a steady stream of "tar pits", "quagmires" and "quicksand", i.e., moribund companies that can not stand up under economic pressure. Bankruptcy became a last resort for "retiring debt"— albeit not without economic costs (B10). In 1990 cash was king: as US tender offer activity declined to its lowest level since the early 1980s, cash continued

---

[12] One deal involved a group led by Merrill Lynch Capital Partners Inc., which failed in a proposed $684-million buyout of Philips Industries Inc. Philips was eventually acquired by Tomkins PLC for $527.8 million. The difficult financing environment affected strategic buyers as well, including Ball Corp., which backed out of a deal to acquire the European operations of Continental Can Co.

to be the preferred acquisition currency in tenders, with 49 of 60 bids being straight cash offers (A4).

———— .***. ————

As the 1980s gave way to the 1990s, the US and European merger and acquisition (M&A) markets seemed to be headed in opposite directions. In the US, the decade-long takeover binge subsided in 1989 as the number of leveraged buyouts decreased and prices became more realistic. At the same time, in Europe, the volume and prices of deals continued upward as corporate dealmakers intensified their restructuring efforts. In the process, the competitive lineup in key European sectors underwent some dramatic changes: 1. The food sector registered 101 crossborder deals. 2. Banking and finance underwent nearly 100 crossborder transactions. 3. The chemical and pharmaceutical industry accounted for some 120 deals, totaling over $4 billion. A new trend in 1989 was a sharp increase in acquisitions by US companies abroad, especially in Europe. The M&A Data Base of ADP/MLR Publishing's shows an increase from 180 to 243 completed transactions around the world, with the total value doubling to $14.4 billion.

Global, crossborder M&A activity declined by 13% in 1990 from $131 billion to $114 billion, of which 32% was in the fourth quarter alone. French and US purchases were particularly affected: US acquisitions in the EEC dropped down from $13 billion to only $4 billion, although the US was still a popular target country. Japan, Sweden and France were the only countries to increase acquisition spending over 1989. The number of companies sold in crossborder acquisitions increased in the UK, Germany, France, Spain, the Netherlands, and Italy (B37). There is still no shortage of European acquisition candidates. Many big European firms that grew fast in the late 1980s are now selling businesses. State-owned enterprises continue to be privatized. Finally, the owners of many small businesses set up after World War II are retiring with no successors. In the final quarter of 1990, crossborder acquisitions of EC companies bounced back from a downward trend to provide the UK £ 7.85 billion (roughly US $14.5 bn) worth of deals. The number of acquisitions in the EC dropped to 420 purchases, compared to 531 in the first quarter. The highest number of bids per country was in Germany, 119 in all. The UK, France and Spain were also popular target countries (B18). Three-fourths of the world's 1000 largest companies made no crossborder deals in 1990, although British companies spent $1 on foreign acquisitions for every $3 invested in new plant and equipment (B37).

Over half of the big buyouts and buy-ins in 1989 and 1990 were in Europe, two-thirds in Britain alone. In Germany buyouts dwindled down to 25 MBOs in 1989. With less large deals to aim for, competition between banks and buyers is more intense than ever before, although European deals are steadily larger and more complex (B14).

2.3 CONTINENTAL EUROPE TAKES FRONT STAGE

FRANCE. In 1989, the year of new takeover regulations, France made one-third of all acquisitions in Western Europe (B33), primarily of companies in Spain, Germany, Italy, the UK, Belgium and Luxembourg spending US$ 9.2 billion on 329 EC crossborder acquisitions. French buyers spent a further US$ 6.2 billion in the US—trailing only UK buyers who invested US$ 141.3 billion (B12).As a result French companies now hold leading global positions in steel, cement, tires, packaging, and hotels. High volume acquisitions as a strategy may pay off in the long run, although current resulting problems include falling stock prices, rising debt and excessive losses (B7).[13] Perhaps the French appetite for aggressive US megabids is satisfied. French acquisitions in Europe have become more aggressive, although the emphasis in the future may be on smaller fill-in acquisitions in Spain, Italy and to a lesser degree in the UK (B12). With cheaper prices, France also remains attractive acquiring territory.

GERMANY. Much of European merger activity has focused on Germany, now the largest single market in Europe and one of the most rapidly growing regions in the EC and the industrialized world. Germany now accounts for one-third of the total GNP of the Common Market, compelling companies with European pretenses to "buy Germany". In contrast, many smaller,

---

[13] Compagnie de Suez tripled its assets in only 3 years. However, weak commodity prices, declining arms sales, and a slowing real estate market are causing its 55% stake in Société Générale de Belgique (SGB) to plummet. Suez's stock has lost 40% of its value since April 1990. With a market capitalization of only $7.8 billion, the group itself may now be a takeover target. Another French company, Michelin, the world's leading tire manufacturer, has forecast a $460-million loss for the year. To offset its losses, Michelin slashed capital spending 60% in 1991, to $600 million. While Michelin's debt has risen to $6.7 billion, it still has $2 billion in cash and unused bank-credit lines.

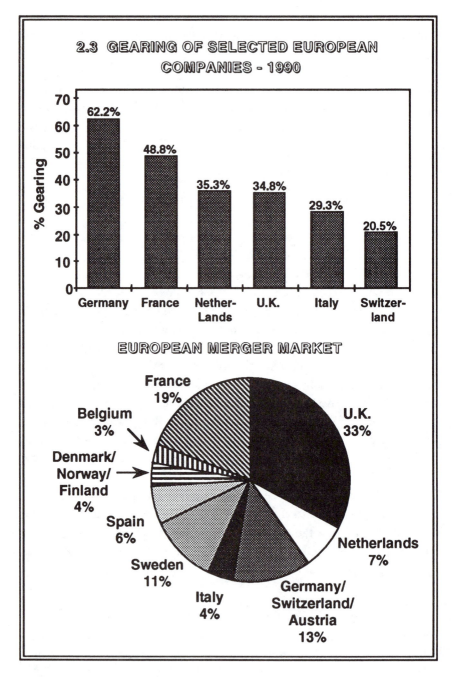

2.3 GEARING OF SELECTED EUROPEAN COMPANIES - 1990

EUROPEAN MERGER MARKET

Source: M & A International.

private, German firms can not raise enough capital to position themselves in the larger European market,[14] and are therefore potential sellers.

In 1990, 1,412 majority acquisitions involving German companies were reported (B28). After official integration on October 1991, it is anticipated that eastern Germany will account for about one third of all takeovers in Germany. Like Italy, there is still a general absence of takeover rules and disclosure requirements. For example, a bidder can claim to hold 50% of a company's shares whether or not it is true. According to recent reports, only one hostile takeover has succeeded in Germany. Controlled auctions with several potential acquirers have gained in popularity, as in France. Like Italy, only a small minority of companies are publicly quoted (about 500). Major sources of future acquisitions are divestments by German multinationals eager to scale down, and the sale of firms in the "New Five Lands" (NFLs) by the German "Trust" or Treuhand. There are currently 6,000 east German companies on offer. This figure may double when companies are split up into more viable economic units (A18).

NFL firms remain to be properly capitalized, registered and manned with a board of directors and proper management structure as well as endowed with proper infrastructure. However, the potential lucrativeness of having an early seat in emerging central Europe has led buyers to acquire 2,000 companies before the first anniversary of German reunification!

SCANDINAVIA.   After booming domestic stock markets and active acquiring abroad in the 1980s , notably by Finland[15] and Denmark as well as Sweden and Norway, corporate acquisitions now are seriously curtailed by recession—causing retrenchment and restructuring due to higher costs and lower profitability. Nordic companies are deleveraging, focusing on core

---

[14]About 75% of all German companies were sold due to financial problems of the sellers. Thus most owners will request absolute confidentiality when discussing a potential sale.

[15] In the 1980s Finland underwent a period of unprecedented change. A consistent OECD growth leader, Finland's major companies were active acquirers in fields such as forest products, mining, telecommunications and financial services and have become world participants and competitors.

sectors and selling diverse interests to pay for their recent acquisitions. Furthermore, driven by possible entry into the Common Market.

Major shareholders are embarking on a consolidation of their holdings 'in the next few years and by the local relaxation of laws concerning foreign ownership coupled with undervalued markets.[16]

SPAIN. Many sectors are restructuring in order to do in five or six years what other European countries have done over a longer period. Spanish firms reportedly need to merger to combat fragmentation and grow to the size of an average European company. In 1990, France, the Netherlands and the UK have made some $8 billion of investment in insurance, service and rental companies followed by $ 2.7 billion in mining $1.7 billion in manufacturing (A17).

ITALY. Another growth market for mergers and acquisitions is Italy. This market has a lack of regulation and a lack of company financial information, as well as a paltry number of publicly listed companies (231 on the Milan Stock Exchange). The corporate market is divided into three parts:

1) the state-owned sector which controls nearly 25% of total market capitalization. Although threatened by competition from European and private Italian groups, this sector has failed to form joint ventures with the private sector.

2) In 1990—1991 the large private conglomerates increasingly diversified outside Italy having reached quasi-monopoly positions in most sectors domestically, and because of difficulties in dealing with the State.

3) Medium- and small-sized family companies, the real motor of the Italian economy, will continue to be a focus for acquisitions (A14).

THE NETHERLANDS. An interesting case in the world of European mergers is the Netherlands. Asset stripping, short-term financial gains, junk bonds and leveraged deals, and megasized transactions have been largely absent, perhaps due to a naturally cautious mentality and a conservative

---

[16] This holds especially true for Finland.

business ethic. In contrast, on a GNP size-adjusted basis, the Netherlands has been the largest and perhaps one of the earliest MBO markets in Europe, stabilizing when the MBO markets in the UK and USA were taking off during the second part of the 1980s (A16). Perhaps because of this volume almost every Dutch company has antitakeover measures built into its company laws (A10).[17]

2.4 THE NEW PLAYERS: JAPAN AND THE EMERGING ECONOMIES

JAPAN. Perhaps due to their behind-the-scenes approach, surprisingly little attention has been devoted in the literature to the omniscient presence on the global M&A scene of the Japanese. Until recently, mergers have been surprisingly unpopular in Japan. A psychological distaste for M&As persist. Responding to a questionnaire by the Ministry of International Trade and Industry, 70 percent of companies polled believe that a company is an organic body including employees and other parts that should not be bought or sold as a mere commodity. However, Japan may be on the brink of a series of forced mergers in the banking sector where smaller financial institutions are feeling severe pressure from some of the strongest banks in the world (A3). Although potential foreign acquirers in Japan are thwarted away by stock and land prices, the Japanese appetite for takeovers abroad has not subsided (B8). For example, in 1991 Toshiba and C. Itoh invested $1 billion in Time Warner. During the same time Mitsubishi Estate increased its stake in the Rockefeller Group by $416 million. Sony bought out its RCA/Columbia home-video joint venture for $300 million. Mitsui & Co. with Nippon Soda purchased an animal feed division from Monsanto for $250 million. Transactions in the USA ranging from $80—159 million were also undertaken by Dai-Ichi Mutual Life, Dai-Ichi Kangyo, Yuasa Battery, Mitsubishi Motors, Yamanouchi Pharmaceutical and Sony.[18]

---

[17] E.g., limited shareholder rights, power concentrated in management, voting shares held by management-friendly administrator or non-voting shares, the issuance of preferred shares to management-friendly foundation, and priority shares with far-reaching voting rights issued to a management-controlled foundation.

[18] "The Top Ten Deals of 1991," *Business Tokyo*, June 1992, p. 19.

THE EMERGING ECONOMIES. The M&A market is growing substantially in developing economies. Brazil is a good example. Subsidiaries, alliances and joint ventures tend to precede acquisitions as a way to enter emerging economies. For example, to penetrate the US processed food market, Japan's Ajinomoto Co., the world's largest producer of chemical seasonings, constructed a plant in Brazil exporting 100% of production. Monsanto penetrated the Brazilian market by forming a joint venture to produce PVC sheeting with Norquisa, a holding company of 17 Brazilian companies. Brazil is aiming at a major expansion domestically in order to attain world market status. For example, six of Brazil's leading petrochemical conglomerates formed a consortium called Braschem with Japan's Mitsubishi Kasei in order to bid for the Portuguese Sines Olefin Complex.

Despite Brazil being the world's eighth largest market with an articulated foreign investment and acquisitions regulatory environment, M&A activity has been modest. Acquisitions are constrained by culture, size, the control characteristics of companies, and the lack of an extensive service and financing infrastructure. However, recently M&A activity is picking up. Compared to US companies, Brazilian firms are small. Amongst the leading three hundred Brazilian firms 94% are family-controlled. Similar to Germany, most companies are run by founders of retirement age or their children. The pool of acquisition target firms is thus substantial.

Similar to Braschem, Indonesian tycoon Liem Sioe Liong's Salim Group bought for a small cash outlay the controlling stake in the United Industrial Group and Singapore Land, Singapore's ninth and tenth largest companies. Salim Group thus opened a second front in its campaign to build a durable international presence on the Pacific Rim where M&As are relatively rare, by linking up with nearly all the prominent business families in Singapore (A19).

2.5 SUMMARY

Based on the Grimm data series for M&A, Weston maintains that mergers have steadily increased in both size and value since 1969. The constant dollar consideration in M&A during 1985 was 40% higher than in 1968 (although in 1984 it was the same). However, the net number of announcements in 1985 was only about half that in 1969.

Taking the USA as an example, the importance of M&A can be assessed as follows. From a peak M&A year in 1968 until 1988 the dollar value of M&A constituted:

- 1.00—05.00% of GNP
- 0.25—01.75% of total assets of all corporations
- 1.20—06.90% of total equities (which roughly equals the shrinkage factor of the stock markets every year)
- 0.80—57.50% of total expenditure on plant and equipment, a figure that has continuously been rising since 1977 to 57.5 %.

Since 1968 M&A appears to parallel the growth of the economy. M&A activity accompanies or follows spurts of economic activity and is boosted by notable changes in technology and economic infrastructure. One example is the drop-off in large public takeovers during the 1989—1990 recession. The financial and strategic causes and global effects of merger waves are explored systematically in Chapters 4 and 5.

———— .***. ————

CHAPTER 3
THE M&A PERSONAE

"Commit the oldest sins the newest kinds of ways."

SHAKESPEARE, HENRY IV PART 2, 20, 124.

A prevalent view is that *investment bankers* create and promote M&A in order to secure *horrific fees* by providing expensive debt finance to *corporate raiders* so that the latter can grab up the undervalued assets of innocent firms. Others consider acquirers as leaders who by rationalizing are making the crowded business floor more efficient. The merger landscape of the last three decades is undoubtedly populated by villains and heros. Can we smash this mythology and break it up into meaningful bits? Probably not. The M&A atmosphere is already overloaded with political venom and "a new language, a lurid vocabulary so rife with terms of 'predation, crime, and war' that its 'lexical violence' alone may be evidence of need for reform".[19] The best that can probably be done is to segregate fact from fiction. Who done it?

3.1 BENEVOLENT AND LETHAL BUYERS

In 1973 and then again in 1978 the "energy crisis" served to drive up the prices of oil and other natural resources. Conoco was the ninth largest oil company and second largest coal producer in the USA. In 1973, the value of Conoco's oil, coal, natural gas and uranium reserves was $2.6 billion. By 1981, inflation

---

[19] Moira Johnston, *Takeover: The New Wall Street Warriors: the Men the Money, the Impact*, New York, Arbor House, 1986, p. 9.

had pushed this value up to $14 billion. Conoco's assets included almost 400 million barrels of oil. Domestic oil was selling for $30 a barrel, and the costs of drilling was between $11 and $15 a barrel. The company's shares were trading at $50, when asset-reflecting share value was probably more like $160 per share! Consequently, whoever purchased Conoco would be acquiring oil at $4.50 to $9.00 a barrel, plus manufacturing facilities, a research facility and resource reserves thrown in for good measure. So-called corporate raiders rose to capture the hidden values, much of the mergers activity in the late 1960s and 1970s centering around the undervalued oil sector. Conoco's shares were driven up to $85 per share by Dome, and then by Dupont, Seagram and Mobil.

In the United States, Britain and Australia during the sixties and seventies a new financial door was opened for aggressive or "hostile" large public takeovers. Other examples of mid-seventies oil and other resource deals are Shell Oil's $3.6 billion buyout of Belridge Oil; Fluor Corporation's $2.7 billion bid for St. Joe Minerals Corporation; and Exxon's $1.7 billion purchase of Reliance. The stage was set for assaults of T. Boone Pickens backed by Mesa Petroleum from 1982 to 1985 on UNOCAL, and on Getty Oil by Pennzoil and Texaco in 1985. The four largest mergers in 1984, with a total value of $33.6 billion, were acquisitions of oil companies by other oil companies (F3). M&A transactions in America dwindled in total numbers from 6,107 [20] in 1969 to roughly 3,000 in 1985. Total dollar volume, however, rose from $10 billion in 1975 to $200 billion in 1985! Size was no longer a means of sanctuary; companies of $5 billion and more were no longer immune to takeover.

Corporate raiders had tapped an undervalued asset: oil reserves and other fixed assets were like gold nuggets. Whole divisions could be sold off separately at better prices than the total acquisition price.

Secondly, laws designed to limit the reach of early twentieth century robber barons were allowed to go lax as more international competition required larger domestic firms to keep a foothold in international markets. What began in oil spread to the airlines, trucking, banking and securities, television networks and telecommunications as corporate raiders followed the tracks of deregulation. T Boone Pickens, Carl Icahn, Ted Turner and Tiny Rowland

---

[20] To demonstrate the variability of the mergers data, other sources say there were 3,012 transactions in 1969

made their mark in the 1970s and 1980s as well as Henry Kravis and George Roberts of KKR, Lord Hanson and Gordon White of the Hanson Group, Alan Bond, Kerry Packer, Robert Maxwell, Rupert Murdoch, Robert Campeau, Sam Belzburg, Robert Holmes à Court, Donald Trump. All succeeded to build empires in the 1970s and 1980s. Frank Lorenzo was particularly active in the airline sector. From his corporate base at Texas International, he bought National Airlines stock before it was sold to Pan American. Some say that the beginning of the final demise of Pan American at the end of 1991 was from paying too much for National, and not being able to downsize staff. Lorenzo founded New York Air which was acquired by Pan American and then by Delta. He also bought into Continental, using his position as a base to buy into Eastern, which was sold out in part to Trump. However, in five years effective control may very well pass on to Northwest, itself subject to a junk bond takeover.

Up until recently, the largest portion of mergers and acquisitions were initiated in English-speaking countries. Now hardly any of the major Anglo-Saxon acquirers such are coming out of the 1980s well. Even KKR is feeling the pull of debt. Most others have sunk into self-built debt pyramids. At the same time new acquirers such as Yuk Sui Lo and Li Ka-Shing of Hong Kong, and Oei Hong Leong and Boon Suan Lee of Singapore continue to expand. Thailand and Korea have joined the acquirer gang.

Many of the global takeover elite know each other personally, often working together. Drexel Burnham Lambert backed most of the corporate raiders as well as smaller LBO players. The Canadian Reichmann brothers offered potentially fatal support to countryman Robert Campeau. Normally it pays operations managers to know their equivalents in other firms. Thus, due to a uniformity of basic information sources and the intimacy of key players, perceptions of financial opportunity are not diversified. They are homogenized. Merger waves occur within the timeframe of the financial, legal, economic and technological developments. They are pulsated by the "motivational synergy" of the league of big acquirers.

As described above, the prime movers of M&A do not respond specifically to inflation, increased capital costs, nor to technological or legal changes alone. They react rather to a full range of variables in the business environment that determine the availability of improved financial and market windows of

3.1 1920s STOCK MARKET PROFESSIONALISM AND 1980s GREENMAILING COMPARED

1920s Pool	1980s Greenmail
New products: leveraged investment trusts	New products: loans repackaged as securities and junk bonds

. . . .

1920s Pool	1980s Greenmail
1. Pool group, through pool manager and stock market floor specialist, quietly accumulates large block of target stock.	1. Raider, through various brokers, quietly accumulates a block of target's stock.
2. Pool group, through sales and planted publicity, generates stock activity to draw public into the target stock.	2. Raider announces 5%-plus holdings and intention to take-over cause arbitrageurs to rush into stock.
3. Stock price rises sharply.	3. Stock price rises sharply.
4. Pool group suddenly "pulls the plug", taking profits through open-market sales and leaving public holding the bag.	4. Raider negotiates sale of stock back to target company at above market price, in exchange for promise to desist from takeover attempt.
5. Pool group dissolves with huge profit.	5. Greenmailer desists with huge profit.
6. Stock price collapses.	6. Stock price collapses.

Source: John Brooks, *The Takeover Game*, Hutton, New York, 1987, p. 341.

opportunity. Mergers occur when key players perceive that new investment opportunities via the M&A path are at hand. Otherwise, other profitability paths are pursued. To measure the motives and the impact of the motives of the M&A prime movers one can sample M&A failures compared to successful transactions. M&A is a highly signaturized sector. Since people and people's decisions make mergers and acquisitions happen, the sample can be analyzed by type of acquirer - financial, corporate strategist, tax dodger other. Furthermore, as explored above, capital market conditions at the time of merger may also be added.

A special sort of egocentrism is required to gain the support of a militia of lawyers, accountants, bankers and other intermediaries who will be paid fees often surpassing the hundred million dollar mark in order to undertake what ranks amongst the largest single undertakings in financial history. This frequently occurs without initial capital to pay for even a small part of the corporate asking price.

The acquisition process depends highly on the availability of a lead corporate acquirer, Also required is the formation of a cadre of support. Yet the occurrence of merger is not assessed in the technical literature in terms of its key and principle actors. CEOs, CFOs and other corporate managers are sometimes described in academic studies as "agents", or value allocators and representatives of shareholder vested interests. The popular press also contains bibliographies of the corporate acquiring elite. Yet the only merger attempt we came across that describes acquirers in a categorical way was prepared by David Mitchell of Business International London.

Mitchell allegorizes the business environment as the large Serengeti Plain filled with game targets and predators in six categories:

> 1. **The Carnivores,** or habitual acquirers, for example Unilever which has bought about 50 companies in the last five year, or Esselte, the Swedish publishing and office products company, that buys about 10 firms per year. These companies relentlessly integrate new acquisitions into their system, unfazed by organizational and restructuring problems and the human implications, rarely retaining existing management.

2. **The Dairy Farmers,** or value extractors, milk the companies without interfering extensively in the running of the companies beyond basic nurturing. Management is left intact. Unsuitable beasts that do not fit the herd are sold off. Sir Gordon White and Lord Hanson of the large-scale acquisition and holding company Hanson Trust are examples.

3. **The Vegetarians** nibble at the acquisition market with objectives that are less clear. The new fashion for refocusing on core businesses rather than diversification has made them less visible on the acquisition scene. Management is usually left in place, with subscription mainly to corporate maxims and culture.

4. **The White Hunters** raid for profit. They audaciously gun for targets much bigger than themselves. An unknown UK supermarket-trolley maker aimed for and shot the US advertising giant JW Thompson (see the Saatchi&Saatchi case study). Shooting forays are justified by claims of invigorating lazy managements to put under-used and undervalued assets to better work to dispose of them. These hunters make a catch even if there is not a kill: Sir James Goldsmith netted $90 million for failing to acquire Goodyear. After purchase acquisitions frequently plunge while awaiting eventual dismemberment or disposal.

5. **The Gentleman Shooters** are the most common of European acquirers, buying rarely, but in a friendly and civilized manner for good strategic reasons. Occasional acquisitions are difficult to implement, as managers accustomed to the distinct nature of mating problems are in short supply. Consequently, companies often have depressed performance for one year or two. Burroughs bought Sperry Corp, becoming Unisys, for market share pure and simple, and was prepared to accept the integration problems associated with incompatible product lines. The Economist

acquired Business International to position itself as a global
business information supplier.

6. **The Cross-Breeders** are a new set of Eurohybrids uniting
national companies across national borders. Examples are
the mergers of Asea of Sweden and Brown Boveri of
Switzerland in heavy electrical equipment; the Italian SGS
and French Thomson in semiconductors, and between
French CGE and American ITT in telecommunications.
Earlier Trans-European alliances frequently have sunk into
the bog of national rivalries. Whether global competition will
keep the cross-breeders together (D37).

3.2   THE CAST: BANKERS, INVESTORS, ARBS AND ATTORNEYS

In the 1980s arrived the financial "department store" offering the services of
many financial "boutiques" under one roof. At the same time in London and
New York hotel lobbies where financial executives stay, exotic flowers with
increasing height and stature were added to central lobby bouquets.

Recessionary restraints in the 1990s have led many to recall that the primary
business of banks is to lend to firms with at least somewhat promising credit
ratings. Eager to capture a portion of the massive cash flows of global
corporations and newly emerging firms, bank rating standards were stretched
in the 1980s parallel to the issuing of lower quality bonds (B24). After the third
world lending fiasco of the 1970s, LBO finance was one way of increasing bank
business.

Senior investment bankers on Wall Street most involved in LBO expansion
characteristically graduated in the late 1960s. College friends became financial
colleagues. They hired young recruits proliferating at rapidly expanding
business schools to man the new "one-stop-shopping" integrated financial
services houses as well as global accounting houses such as Arthur Anderson,
Coopers&Lybrand and probably the only company in the world with
interchangeable name parts, depending upon what country they are in: Deloitte
Touche, Ross and Sills. "Financial engineers", mathematically-oriented

accountants as well as gifted attorneys were also contracted or hired to create new types of "financial and legal architecture" (see below). The new models were set up to allocate risk and reward by the untying and redistributing of each to willing separate recipients - one party seeking security, the other seeking higher returns. The old rules of common-sense banking conservatism were frozen as new products shouldered by new players proliferated.

Surprisingly little attention has been devoted to the impact of business schools on the emergence of creative financing. The explosion in North American business schools in the 1970s and 1980s is now happening in Europe. The leading triumvirate of INSEAD near Paris, LBS in London, and IMD in Lausanne/Geneva, are encountering new competition from a bout of private and government-sponsored schools in Britain, Belgium, Germany, Switzerland and elsewhere. The financial impact of business schools has been engineered by professors - Hicks, Modigliani, Miller, an many others - the production of a cadre of trained accountants and managers with standardized approach and rationalized technique, particularly with regard to company valuation and cash flow and risk analysis (DCF, IRR, CAP-M) as well as strategic marketing models. Furthermore, the new emphasis in economics and elsewhere on nonlinear and chaotic approaches can also be expected to yield a new generation of analytical models.

The breed of investment bankers during the 1970s and 1980s served clients not necessarily strategies that ensured corporate survival. also served themselves in the form of fees and equity participation in the client company (B24). They were sustained by corporate debt salesmen who were cutthroat, competitive, inebrious and often paranoid (B7). Whether pushing junk or pushing fees, the managers of Wall Street and London's City added a strong flavor to 1980s finance.

Oddly enough, a parallel crash in pension fund and insurance companies has not occurred. which have also been avid buyers of junk bonds, although there has been a certain of consolidation (e.g., Allianz of Germany's takeover of US Fireman's Fund). KKR's financial backers, particularly New York State and Local Retirement - have been especially vocal dissenters against the RJR Nabisco takeover. Met Life holdings of RJR have substantially increased in value, at least until recently. Public funds in general have been particularly sensitive to the popular backlash against LBOs. In several US states, public employee funds encounter portfolio limits on LBO investing and hesitate to seek approval to expand them. Public pension fund investment can not be easily replaced since very few states are diversifying into LBO investing. Scandals have led to the upgrading of professional credit review services. Already suffering from failing real estate holdings in early 1991, institutional investors swapped depressed, illiquid junk bonds of troubled companies for other assets, and diversified portfolios internationally.

The rise of pension funds represents a startling power shift in economic history: US pension funds - now the most mighty of shareholders - control total assets worth $2.5 trillion. Institutional investors own more than 40% of all US stock. These are unwilling owners as they can not sell their assets with any degree of ease. Nor can they effect directly management outcomes. More recently, however, funds actively lobby at stockholder meetings, and influence boards of directors and governments on issues effecting their investment portfolios. New laws may facilitate mutual funds acquiring share votes.

Lewis insists that the leaders of LBO syndications were able to have their cake and eat it too, or no risk and all reward. Through the mortgage-backed security and the junk bond, risk was re-circulated back into the system, falling primarily upon the shoulders of seemingly benign institutional investors such as the savings and loans associations, pension funds and insurance companies. The last investor takes the risk. More precisely, by protecting the mortgage holder and private bank client with insurance coverage for the collapse of lending institutions, the guarantor of end investor risk, for example the United States the Government assumes default risk. In fact, the US Government is hit twice over - once through the loss of uncaptured tax revenues (nontaxable interest payments took the place of tax-bearing stock dividends and capital gains taxes), secondly through deposit insurance compensation payments.

LBO firms with sufficient political clout to lead management buyouts were financed with bank debt and monies raised for them by banks (and LBO firms) from private pools or the public sale of securities, thus providing banks with fees. Commissions comprised not only loan fees, but also commissions for acquisition and subsequent divestment consultation.

As bankers and other intermediaries stepped in, takeovers during the late 1980s were increasingly driven by the pursuit of fees[21]. For example, in the R.H. Macy & Company buyout, Goldman Sachs received US $31.25 million plus a 2% equity stake, valued at the end of the decade at $50 million. However, note that of all the transactions undertaken by M&A intermediaries including banks and accounting firms, only a small fraction result in completed acquisitions or mergers. Since most or all of the payment for merger broking is payable only upon successful closure, the intermediary is obliged to assume all or most of the non-completion risk. With increasing competition in this area and fewer deals, acquiring monthly retainers from clients companies has become increasingly difficult. Many of the banks and other intermediaries therefore offer their services without payment, hoping for substantial returns perhaps months or years later when the transaction is finalized and bills are hopefully paid. M&A broking in not a career for the faint of heart.

A bank is paid down with cash from company's operations and revenues from selling parts of the business (B24). Most important in determining the viability of a takeover is the cash coverage, or the coverage ratio, the critical relationship between cash flows and debt payments. During the 1980s, coverage ratios were allowed to fall as interest rates rose in many countries.

A discussion of 1980s tactics and key players is hardly complete without including the "arbitrager" or simply "arb", the greenmail operation whereby a bid on a company is turned away by the company management with "greenmail" payoffs. Brooks* succinctly summarizes the influence of greenmail and arbitrage on stock prices by comparing greenmail operations to professional stock market techniques used during the stock market boom of 1928-29, "the plaything of insider technicians and wealthy outside investors".The recurring theme of stock price manipulation on the Vancouver

---

[21] For example, for participating in the RJR Nabisco takeover, the largest in financial history, Drexel Burnham reaped $227 million in fees for a $3.5 billion bridge loan, and even more for selling junk bonds. Merrill Lynch earned $109 million for bridge financing. A syndicate of 200 banks collected $325 million for committing $14.5 billion of loans. Kohlberg Kravis collected $75 million in fees from its investors. Morgan Stanley and Wasserstein, Perella earned $25 million each. This conglomeration of fees over one billion dollars does not include payments to a host of other consultants to the transaction, nor the fees for further second-round divestments.

* See John Brooks in Table 3.1.

is almost certain to go through. In spite of prevalent free market attitudes on the US Securities and Exchange Commission, stock price manipulation and the impact of takeovers led to a round of US Congressional hearings in 1985.

3.3 WHY SELLERS SELL

Since World War II and the onset of a new era of firm foundation and build-up, private owner-sellers have divested because of succession problems, i.e., too many children and not enough leaders. Coupled with tax benefits, family successors have also been satisfied to receive personal income from the firm disposal and proceed to develop their own concerns.

A fascinating study recently appeared by Lang, Poulsen and Stulz that attempts to pinpoint financial reasons why firms—both private and public—divest of assets in either partial or total divestments of the firm. Firms sell assets after a period of poor performance. Roughly 40% of the firms they surveyed sold assets to repay debt following poor cash flows. This was typical of somewhat smaller firms with low interest coverage (+3%) and few investment opportunities. Poor performance was coupled with a poor profile and lower prices in the stock market. Selling (non-core) assets in many instances was cheaper than: 1) new security issues—at lower stock price ratings; 2) debt renegotiation; 3) and loss of investment opportunities due to lack of alternatives. The stock market seems to react significantly and positively only when firms use sales proceeds to repay debt. Proceeds were never used by surveyed firms to pay dividends.[22]

3.4 THE UNSUNG SONG OF THE EMPLOYEE

> *"Japan's real secret ... The Japanese seem to have broken down the 'us vs. them' barriers that so often impair labor relations in American and European companies. They do so by creating a feeling that employees and manager share a common fate."*
>
> ALAN S. BLINDER, *BUSINESS WEEK*, NOV. 22, 1991

> *"This is now a social problem. You have the chairman of a major US corporation being paid $12 million, more or less, and firing 60,000*

---

[22] Larry Lang, (NYU), Annette Poulsen (U of Georgia), and René Stulz (Ohio State U), "Asset sales, leverage, and the agency costs of managerial discretion," Working Paper, April 1992.

people. This is simply irresponsible.. .In the US it is in the process of being stopped by the public employee pension funds. The process will take five years. I hope we will not have legislation — I hate legislation —but if it's not stopped by the participants themselves, there will be legislation. "

PETER DRUCKER
DIRECTOR (UK), JULY 1992

Until very recently, surprisingly little attention has been devoted in the literature to the effects of takeovers on the target company employees and their communities. Buono, Bowditch and others have considered the human toll that mergers have taken. The effects of mergers in terms of human costs include the much cited job losses and re-deployment. Psychological effects include trauma, uncertainty, stress, and a wide-held sense of uneasiness concerning job security. Bonds formed between the employee and employer can be ignored by a successor. Furthermore, the secrecy of the private firm is challenged in a public company. Winners revenge on losers. Other symptoms recorded include psychological shock waves, alienation, grief, a sense of loss at termination. alienation, preoccupation, eroded trust, and self-centered work activities. In spite of the illusion of management control, these changes can occur rather quickly. It seems that many firms give only lip service to the saying "people are our most important asset. "

The costs of firing can also be costly to the firm. Recent US evidence suggests that employee turnover can cost as much as $3500.00 to $25,000 per individual, depending on the job. The Xerox Corporation estimates that replacement costs for a top executive are $1 to 1.5 million.

Other labor-sensitive criticisms of takeovers are that aggressive entrepreneurs have too much say over other people's lives, and over where plants and jobs will be located. Entire communities are at risk. All assets and staff not pertaining to the core focus of the industry are imperiled. Some intimate that if an asset can not be sold it is liquidated, with momentous repercussions for staff and families.

A lead technician interviewed by the author joined Memorex in San Jose, California, some twenty years ago. He stayed with the company through troubled times and final takeover by Burroughs seeking world markets.

Burroughs bought Memorex at a good price. Burroughs also took over Sperry and became Unisys. In order to pay for the Sperry takeover, Burroughs took money out of machine assets, pension funds and working capital. According to some, Sperry was more experienced because they drove their stock price up; Burroughs also needed to drive up their stock price in order to perform the buyout. Blumenthal, head of Sperry at the time, is now working for the finance company that financed the buyout of Sperry by Burroughs!

The technician's division was moved to Singapore to secure cheaper manufacturing. His San Jose branch was spun off in a management buyout by three to four highly-placed managers and renamed Sequel. One outcome is that the technician lost his benefits. In February 1990 he was asked to sign up for retirement. He was also invited to take his pension now at US$430.00 per month, or wait two years to receive benefits somewhat over $600.00 per month. Due to retire in the early 1990s anyway, this head of a household with five children is angered at corporate restructurings that severely lowered his career path by several internal corrections to eliminate duplication of function. The meager nature of pension benefits may be due in part to rumors that Sperry and other phases of the company reverted to employee pension funds for cash to pay off debt.

The practice of management dipping into employee pension funds was recently highlighted by the decease of newspaper magnate Robert Maxwell. On December 7, 1991, the *Financial Times* reported that Maxwell's network of private companies devoured £600 million (roughly US$ 1 billion) in cash which he stripped from his public companies and their pension funds between May and his death on November 5th. Some of the cash went to pay interest on bank loans, some for the immediate payment of debts. Much of the private debts were secured on shares of the company MCC. The trouble began in November 1988 with one acquisition too many at far too high a price. All the deals thereafter were money losers. Mirror Group Newspaper pensioners are now out £350 million (about US$ 700 million). Another £50 million (about US$ 100 million) is missing from MCC's UK pension funds. Although the Mirro Group is strong enough to resume pension contributions and fill the hole left by Maxwell's financial digging, MCC pensioners may not be so lucky. Similarly, employees of Midway Airlines recently lost their pensions during the takeover negotiations with Northwest.

Contrary to the common view of the disenchanted employee at the selling firm, a corporate finance executive for British Hoskyns PLC, a facilities management firm, reports a rewarding track record after having been taken over several times.

Sir John Hoskyns, previous head of the illustrious British Institute of Directors founded the firm specialized in facilities management in 1964. Hoskyns sold the private company in 1975 to US Martin Marietta. In 1986 Hoskyns' Chairman convinced Marietta to float 25% of its holdings on the London Stock Exchange so that the firm would profile and benefit as a UK public company. Then Plessey bought Martin Marietta's shares.

In 1988 Plessey paid a 40% premium on the share price. Since 500 employees out of 2,500 owned shares on a save-as-you-earn basis plus stock options, they benefitted greatly from the takeover. Hoskyns was the best performing British stock in 1990 - partially because of the Plessey offering. Six months later Plessey undertook to issue the shares again and floated 25% at a lower price on London Stock Exchange. Employees were now able to buy back the shares at a lower price and make a substantial profit once again.

In August 1990, Cap Gemini of France bought Hoskyns shares at £3.30 (about US$ 6.50), compared with a market value of £2.90. Cap Gemini agreed not to buy the shares outright immediately, allowing the company to stay public for two-and-one-half years on the London Stock Exchange. Cap Gemini agreed to a £4.69 minimum offer price to Hoskyns. States one satisfied employee, the shares are like gilts. Share-holding employees fared extremely well.

According to a Hoskyns mergers and acquisitions specialist, success rules for a seller are:

- Maintain corporate culture and ethics as well as personal integrity
- Negotiate well
- Define takeover objectives and stick to them
- Be Competent
- Most importantly, have fun with your colleagues and work.

The advantages of being acquired by Cap Gemini stated by the Hoskyns' executive 1) are worldwide exposure provided by Serge Kampf, the "Napoleon of Software", and the first major shareholder "who understands the business", and 2) access to the European Community and the Japanese market. The internal international climate has also proven valuable. The Hoskyns example demonstrates significantly that it is possible to negotiate a favorable deal as a seller and to benefit employees at the same time.

The importance and growing popularity of stock ownership is well demonstrated at Relexite, a US company producing retroreflective material that coats highway signs and barricades invented by company cofounder Hugh Rowlands. Employee share ownership schemes called ESOPs provide incentives for staff even at junior levels. ESOPS are *legal devices that allow corporate employees to buy out the owners.* Reflexite's President Cecil Ursprung reasoned that employees want more than money. They want power over the decisions affecting their work lives. Give them that and they would repay the company a thousand times over. His logic may not have been less altruistic than a matter of business sense. Utilizing ESOPS as a vehicle for employee partial or total purchase of the company can be termed EBO (Employee Buyout).

Over several years, the Reflexite ESOP bought stock, borrowed money, and bought more. Management gained liquidity for expansion, and control of the company remained in local and concerned hands. Large corporate ESOPS normally hold 5 to 10% of the company's stock. Reflexite's ESOP owns 34%, and will eventually hold a majority. Dozens of individual employees, moreover, hold another 25% outside the ESOP, bringing the total of employee-owned stock to 59%. The median ESOP account comprises $50,000. The accounts of longterm employees are substantially larger. At the annual meeting —typically the same day as the company picnic—employees vote for the board of directors. Like most corporate shareholders, they have so far dutifully supported management's slate.

Reflexite employee shareholders receive an "owner's bonus once a month, or 3% of the company's operating profit divided by shares. In a good month the bonus adds several hundred dollars to an experienced worker's income, in a bad month nothing at all. Shareholders also receive annual dividends up to 20% of pre-tax earnings, or about $1,000 for a middle manager. Reflexite's ESOP builds loyalty: the longer you stay, the more shares you earn. Experienced employees rarely leave, and the company almost never loses know-how. Importantly, particularly in MBOs, ESOPs reduce the "us-and-them" atmosphere within the company.

The toll remains to be taken of employees that thrived and those that "died" were victims of corporate consolidations. What can be asserted with great certainty at this point is that the increased participation of employees in stock ownership schemes and in management will positively effect corporate policy towards employees. Especially at smaller firms, increased employee participation should be positively correlated with productivity. Moreover, as demonstrated by Hoskyns, corporate policies can be developed by management that put corporate sell-outs to work for the company and its staff.

3.5 WHO BENEFITS? MERGING FOR RETURNS

Corporate strategists restructure via the M&A entry and exit route when it is perceived as the optimal and timely way to enhance economic returns to the firm and to themselves. This is none other than the classic profit motive. The big question is *when* do buyers perceive that is a good time to expand vertically, or to focus on core activity by buying horizontally, or to diversify in conglomerate fashion.

There is a definable "psychographics" to merger waves—sentiments that push decision makers to expand geographically and shift corporate marketing strategies. Fad formation—not unlike bubble jitters and other attitudes slowly being incorporated into mainstream economics—appears here as an economic event (see Chapter Five).

The magnitude of gains to corporate buyers is great. Particular "profitability paths" are chosen in accord with 1) debt/equity financial cycle (Chapter Four), 2) predominating product and business cycles (Chapter Five) and 3) government antitrust cycles (Chapter Six).

Strategic market and financial returns in a given economic and legal environment are reinforce by the **"power and pride" returns** to acquisition executives, or "CEO egos". Yet in the vast forest of M&A research, the simple and classic explanations of firm behaviour do not emerge.

Successful acquiring executives usually benefit from higher salaries, increased prestige and visibility. However, it is usually overlooked that unsuccessful acquirers buy headaches, financial imbroglios and bad reputations. The acquisition team can acquire new liabilities rather than sellable or income-earning assets, regardless of earn-out formulae (e.g., the advertising sector in the late 1980s). Even in successful takeovers, only certain key officers receive extraordinary benefits, unless the acquisition is carefully tuned/structured so that employee interests are enhanced (Hoskyns). *That this is a possibility is not even discussed.*

Divesting sellers also personally benefit from:

> • golden parachutes (financial bonuses for "bailing out")

> • downstream participation in earn-out formulae

> • returns on company shares sold that often increase in the days preceding the acquisition (certainly to levels far higher than when the seller acquired them at company inception or as salary bonuses. The acquisition of target firm shares before takeover earned about one-half as much in 1990 as in the early 1980s, and the yield is still highest when the two companies are in unrelated industries.

Edward K. Finklestein, previous Chairman of the Board of Macy's Department Store provides an example of the extent of personal rewards available through corporate restructuring. Together with other top executives Finklestein bought Macy's in 1986, divested the store of property and other assets shortly thereafter, then offered shares back to the public.

. . .FRINGE BENEFITS

1. As Chairman Finklestein was granted executive bonuses including a $15 million Gulfstream jet.

. . .LEVERAGED BUYOUT

2. Finklestein, the largest shareholder, proposed to buy Macy's out at a bid price of $68 per share - 50% higher than the current market price, 165% of tangible book value, and 18.4 earnings. A reluctant board, however, insisted that the company be shown to all potential buyers. Five other buyers were shown the company but apparently were dissuaded from taking it over in subtle fashion. With restricted, alternatives, the Board then asked Finklestein for $70 per share to buy the company out. The original offer of $68 was then agreed upon as a fair price. Finklstein became "owner-manager". The total price paid by Finklestein and other top executives for Macy's in 1986 was $3.7 billion.

3. Based on a sale price of $68, Finklestein made $9,755,280 profit on share options (the shopping mall property assets had been valued at $100 million book value; Finklestein valued then at $250 million).

Finklestein put back in $4,375,000 for 4.9% of the new, private company's shares and voting rights on ALL the shares (total share value $89 million).

Macy's was stripped of equity and laden with debt. Before the buyout Macy's had a debt-equity ratio of 1:10. After the LBO, the ratio was 10:1. Interest deductible on debt and Macy's need not pay taxes, thus the government as "46% partner" eliminated .

. . .DELEVERAGING INTO BANKRUPTCY

4. The shopping mall assets were resold 3 months after the LBO for $555 million, over five times estimated book value and over two times Finklestein's estimated value.

5. Soon after the buyout the owner-managers registered for a "reverse LBO", or public offering of Macy's.

6. Offered at $2.4 billion (including the assumption of $1.4 billion debt) were 40% of company shares. Finklestein is reported to retain about one-quarter of common stock.

7. The Finklestein stake of $4.375 billion was worth $122.5 billion at the end of the 1980s (B24).

Where did the money go? 1991 Christmas retail sales were too low to sustain cash flow requirements. Macy's was on the brink of filing for bankruptcy under Chapter 11. Laurence Tisch, CEO of Loews Corporation and CBS and already a major Macy's investor, offered to inject $1 billion more to buy out Macy's at bargain prices from shareholders fearful of the company's total dissolution by a Chapter 11 judge. Discussions broke down when major creditor Prudential Insurance Company balked at refinancing $811 million worth of mortgage loans. The shopping malls - once prize gems in the Macy's portfolio, were now contributing towards the company's demise by requiring substantial cash outflows for interest payments on debt. Finally, on Monday, January 25th, Macy's filed for bankruptcy.

———— .***. ————

Chief planning or development officers and other staff of large public corporations such as Shandwick PLC undertaking repetitive, serial acquisitions probably do not reap the same benefits as sole players in more aggressive or one-off deals. A study is required to substantiate differences amongst officers in wages, earnings and bonuses associated directly or indirectly with takeovers. The subject of executive benefits may require public exposure. Consultant fees of investment bankers, attorneys and others may also be deemed subject to public surveillance.

Arguments concerning benefits parallel the high cost of capital arguments (B12, B20, C35, I8) stating that firms merge to exploit investment opportunities when the capital costs of acquiring are high. The argument also approaches Gort's expectational disturbance theory maintaining that the differences in firm price valuation between buyers and sellers are due to economic disturbances such as rapid changes in technology and the volatility of securities' prices which make the future less predictable.

Are mergers superior to organic growth and internal expansion, which intrinsically promises "right or close fit" between business and community, centralized control (in privately held companies), and a less debt burden? The distinctive characteristics of the M&A phenomenon have been established within the parameters of capital availability for acquisitions finance, markets in which to expand, and the availability of a sufficient pool of managers to lead acquisitions.

3.6 BUYOUT MANAGEMENT: A SPECIAL CASE OF ENHANCED RETURNS

MBOs provide a vivid example of enhanced personal returns - at least in the short term. Unlike Auerbach and Reishus' assertion that the tax gains do not seem to be the *sine qua non* of mergers and acquisitions (D6), Shleifer and Vishny find the magnitude of tax gains from MBOs to be substantial. For example, the oft cited Dan River Co used an Employee Stock Ownership Plan (ESOP) to buy 70 percent of the new company's equity. Out of the total purchase price of $151 million, $100 million could be ascribed to various tax savings, the premature liquidation of pension plans and other sources unrelated to the company's operations (D49). Thus they conclude:

> Whether or not management buyouts are a good thing depends on whom you ask. To the investment bankers who earned both high fees and 50-60 percent annualized returns on their equity positions, MBOs are a good thing. To the shareholder who got out of poorly performing firms at a 50 percent premium, MBOs were probably a good thing, although they may have advised that they could have stayed on to receive a bigger portion of the tax and efficiency gains and, with the benefit of hindsight, to profit from the enormous rally in the new issues market. MBOs were probably also a good thing for managers who traded a good deal of sweat for valuable equity positions, and perhaps more important, for the opportunity to escape hostile takeover. To the banks, MBOs were probably also a good thing, in contrast to many of their other above prime loans. The principal loser in MBOs may very well be the taxman (D49).

Shleifer and Vishny also point out that in exchange for 5 - 10 percent of the equity of the firm (acquired for virtually no money - the manager loses much control over free cash flows as well as the ability to run the firm without outside interference, particularly from investment bankers with perhaps even larger stakes in company equity (D49). Advocates claim that managers with equity stakes after LBOs can devote more time to running the business instead of endlessly justifying themselves to stockholders and analysts.

The huge importance in M&A research given to cumulative "abnormal" returns (CARs) to target and acquirer **shareholders** may be due to the relative accessibility of time series data on stock market prices and earnings, and to the positive value normatively assigned to maximizing shareholder returns. Shareholders may be assumed erroneously to represent the longterm interests of the firm and the public, as opposed to the special interests of owners, board members, and chief executives, especially those who are acquiring. Alternatively, CAR researchers may assume that buying a company is a financial market play, perhaps typical of early corporate raiders, but less true of perhaps the bulk of takeovers today. The latter actually may be major shareholders, too, or opposed to the short-term interests of the shareholders who are speculative investors or stock accumulators. The stakeholder issue is confused and overlapping. Shareholders in any case do not have the centrality and importance assigned to them by fifteen or more years of exhaustive research.

Lord Gordon White of Hanson Industries, the acquiring US arm of British conglomerate Hanson Trust, and one of the remaining (to date) successful acquirers firms, goes even further in stripping away the supposed power of the shareholder: " The absolute power that the directors have over companies in the U.S. . . [has] got stronger and stronger. I think the shareholder in this country has no rights at all. Everything has been done for the benefit of the incumbent directors and management - which broke up companies and paid off shareholders not to be taken over, earned lots of money and leveraged the companies up."

"Whenever you go to make a bid, you say to the chairman, 'Look, we think we can offer you a very good price for your shareholders.' But then he calls his lawyers, calls his merchant bankers, and he spends an enormous amount of money to avoid a big debate with the shareholders. . .The shareholder is the last person to be considered. Shareholders in the U.S. are low, low on the totem pole."

Non-executive directors are also falsely assumed to better represent the interests of shareholders, They are not remedies to managerial abuse, as they quickly assume the interests of the board. Lord White insists that institutions own companies in the U.S. and to a growing degree in other countries. But "institutional investors don't want to do anything about anything. If institutions wanted to go to the trouble of combining their power, then they could whip every management . . .and have the company run for the benefit of the shareholders and not the benefit of management.

The takeover environment may not be as hostile as implied above, particularly in the vast majority of smaller, private acquisitions and mergers where target share ownership is closely aligned with target firm management. The earlier financial motivation synergy approach described above fits in well with the investment opportunity view, and to a certain degree with Opler's thesis that merger waves may be explained by *differences in opinions and expectations of share values and other variables.* We suggest that an overwhelming *homogeneity of opinion* builds up amongst top corporate decision makers concerning periods when M&A is considered worthwhile. In fact, it is this homogeneity which focuses financial forces into what may be considered a merger wave. A consensus develops and even spreads globally concerning what type of merger is preferable (eg., 1960s conglomerates; 1990s core focus). A common view also unfolds concerning the globally preferred method of finance (in the first half the century through internal cash flows and stock issues; in the 1980s debt financing, LBOs, or even dipping into employee pension funds, a custom broadcasted recently by Robert Maxwell's demise. This matter is discussed further in Chapter Five Section 5.5 "Strategy Mood". Opler's view may be more aimed at price settling in the M&A negotiating process. Buyers and sellers have different views of price. Buyers and sellers may maximize individual price gains while *concurring* on the mutual benefits of merger or acquisition in a given environment where oligopoly, rationalization and diversification benefit both sides.

Laying down negotiating cloaks and daggers, both buyer and seller may *agree* about the fair value of a firm although views of specific terms may differ: The seller may seek to retire under a generous golden parachute, or specialize in another product, while the buyer may want to expand the given product line. A harmony of interests and perceptions - not the much cited differences - (see B32 for references) is the end objective of merger negotiations. Divergences apply more to third party or "outsider" stock market speculators. Even when management and parent are in agreement and there are no rival third-party bids, finance may be hard to source, or prohibitively expensive. A successful buyout probably depends less on negotiating terms and more on factors such as strong and committed management; a steady, predictable business in a non-cyclical sector; a substantial market share, and the ability of two corporate cultures to combine. In addition, most capital spending should already have occurred by the time of merger. However, several M&A transactions fail to get off the ground because of the price issue, particularly in the late 1980s and early 1990s: uncompromising vendors insist on excessive prices, and managers have been eager for bargains. More often, however, the contest is between the managers who have put a company into play, and a rival bid from a trade buyer, with the odds in favor of the latter because of wider sources of capital. However, trade bids diminished greatly after the Crash as quoted buyers were no longer able to offer their own highly valued paper in lieu of cash for acquisitions. Bidding managers have also been assisted by the ascent of mezzanine financing.

——————— .***. ———————

CHAPTER 4
CREATIVE FINANCING:
THE NEW TECHNIQUES

"Nothing focuses the mind so much as a lot of debt."

KARL VON DER HEYDEN
CFO, RJR NABISCO

4.1 CAPITAL COSTS

Explanations of merger waves often assign a central place to the costs of capital and the availability of acquisition finance. However, one variable divides researchers into two camps. Low interest rates are asserted to encourage more acquisitions, especially in pure conglomerate mergers which are more financially driven than strategic "product or market extension" mergers. Low interest rates make available low-cost acquisition finance. For example, Becketti found statistically significant correlations at the 10% level between mergers and the US T-Bill rate (F3). Yet, Weston, Chung, Golbe and White and others maintain that merger activity *rises* when the costs of capital are *high* as firms without easy access to capital sources seek merger partners to exploit investment opportunities (B32). High capital costs often reflect high interest rates, real or expected inflation, and an over-heated economy which has become subject to governmental tightening of the money supply.

Three issues in acquisition finance must be resolved by the buyer:

1. How to pay the present target owners.

2. Where to raise money to take over the target.

3. Choosing the *type* of acquisition (private or public tender offer, auction, proxy fight, raid).

4.1.1 PAYING FOR THE ACQUISITION

Acquisitions are financed by (1) *share swaps* in friendly mergers between acquiring and target firms at a mutually agreed price or *stock-for-stock* of the target's shares for acquirer's shares, (2) *debt*—loans, bonds and convertible instruments, and (3) *cash* for all outstanding shares—the simplest and most effective way—on the basis of the creditworthiness ("the free cash flows") of cash-rich companies.

4.1.2 CASH VERSUS DEBT

If cash is paid for the acquisition—even if generated internally—the acquirer's balance sheet can appear overstretched, at least until capital is raised through disposals. On the other hand, if the company issues shares, earnings are diluted in the short run. In addition, longterm projection of profits and earnings with any degree of accuracy of the new combined group is painstaking, if not impossible.

The acquirer can also borrow funds, say up to 2½ times shareholder funds plus written-off good will. In recessionary times, however, it may be difficult to raise money from the investment banks or other sources to finance a cash bid, especially if the target is also a client to the banks and conflicts of interest are involved. Banks evaluate the likelihood of a successful takeover, including government pressures. Even if banks put up the cash, there is a strain on net assets for balancing net debt as the difference in goodwill is written off. One solution is to revalue target assets upwards to compensate for goodwill write-down.

The acquirer can also issue shares to pay for the target, say 6 shares and $1.80 in cash, convertible stock or loan notes. The consolidated balance sheet of the merged group then appears relatively low-geared, although earnings dilution is now a factor. It is interesting to note that for 3,884 transactions covered by AMDATA (UK) in the first nine months of 1992, the mean for company sales price as a multiple of net assets was 4 and the median 1 2/3—a far cry from multiples of 8 and even higher in the late 1980s. The mean price/earnings ratio was 27 and the median 14.

There may also be a need to pay dividends on the extra shares. One solution is to finance with debt the money intended to be raised from disposals, which can be pre-sold, using shares for the part of the target the acquirer plans to keep. The Hanson Group and many others use this strategy (A2, B16, D12).

4.1.3 SOURCING ACQUISITION FINANCE

New forms of "creative financing" emerged during the last two decades that facilitate expansion and return maximization via M&A. The new "financial packages" re-address traditional corporate accounting as well as the assignment of risks and returns. For example, the need for billion dollar loans for offshore oil and other large-scale projects during the 1970s made multibank loan syndication a prevalent form that allowed a large number of lenders to share the risks and rewards of one project. The corporate acquirer has been given more choice in accessing finance, often at lower capital costs. In spite of a general recession and lay-offs in the banking sector, M&A departments thrived until very recently. As competition for merging and divesting clients increases in the 1990s, corporate finance departments of banks and investment houses worldwide will offer more advisory and packaging services to clients. Mergers and acquisitions is a permanent entry on the agenda of investment finance departments.

Creative financing aims at improving the accessibility and lowering the capital costs of acquisition finance. By strip financing, i.e., by providing equity or lower-grade "junk" finance to acquirers—at the same time protecting own interests with debt covenants, i.e., special clauses concerning the future use of funds—venture capitalists, banks and other financial groups have enabled individual and corporate acquirers to undertake massive takeovers as well as smaller MBOs.

A conventional financial mix is 80% per share in cash, 16% PIK or other preferred stock, and 4% in convertible debentures. Average sourcing of takeover finance might be:

- 60% commercial bank loans (attached with covenants to protect the banks)

- 10% from the buyer-principal (a thimbleful of cash and a wheelbarrow load of debt)

• 30% direct from slow-moving major insurance and pension companies (up until the arrival, at least, of speedier junk bond intermediaries)

In the eighties financial packaging coupled with capital abundance at relatively low interest rates encouraged the popular rise of the LBO, or leveraged buyout and its in-house form the management buyout (MBO). The new debt instruments allowed company managers and third-party entrepreneurs to finance acquisitions. Like a mouse that roars, small groups are thus enabled to take over large public companies.

Furthermore, the 1980s bond and particularly Eurobond markets were replete with new instruments. As atoms smashed into sparks and quarks and muons, new financial instruments with equally bizarre names appeared as unemployed particle physicists apply advanced mathematics and computing skills to new banking careers. The new financial instruments similarly "dissemble" debt and debt-like instruments as well equity and currency contracts into their component parts, and re-assemble them through time to different holders with different risk-reward profiles, thus customizing returns for conservative and risk-taking investors alike.

Lending not against assets but against cashflows is another approach that started in the USA, was accepted to a lesser extent by Japanese bankers and with greater reluctance by European lenders. LBO and MBO candidates have tended to be companies with substantial physical assets that can be sold to generate cash, or against which debt can be secured. In the case of the MBO of Britain's MW Marshall, a money brokerage "cash flow business", asset cover fell far short of required debt funding. The final financing of £184 million (very roughly US$ 350 million) comprised three components: £34 (US$ 65) million of equity, £20 (US$ 38) million of mezzanine debt, £130 (US$ 250) million of senior debt, backed only with £40 millon of conventional assets.

Furthermore, as new futures and options contracts open at the Chicago's Chicago Mercantile Exchange and CBOT, London's LIFFE and LBOT, Paris' MATIF and Frankfurt's DTB exchanges, there are increasing numbers of opportunities for hedging the interest rate and the exchange rate risks of merger packages. This trend will increase in the future. Interest rate swaps and other methods for hedging interest rate risk also have blurred the traditional distinction between short-term and long-term debt. Buyout debt has generally been at the long-term end of the market implying cheaper borrowing rates and well-hedged borrowers. Recent developments, however, imply that long-term debt shall be far dearer in the future. Recently, medium-term notes have become a growing source of funds. In the case of MW Marshall, the financial package was structured in a number of different currencies to lower the interest rate base, also minimizing currency risk by layering in those currencies in which the income streams occur.

What kind of mix can be anticipated in future takeover financial sourcing? It is difficult to say, although the bank portion will shrink materially unless warrants (incentives) are legally available.

4.2 A FINANCIAL CYCLE: THE DEBT-EQUITY CLOCK

An interesting aspect of mergers and acquisitions is the rigor of valuation required in all aspects of corporate activity in order to correctly assess the selling price of a company. Corporate price is generally based on current cash flows adjusted for risk, plus projected future cash flows - based on market demand for products or services, as well as asset replacement values. Price is an outcome of the capital structure of the transaction as expressed by interests most at stake (senior and subordinated debt holders, top management and key equity holders) and what their recourse to the project is in times of distress (i.e., the terms of repayment, or who will be paid back first). An underlying ethical issue is whether those receiving large payments and control at the time of acquisition settlement are also those who bear future risks, for example, the new manager-owners of LBOs.

In this context one can delineate a cycle of causalities triggering or dissuading mergers and acquisitions. *Equity takeovers are more likely to occur.* 1) When money is made cheap and abundant to counteract recession such as in early 1991, or alternatively, 2) when the stock prices of the acquirer are high relative to target stock prices, thus encouraging stock-for-stock exchanges.

A simple causality model can be formulated: the Debt/Equity Clock. When the equity proportion of the total capital structure is high then it is "time to borrow". When the debt proportion is high, then it is time to issue equity. The probable debt-equity ratio for any one period is described by the rotating diameter of the clock, which "ticks" according to shifting or gearing in interest

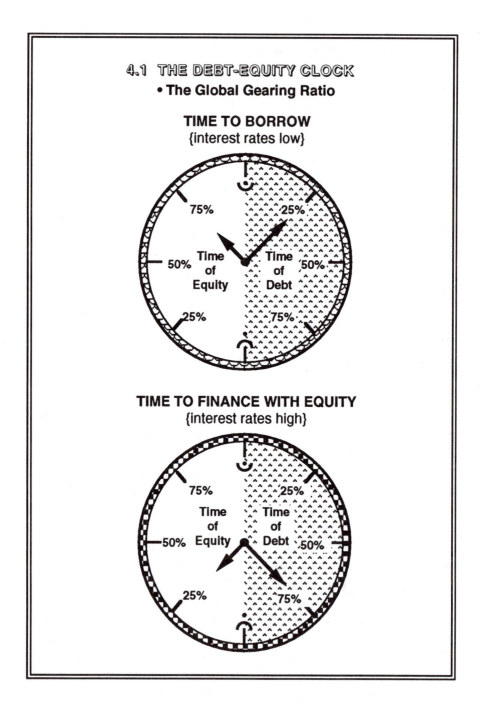

4.1 THE DEBT-EQUITY CLOCK
• The Global Gearing Ratio

TIME TO BORROW
{interest rates low}

75%   25%

50%   Time   Time   50%
       of   of
       Equity Debt

25%   75%

TIME TO FINANCE WITH EQUITY
{interest rates high}

75%   25%

       Time   Time
       of   of
50%   Equity Debt   50%

25%   75%

rates and rates of inflation, and to a lesser extent due to changes in the volume of money supply.

4.2.1 THE HOURS OF EQUITY

When a company is highly leveraged, especially with *new* debt, then a new round of equity issues can be expected. The debt-equity clock correctly predicts that after the long period of borrowing and high levels of debt during the 1980s, equity issues should abound during the 1990s. In 1991, there was substantial activity especially in the IPO market. According to the Securities Industry Association, after a long downtrend beginning in 1987, the level of new stock issued reached a new high in 1991 of $71.9 billion, over three times more than the preceding year. IPOs increase with the popularity of the stock market as a "last best" investment, with interest rates now lower due to central bank easing to stimulate the sluggish, over-indebted economy, the popularity of the bond markets may decrease. Whether the debt-equity clock has merely illustrative value to demonstrate shifts in cumulative debt-equity ratios, or whether it has predictive value can be determined by regressions analysis.

The fragility of the clock is manifested by the purpose of financing: in recent months, initial public offerings (IPOs) equity and junk bond issues have been undertaken in order to service old debt. In fact, some companies offer equity to creditors in private restructuring where debt holders are paid stock rather than cash for all or part of the positions. Although the clock ticks on, the overall *quality* of corporate borrowing has, in this instance, eroded.

As stock prices rise, corporate debt-equity ratios shift in such a way that firms are able to support more debt financing, at least ostensibly. More debt financing at lower interest rates is made available, as low inflation encourages central banks to lower interest rates which in turn expand liquidity. As bank lending capacity is allowed to expand, cheap debt financing is available for acquisition of assets bearing prices that have been suppressed by a previous recession induced by earlier inflation fighting. Internal cash flows are also made "free" for acquisitions. The attractiveness of acquiring is thus "regulated" or determined by a **"slippage factor"**, or the negative correlation between price increases for depreciating old assets and the inflated prices of new assets (see Tobin's q below).

62

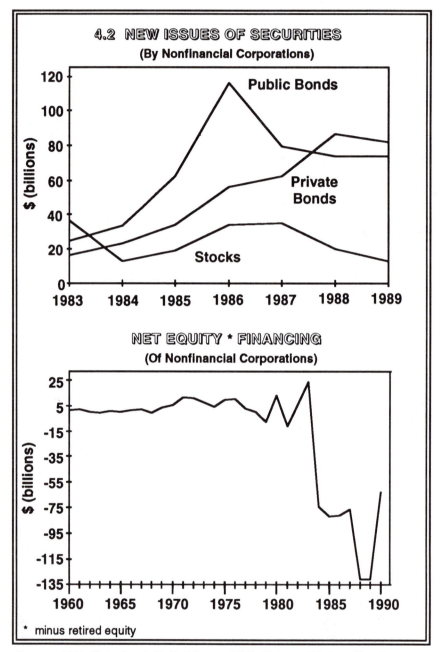

4.2 NEW ISSUES OF SECURITIES
(By Nonfinancial Corporations)

Public Bonds

Private Bonds

Stocks

$ (billions)

120
100
80
60
40
20
0

1983 1984 1985 1986 1987 1988 1989

NET EQUITY * FINANCING
(Of Nonfinancial Corporations)

$ (billions)

25
5
-15
-35
-55
-75
-95
-115
-135

1960 1965 1970 1975 1980 1985 1990

* minus retired equity

Source: M.H. Pickering, L.E. Crabbe, and S.D. Prowse, "Recent Developments in Corporate Finance," *Federal Reserve Bulletin*, Aug. 1990.

Importantly, however, as stock prices rise, the acquirer's debt-to-equity ratio decreases, and the company is capable of supporting more debt financing. At the same time, creative financial manoeuvers with convertible, stripped and covenant features also increase as the corporate finance departments of large banks vie for M&A corporate clients. These departments also become more involved in servicing the strategic planning and other ancillary requirements of their corporate clients. The debt-equity clock ticks forward into the hours of debt.

Surprisingly, according to Crabbe, Pickering and Prowse of the US Federal Reserve, since 1982, rising equity prices have largely countered the rise in corporate indebtedness (B33). Merton Miller substantiates this point by reportedly asserting that "there's less leverage than people think because debt to equity book value is As stock prices increase, mergers also increase, thereby reducing total market capitalization until stock market indices and market p/e ratios reach all-time highs, credit tightens, and/or inflation drops more than debt to market value."[23]. Similarly, the D/E clock demonstrates that the debt-equity ratio seeks an elusive equilibrium across time. What the D/E Clock does **not** reveal, however, is declining financial health. This occurs when new stock issues are used to service debt. For example, the ratio of interest expense to cash flow has deteriorated in recent years. It is estimated that 40-60% of new issues are consumed by interest payments. In comparison, according to the Federal Flow of Funds and Moody's estimates, net interest payments consumed 22 cents of each US dollar of corporate cash flows in 1981, dropping to a low of 18½ cents in 1985, and rising to 26 cents in 1990. Interest expenses of nonfinancial corporations declined in 1991 for the first time in years. Merton Miller, similarly asserts that markets are self-correcting mechanisms. If corporations issue more debt than the public wants, then interest rates change to discourage it. About 40% of all outstanding bonds have been downrated because of leverage increases; one-fourth of the rating reductions are related to restructurings. The clock ticks on.

The debt-equity clock also does not reveal shifts in the levels of *internal* cash flows and internal financing. It would be interesting to add a third dimension

---

[23] *The Wall Street Journal*, Dec. 16, 1991, A8.

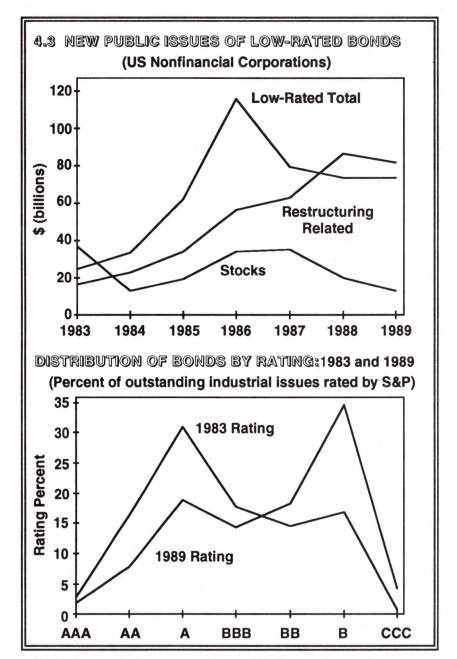

4.3 NEW PUBLIC ISSUES OF LOW-RATED BONDS
(US Nonfinancial Corporations)

Low-Rated Total

Restructuring
Related

Stocks

$ (billions)

DISTRIBUTION OF BONDS BY RATING:1983 and 1989
(Percent of outstanding industrial issues rated by S&P)

1983 Rating

1989 Rating

Rating Percent

Source: M.H. Pickering, L.E. Crabbe, and S.D. Prowse, "Recent Developments in Corporate Finance," *Federal Reserve Bulletin*, Aug. 1990.

to the clock (like an independent second hand) on a case-by-case basis to reflect shifts in retained earnings and internal investment.

Asset availability is in part determined by: (1) The desire of managers to sell and benefit from golden parachutes, "windfall" profits and other "surplus returns"; (2) the degree of distress in the recession-insolvent firm, and (3) the degree to which assets have already been written off by the original owner. Depreciation schedules determine the life of a turnaround.

An increase in merger activity was readily observable during the 1980s when interest rates were raised to combat 1970s inflation. The D/E clock was heavily weighted towards equity during the 1970s and 1980s. To take advantage of low asset values through acquisitions, acquirers first tended to resort to cash buyouts, then stock swaps, and earn-out formulae.[24] Finally, as the clock ticked on, high yield or "junk" financing during the 1980s tapped available liquidity by promising attractive returns.

As interest rates rise, debt-financed mergers tend to decrease because of the higher costs associated with raising acquisition finance. The 1980s bond boom—with positive correlations to a merger wave and a long period of high interest rates—was followed by a decline in interest rates, in the number of high-yield bonds and in mergers during 1990-1991. This suggests that high bond yields attract investors who provide acquisition finance without being fully aware of the high risks involved. However, the positive correlation of decreasing junk bond sales and mergers may be more due to the unpopularity of junk bonds after the widespread collapse of that market in 1989-90 than to diminishing coupon rates.[25] Junk bonds are more sensitive to financial distress than ordinary bonds, as aptly proven in the first half of 1990. In fact, not until mid-1990 when bond yields rose to phenomenal levels (20 - 100% was not uncommon) did massive responses from less risk-averse institutional investors provides for corrections in risk-reward ratios.

---

[24]I.e., stock and/or cash payments in stages to the seller depending on the level of performance in the larger group.

[25]Some maintain that only public junk sales have dropped off. The private junk market continues to thrive.

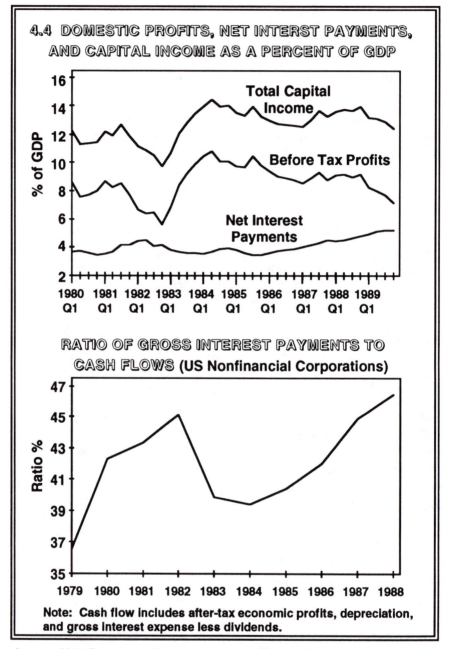

4.4 DOMESTIC PROFITS, NET INTERST PAYMENTS, AND CAPITAL INCOME AS A PERCENT OF GDP

Total Capital Income

Before Tax Profits

Net Interest Payments

RATIO OF GROSS INTEREST PAYMENTS TO CASH FLOWS (US Nonfinancial Corporations)

Note: Cash flow includes after-tax economic profits, depreciation, and gross interest expense less dividends.

Source: M.H. Pickering, L.E. Crabbe, and S.D. Prowse, "Recent Developments in Corporate Finance," *Federal Reserve Bulletin*, Aug. 1990.

This trend was heightened in the US after October 1979, when Paul Volcker allowed interest rates to float in response to 1970s inflation and stagflation (i.e., inflation combined curiously with no or low growth). Mortgage rates—already subject to change due to high and fluctuating interest rates, were now more prone to repackaging in the form of new instruments and issues due to take-off in the bond markets, in turn riding on the back of speculative windows created by the new volatility in interest rates. The end result may be termed "leverage saturation" characterized by: 1) high debt-equity ratios; 2) banks lent out to the limits of their reserve requirements, and 3) multiple corporate insolvencies as persisting high treasury (or gilt or lombard) rates remain in a continuing battle against inflation. Leverage saturation occurred in 1990 and 1991. The incremental drop in interest rates driven by central governments attempting to stimulate the economy that began in August 1990 reached its lowest level by the end of 1991 since 1973. Weak M&A transaction rates have encouraged investment bankers to seek alternative income streams from consulting and distribution deals. When the stock market falls stagflation may be supplanted, at least in the short run, by a classic Keynesian liquidity trap.

Up until now the debt-equity clock on the wall of finance has been viewed largely from the angle of the borrowing company. Entering the room behind the wall where assets become liabilities, one can observe the D/E Clock from the banker's point of view.

When interest rates are low, banks want to borrow and lend, but there is little to borrow because few of the bank's clients are saving as interest rates are too low to save money in banks. When interest rates are high, people want to save, but they don't want to borrow. However, if everyone *starts* to borrow, the interest rate goes even higher. What is important to the banker is the margin or the "spread" between the average cost of funds (the savings rate or the rate at which banks borrow, often defined as the rate in the 12th district of the Federal Reserve System of the western states) and the lending rate. The spread is how banks make money. The spread must usually be 2—3 percent for a reasonable profit. It is squeezed hard at the top and the bottom of its cycle—at the top because banks can't afford to borrow, and at the bottom because the banks must pay up to acquire money to lend. The depth of the spread also depends on whether interest rates are going up or down. When interest rates drop, the spread is typically greater and bankers make more money. Thus the

Maschmeier or banker's dilemma is that when bankers want to lend there is no money, and when money is cheap and available no one wants to borrow. If interest rates didn't drop rapidly from time to time, thus creating a very profitable spread for bankers, they would probably go out of business, as many of them did in the late 1980s when interest rates were still very high.

4.2.3 RICH MAN POORER MAN

Monetary stringency and higher capital costs create higher risk premiums for less profitable firms.[26] At the same time, during periods of tight money, new, cyclical or mature companies with lower cash flows and higher leverage ratios are hit hard by high capital costs. Taking late 1989 and 1990 as examples, many new and mature firms in increasingly competitive yet standardized and proven markets became financially insolvent. The pool of firms suitable for acquisitions increased. These firms are more vulnerable than ever by "cash cow" acquirers with strong internal cash flows, lower risks, and relatively enhanced borrowing power.[27] We then witness the "rich man - poor man" scenario: the rich get richer, and the poor are acquired. Cash kings use retained earnings and equity financing to pick up cheap corporate "steals" through merger deals.

After a period of cash stress, merger activity has a tendency to slow down (1989/1990). The decrease in merger volume is amplified by public outcries against corporate raiders, insider malfeasance, and junk bonds. Investors complain as savings and loans associations and even banks collapse. Low inflation coupled with low interest rates encourage asset investment as opposed to asset acquisition, especially for companies requiring significant asset upgrading that are also eligible for government tax and other incentives. As capital costs and construction costs drop relative to previous periods, external

---

[26] Throughout most of western history interest rates were usually fixed and rarely exceeded five percent! Hyperinflation and high interest rates are predominantly a phenomenon of the twentieth century. Important here is that interest rates were less demanding on future income streams, and they were easier to predict.

[27] Siemens of Germany, for example, sat in the financial sidelines well into the 1980s. Rather than finance expansion, Siemens chose to invest retained earnings in the financial markets, earning higher returns there than from actual operations. When opportunities emerged to acquire assets through acquisitions of other companies, Siemens was subsequently well-positioned.

expansion no longer appears easier, cheaper and quicker. Furthermore, awareness increases amongst entrepreneurs that releasing control to bankers, LBO firms, venture capitalists or even shareholders as required by externally financed expansion exposes the firm to the external risks of the financial environment and the lenders' whims. In 1990/1 even working capital requirements were often externally financed. Other methods for financing mergers besides debt are sought.

In the second quarter of 1990, the debt-equity clock ticked on: Interest rates began to drop. Low interest rates predictably stimulated stock market activity as investors (borrowed and) migrated from the bond and money markets to the stock markets in search of higher anticipated returns.

The correlation between interest rate changes and merger activity can be exemplified. Lord Hanson, one of the last western acquisition barons to remain solvent, is reported to maintain his UK£ 7.5 billion Hanson Group (Britain's "seventh largest empire" with 20% per annum growth) by a seemingly simple strategy. The Hanson portfolio is based on businesses that are low-risk and require little capital investment, but generate considerable cash with improved management (A40). Low-technology companies are bought cheaply and turned around with strict cash management. Superfluous parts of the business are sold off, expectantly successful at a healthy profit. Characteristically, Hanson quickly sells off parts of newly acquired businesses to buyers willing to pay a premium price. Local managers of companies Hanson acquires are given considerable autonomy. They are told to run the companies as if the money were their own. A pre-tax payback on investment is expected in about three years. Some executives complain of negative management because the hurdles for having capital projects approved are so high. One former Hanson executive maintains that profit today is overriding reinvestment tomorrow (D12).

Perhaps the main key to the Hanson formula is arbitrage. The Hanson Group reportedly borrows at low interest rates in the United States for re-investment in the UK. In this case, solid asset-based acquisitions serve to expand the credit base for further borrowings. The current economic environment encourages the Hansons of this world to acquire: after being a net seller of companies in 1988/89, new acquisitions by the Hanson Group may be back on the agenda.

As mentioned earlier, merger activity increases when interest rates are high, but also when interest rates are low! Let us account for this anomaly. The externalities that drive the interest rate engine - inflation, the money supply, the interest rate, GNP shifts, and changes in the legal and tax environment - are critical in determining the *type* and *level* of merger activity.

Low interest rates are usually associated with increased trading volume and rising prices in the stock markets. This explains why low interest rates lead to more acquisitions, as companies relying heavily on borrowed funds take advantage of the low capital costs for financing public takeovers at (share) prices that are anticipated to rise. If the merger is financed with acquirer shares, central is the *relative value of target shares to acquirer shares* - based on value ratios such as Tobin's q-ratio of asset values to share prices (see below). If an external factor such as 1970s inflation occurs, asset values are inflated. Opportunities to acquire another company's assets at relatively lower *share* prices and to depreciate acquired assets arise. At the same time debt ratios of the highly leveraged acquirers are reduced. Then it is cost effective to acquire growth, rather than build up a new company or branch. The debt-equity clock moves on.

Chapter Five addresses more closely the *kinds* of change that trigger certain forms of consolidation, and the *types* of company formation emerging as a consequence. For example, in a recession, are companies more inclined to collapse, or to sell out? During a recession both buyers and sellers alike perceive that there are more companies to buy. Thus, setting aside cloak and dagger negotiating strategies, both buyer and seller may actually *agree* about the fair value of a firm. The seller, however, may prefer to retire under a golden parachute, or start a new business. The buyer may be primarily interested in expanding product line. A harmony of interests and perceptions is easier to manage in the fraught and enduring postacquisition phase than a prickly forest full of bitter deceptions. The oft cited divergence of interests (see B32) may be more applicable to third parties, "outsiders", and stock market speculators than to merging marriage partners choosing the pr frosting for the new corporate cake.

Moreover, corporate buyers and sellers are no less vulnerable to lemming behavior than bankers or stock market speculators. Styles of corporate expansion are as trend-ridden and volatile as skirt lengths. Successful negotiation of merger transactions is a process of drawing out compatible interests and dissuading interest conflicts.

4.3 STOCK MARKET MOVEMENTS AND MERGER WAVES

4.3.1 THE M&A BAROMETER

According to several studies (see Checklists 7.1.2) merger waves peak before stock markets by one month (I34). Others claim that the stock market peaks (or bottoms out) three months before the merger wave peaks (or bottoms out) I26. Merger waves also climax before business cycles (GNP and industrial production) by five months. Merger waves also precede overall economic activity. Furthermore, stock markets bottom out and begin to turn up well before the end of a recession (four months in the US). The trough of the merger wave is also reported to lag by a three month average behind the stock market. Further studies are needed to refine the correlations between the number and value of mergers in any one period and broad economic indicators. Let us say here that mergers waves serve as a barometer of the economic climate. Similar to the level of start-ups, M&A waves indicate shifts not only of the business cycle but also of the overall economic environment. Mergers, acquisitions and divestments regulate the **pool of business firms**.

The fact that M&A correlates positively with stock market expansion (what is termed here "boom mergers") and positively with troughs in the GNP ("bust consolidation") suggests to us that merger activity may be a **magnifier** of current trends, at least an indicator of economic change. Mergers and acquisitions increase in boom periods. Yet mergers also increase in recessions. To explore the M&A Barometer in more depth let us further distinguish merger activity in good times and bad.

Recession mergers follow previous high inflation, taking advantage of currently suppressed stock market prices. If interest rates are held low by the central government in order to stimulate the economy, the acquirer borrows takeover funds. The adjoining table demonstrates the relationship between inflation, interest rates and merger trends.

If company prices are high and the acquirer has low earnings, earnings will be acquired to enhance the corporate price-earnings ratio. The acquirer with high debt levels and no equity will acquire assets with low debt in order to improve the debt-equity ratio. Companies with high earnings and debt-free assets and equity are thus especially prone to being taken over. Such companies take "poison pills" to repel suitors. For example, they acquire debt and stash away or sell off "the crown jewels", valuable assets that attract acquirers.

4.3.2 RECESSION MERGERS

A variety of factors come together to make M&A lucrative during periods of economic slowdown. High interest rates employed to cool off a previously heated economy have a devastating impact on highly leveraged companies. This phenomenon was particularly observable from 1989 onwards as many highly leveraged corporations with diminished revenues fell into bankruptcy. Falling stock prices present excellent buying opportunities for "cash cows", e.g., food companies with strong cash flows, or for companies in growth sectors with stock prices buoyed by earnings strength and growth potential, e.g., parts of the computer and electronics industries. The rich man—poor man syndrome goes into action: the rich go shopping and the poor are acquired. During and after a recession there is a pool of acquirable firms (Bank of New England and other banks, S&Ls) for which more solvent buyers (KKR, Norstar, Bank of America) vie. As demonstrated in 1990/91, new acquisitions during a recession tend to focus increasingly on the acquirer's core business. Likewise, non-core operations tend to be sold off as part of corporate rationalization programs.

The willingness of the seller to sell often is amplified by budgetary constraints that prohibit the technological and other improvements necessary to survive in an overcrowded sector. During a recession, tired and disenchanted managers are prone to consider selling the company rather than wading through debt burdens that recently consume as much as 40 - 60% of gross earnings. Increasingly during 1990/91 in the UK and the USA, selling the firm has been the single alternative to foreclosure.

The combination of vestigially high prices for new assets due to the preceding inflationary period and the low costs of borrowing associated with a government ease on interest rates to stimulate the economy creates a prime period for acquiring (old depreciated) assets through acquisition, as many targets still suffer from inflation government controls.

Sellers, however, recall the higher price multiples of the previous period. For example, in the advertising sector, corporate price multiples of eight times annual earnings available only two years ago have recently dropped to two or three! Consequently, it is likely that sellers must be *lured* by buyers through payment of premiums to market prices. But, as in other markets, price inelasticities do not allow full responses to demand shocks.

During recessions, managers with a flair for self promotion are able to elicit financial backing at low interest rates to buy out firms at distressed prices. The task is difficult, however, as general market sentiment is not susceptible to new endeavor and risk-taking in deep troughs. Banks and venture capitalists already suffer from defaults and failures. The debt-equity clock "ticks" deeper into the equity quartiles. For example, initial public offerings were profuse during 1991 and early 1992.

As used asset and property values fall and interest rates decrease even further, the deep trough of the business cycle presents some of the greatest opportunities for corporate takeover. For similar reasons, during the inflationary 1970s, a consensus developed throughout North America, Western Europe and elsewhere that the individual or corporate credit base was best stretched to the fullest through maximum borrowing. Even if interest rates went up, monetary inflation significantly lowered the value of interest and principal payments. In sum, it became ridiculously cheap to acquire assets through borrowing. In the hands of the financially adept, debt was used to turn slow growth equity into high octane. We categorize M&A that captures capital market anomalies as financial mergers, as opposed to the strategic mergers discussed in Chapter 5.

4.3.3 BOOM MERGERS

To examine the break away from recession standard, arguments from Schumpeter and Kondratieff[28] can be borrowed. Some entrepreneurs retain sufficient fortitude and morale to perceive new growth opportunities due to new cost savings and alternative technologies that debut in recession. Unemployed engineers and venture capitalists look for new ways to survive. Relatively low asset values, low property prices, reduced or cheaper

---

[28] See footnotes in Chapter Five and its appendix.

inventories, and low interest rates conquer sentimental depression. As witnessed in the early years of the 1990s, bankers and other financial bankers think hard about new core technologies that will lead to the future. Stomachs are hungry. Labor is restless and shifting to new industries and new geographic locations. Many capitalists "go bust". Factories as well as distribution centers and administrative facilities close down. Just as the only way up for new merger business in the boom period of the 1980s was into larger and larger deals (followed by smaller and smaller ones when the pool of firms diminished), the only way out of the recession is to go forward by taking advantage of *favorable factor costs.*

Incremental optimism brings incremental success, breeding further optimism. The mood and mode of expansion returns. Economic growth in new technological and market terms causes more investment opportunities. As economic sentiment shifts, so does the general proclivity towards risk. The boom is on. Financial and economic accelerators and multipliers are put in gear.

Acquisitions to increase market reach cause vertical or conglomerate migration out of the core sector. As success breeds success, the acquiring firm expands towards suppliers and end consumers in order to provide "one-stop shopping". The vertical trend was especially prevalent in the 1980s in the financial services sector as banks integrated a full range of services under one logo. Finally, as markets become saturated and weakened by the arrival of new competition, the corporation attempts to diversify risk by entering new sectors.

The conglomerate-building trend in the mature product phase is particularly vivid in the automobile industry. BMW and Daimler Benz, for decades the hallmarks of high quality automobiles, witness their markets threatened by the Japanese Lexus and other brands. Both companies are actively acquiring and investing in electronics, telecommunications, sonar imaging and other non-core sectors.

During boom periods sellers tend to bail out with good stock prices and rich incentives, often under the now optimistic assumption that they can start other ventures in related or other sectors. The smaller company anticipates further growth and earnings within the context of a larger group. Premiums increase as the pool of companies available for purchase diminishes with the boom.

However, a rising stock market and growth-related inflation spell out its demise.

Of 512 chief executives surveyed by Fortune Magazine in the mid-1980s, 9 % owned none of their companies' stock and 5.9 % owned less than $100,000 worth. By the end of the booming 1980s, LBO managers often owned four times as much equity upon transaction completion. However, the management share of net worth, i.e., the amount invested from personal funds, actually declined. Concomitantly and especially after 1985, as returns to managers increased, so did upfront fees to their advisors. As leveraging increased, the proportion of bank-originated debt decreased relative to public debt. Moreover, the average corporate selling price increased relative to cash flows, although *not* relative to market valuation.

We have observed that merger opportunities arise due to surrounding macroeconomic conditions such as shifts in the money supply and the type of money available; interest rate volatility and shifts in the GNP. By the late 1980s, the conditions that favor boom mergers—low real interest rates and low inflation—had largely disappeared. Therefore, the incentives for boom mergers that drive up asset replacement costs as well as stock prices—were gone.

4.3.4 A TIME TO BUY, A TIME TO SELL
An underlying theme of the stock-event literature is that welfare issues, or the "goodness' of mergers, should be weighed in terms of returns to shareholders, or what is "fair" for the shareholder. The average shareholder, however, may be more migrant than the corporate acquirer and as profit-oriented as the deal arbitrageur. The market shareholder may retain stock for a far shorter period of time than the founder-owner, managers, and other employees receiving company stock bonuses or warrants (see ESOPs in Chapter Five). We are not aware of a study that attempts to quantify the average shareholder "life" and expectations.

From a motivational standpoint, shareholders often are not the key decision-making elements of a takeover. The majority of worldwide takeovers are friendly or private. Corporate founder-owners sell for monetary return or for market centrality, or for executive benefits. Non-raiding strategic buyers purchase not for windfall market gains (to the contrary, the winner's curse suggests that successful bidders pay success premiums), but rather to acquire an asset or market necessary for expansion. Specific assets include distribution channels, new markets, technology, a research capacity, a logo, good will and other intangibles, or rich cash flow streams. Although acquiring for profit-maximizing reasons may not benefit shareholder returns in the short term it may in the long run, although recent takeover speculative behavior suggests more short-term gains.

One acquisition scenario is of particular interest in this regard. Acquirers use their own appreciated stock as acquisition currency, as sellers in strategic sectors still command high prices. Stock swaps become attractive. The seller is able to disburse of, say, 10 - 20% of the firm in the stock market, instead of selling off the whole company in the private market.

If there is a total or quasi-liquidity trap concomitant with high stock prices, low interest rates and stagflation in a lean and pessimistic economy, the availability of low-rate financing will *not* incentivize mergers by stock purchase. For example, in mid-1991, merger prices were discounted 10.7% compared to stock market prices. By comparison, during the first three quarters of 1987, acquirers paid a 48.9% premium for companies when the S&P 500 traded up to 23 times earnings (A1).

Similar to buying stocks and bonds, there are good times to buy companies and there are bad times. In the late 1980's the conditions that encouraged M&A - previous high interest rates and inflation driving up asset values - disappeared. Those same disincentives for long term earnings that had also driven up asset replacement costs and dropped stock prices were gone.[29] Do corporate *buyers* worry about making more profit from a cash, stock or mixed offering? The gains to *shareholders*, if any, have proven hard to define;

---

[29] According to Barrie Wigmore, limited partner at Goldman Sachs, 38% of the rise in the S&P indices in the 1980s remains unaccounted for. Corporate performance is ruled out, higher earnings accounting for only 24% of the rise, and overly optimistic earnings for a mere further 15%. Lower interest rates account for 11% of the upwardation, and mergers for only 12% - although many stocks rose on the "mere whisper" of a takeover until the high-stakes merger game "washed up" by the end of 1989. The S&P was not distorted by a few new industries, nor did cash flow grow much more than earnings. Both 1979 and 1989 were preceded, however, by prolonged economic and earnings growth (ROEs of 15.8% and 15.6%, respectively) and anticipation of an approaching recession (B39).

studies indicate that target (seller) gains range from a mere 2% to a grand 35%. Studies (B82) show higher abnormal returns for cash (29-34%) than for stock offers (14-17%), or for mixed cash-stock offers (12-23%). *In about one-half of all takeovers acquiring shareholders actually lose wealth, at least in the short term.* The benefits of acquisition are not reflected in the buyer's share prices, at least in the short term.

Since the 1970s it seems that buyers are pro-active, aggressive, and price-motivated, and that sellers are more passive, particularly in hostile acquisitions not sought by the seller. However, stock-event studies almost universally conclude that the shares of target sellers fare better than shares of acquiring buyers. This would suggest that target decision-makers (especially when they are shareholders) are concerned with payment. Buyers, on the other hand, are more inclined to look towards longer-term synergies and profitability. Even in the case of resale asset-stripping, more important to the buyer than high "abnormal returns" are the *values of earnings and future income streams.* As greenmailer Sam Belzburg stated, we are entrepreneurs, not stock players. Many takeover experts are probably less concerned with immediate stock price returns as with longterm corporate growth; the emphasis of the stock-event literature on immediate to five year gain does not reflect the other interests of the acquirer. The time frame of the stock-event studies may not be long enough.

Stock-event study outcomes must be weighed against the impact of aggregate small investors and institutional traders (large brokerage houses, banks, and pension and insurance funds). Individual portfolios of giant institutional investors are often much larger than the total price of the company for sale. This fact offers negotiating clout to large institutional buyers (see Chapter Five).

In addition, as an exogenous and exponentializing factor, high-volume program trading must be weighed in stock-event studies. To our knowledge, the potentially amplifying impact of program trading on stock prices during an acquisition has not been fully assessed. To the contrary, the only reference we came across discusses program trading as an "assessment of expected fair value by the market place"!

Along the same lines, Opler finds evidence that "bad" acquisitions with high price penalties imposed by the market may not be negative NPV investments; a bad acquisition may lead to a bad stock price (B32). In this instance, the final acquisition price at completion - perhaps inflated by an anxious buyer with winner's curse - may not reflect the full price cycle of the stock. At later phases, "abnormal" acquisition costs may be absorbed as forecasted synergies boost revenues.

The stock-event studies also do not seem to distinguish amongst *types* of buyers and sellers. For example, divestors in a distress sale with disgruntled creditors are less likely to achieve the highest price. A retiring president who sells his private company built up into a cash-rich empire, might.

Furthermore, stock-event studies do not to give sufficient weight to the *high level* of debt financing which predominated in the 1980s. Although stock payment is a critical issue, it may not be the driving consideration of either buyers ar sellers.

4.4 TOBIN'S Q: THE SPECIAL CASE OF ASSET ACQUISITION THROUGH MERGERS

Growth by acquisition of physical, technological, management and intangible assets of other firms predominated in the 1980s. What factors led to the transition from internal to external expansion both domestically and abroad, and what does this inform us about shifts in the economic and financial environment? Central to understanding firm behavior is how the externalization of growth has effected corporate financial strategy, and how this trend has evolved in recent tumultuous months.

The high rate of spending on plant and equipment through M&A indicates that mergers constitute a significant way to expand through asset acquisition. When interest rates and inflation are high, asset replacement costs are frequently forced higher; arbitrage between stock prices and asset values by acquiring assets through takeover, rather than purchasing new assets, is strategically lucrative. If the buyer is a holding company with primarily financial objectives, the buyer may choose to asset-strip, or acquire a company at a discount for further sale of certain assets which are undervalued, for example, by inefficient management or suboptimal capital structure.

According to this popular argument, investment through mergers is undertaken to capture economic returns, for example, of assets undervalued by inflation, or "hidden" assets such as goodwill that are not properly reflected by book nor stock market values. Tobin's q-ratio is cited in this regard. We can derive, for example, from Wigmore that stocks which were selling for 50% of per share costs of replicating firm assets (q-ratio) are traded in 1990 at a premium to replacement value (B39).

In terms of maximizing returns to the firm and its key decision makers, M&A is micro-driven toward deal returns that are termed "financial". It may be cheaper to buy another company's old assets than to build or buy new assets. Assets may also be acquired for divestiture, that is for further resale on the company market. The Deutsche Bank, for example, is currently making a business of buying eastern German companies from the Government Trust or *Treuhand* and turning them around for resale. Lord Hanson also takes over companies for quick asset turnaround.

Tobin's q-ratio (or just q) is a ratio of share prices and debt to asset replacement costs. Q may be intuitively pleasing although its accuracy is highly dependent upon measurement criteria and exogenous economic variables, and frequently does not hold true with regard to shifts in prices and levels of M&A for any one time period.   Golbe and White have observed that q:

> is a measurement of the ratio of prices to costs at one point in time, whereas mergers and acquisitions activity is measured as a flow over a period of time (a quarter or a year) it is the *change* in q between two points in time that should be affected by the level of merger and acquisition activity during that time period. Further analysis of the components' influences - specifically, the level of real GNP, any unexpected changes in real GNP, the level or real interest rates, any unexpected changes in real interest rates, the capital stock at the end of the period, and the value of q at the beginning of the period - should also be important (D22).

Buy now, pay later: assets are "paid for now" instead of against future cash flows. However, *most* asset acquisitions are paid for today (or leased across time, which is equivalent to the M&A "earn-out" formula whereby after an initial principle payment, future payments for target assets are based on future asset earnings). Likewise, a post-LBO acquirer must sell off enough assets and generate enough cash flow to service a debt burden assumed in order to buy the assets (D5).

Selling assets acquired to pay for their purchase may be an innovation of M&A. The principle of buying cheap and selling dear, however, with or without added value, is standard practice.

4.4.1 UNDERVALUATION

From the seller's standpoint there are several ways of coping with a bad q or company undervaluation besides being acquired. Alternatives are more salient in the 1990s:

(1) Go private like Virgin, Invergordon Distilleries and Magnet in the UK.

(2) Recapitalize the company by raising debt and buying back substantial blocks of shares. Increasing debt will reduce the cost of capital if debt holders expect returns of 10 - 14% and equity holders returns of 24%.

(3) Find new shareholders, for example by listing shares on another stock exchange, probably overseas.

(4) Restructure operationally, for example by selling off non-core businesses.

The disclosure of lacunae in traditional accounting methods coupled with tax changes enabled corporate acquirers to take advantage of undervalued assets. These assets are often at book value without intangibles such as good will, compared with total market capitalization, or share value, of the firm. Serial acquirers by necessity become more sophisticated as the M&A deal flow continues and competition becomes tougher. One consequence are innovative approaches to basic accounting methods. For example, *a new accounting practice that raises borrowing* clout against corporate balance sheets, at the same time steering raiders away, is the capitalization of acquired brands, or making intangibles tangible.

4.4.2 CHANGES IN ACCOUNTING PROCEDURES AFFECTING M&A: THE CASE OF BRAND VALUATION

Britain's Grand Metropolitan, a major food producer that acquired giant U.S. Pillsbury, is a leader in adopting a capitalization policy that records acquired brand names on its balance sheet instead of the common practice of recognizing only tangible assets on a balance sheet (D54). The value of purchased brand names as an intangible asset in the group balance sheet adds UK £ 500 million to corporate assets previously written off as goodwill. The company's *own* developed brands are not valued. The capitalized brands are significant brands only, and the values are not amortized since they should be preserved by extensive brand support. The firm also is having professional valuations carried out on most group properties (D54).

The revival of this old concept has been encouraged by the takeover of brand-rich companies such as Rowntree with high price-earning ratios. The new climate also has prompted companies to reassess internal brands (D30). Other factors increasing the value of brands include the finding that *brand potential generally is underexploited*, especially in view of the costs associated with launching a new brand (D30).

Although the new approach falls in line with historical cost accounting rules, most other major UK companies that own valuable brand names do not place values on them. Various positions are taken on this issue. Grand Metropolitan has stimulated the thinking of other firms (D30).[30]

---

[30] Several UK companies recently have considered having brands listed as assets on their balance sheet. Lord Hanson of the Hanson Group, for example, has declared that the conventional ways of evaluating companies are inappropriate. More attention should be placed on such intangibles as brands and people. While brands are a long-term valuation, the ratio of profits to earnings is a short-term factor. An underlying question involves how to assign a precise value to which everyone agrees. Grand Metropolitan lobbied the Accounting Standards Committee to make it easier to place acquired brands on a balance sheet rather than writing them off against reserves (C49). Cadbury Typhoo has developed a computer program that assesses that impact of different rates of advertising expenditures on a brand's financial returns.

(continued...)

The alternative accounting treatment of goodwill—or recognizing acquired brands as separate assets—may have negative implications:

> 1. A dramatic fall in the acquiring company reserves if the target company was acquired at a high premium over the value of its net **tangible** assets (i.e., the high corporate sales price drains reserves).

> 2. Future reported profits may be affected adversely.

> 3. More valuable assets can be identified and a reader of corporate accounts can assess the brand's continuing contribution to the company's performance (i.e., outsiders have access to otherwise confidential insider information) (D54).

Drawbacks to capitalization include:

> 1. The inconsistency of recognizing brands acquired, yet not recognizing sound, internally generated brands. Valuing acquired brands is very difficult. The task is even more onerous for internally generated brands. Various methods are being proposed to value brand names such as the calculation of the multiple of sustainable earnings contributed by each brand (D54).

> 2. A company may want to run down a brand slowly. However, publishing its declining value is a sure giveaway to rivals (D37).

> 3. Uncertainty remains whether or not brand values depreciate over time like other assets (D37).

Other companies are including the intangible value of trademarks acquired on their balance sheets C50.

However, on a more favorable note, if brands are properly capitalized, they can be borrowed against (D37).

4.5 WHY MORE DEBT: THE INCREASE IN DEBT FINANCING

Traditionally firms endeavor to keep a sound credit rating, a solid level of retained earnings and debt-to-equity ratios as low as 1:1. In the 1970s, however, classic business approaches ended. Creditworthiness was used to extend debt capacity to the maximum limit to increase corporate control by expansion. The single corporate raider did addition in hostile form. The largest stock markets—the US and the UK—were centers for merger activity. Foreign takeovers were influenced by fluctuations in foreign currency rates (note the low value of the US dollar from 1984 until 1991 and the high activity of foreign acquisitions in the USA). Following the wave of large hostile bids, 1980s-style debt financing focused on cross-border product and market expansion, and on privatization by managers of firms once publicly owned by shareholders.

4.5.1 BANKS PRESSURE FIRMS TO INCREASE DEBT

Banks and junk bond underwriters created Humpty Dumpty junk bond kings and dethroned them again when times were tough. In the 1990s a neo-conservatism set in leaning towards classic prudence: low debt/equity ratios and new rounds of financial sourcing through stock warrants and initial public offerings (IPOs), moving the Debt-Equity Clock ever forward.

Why did the early "debt renaissance" occur in the first place? An infatuation with analytical technique combined with expanding markets following new technological advances caused bankers and entrepreneurs alike to wager on optimistic cash flows. Calculations were based on generous assumptions. When rising interest rates led to faltering demand and higher debt service requirements, emerging and even successful companies suffered. Bank pressures on over-extended third world enterprises at the end of the 1970s are now felt in the 1980s by the over-leveraged and restructured corporate world of the Atlantic Rim. The 1970s "bank push" by promotion-seeking frontline bankers competing hard for third world public and private accounts (e.g., the huge oil and gas deals in Indonesia) was duplicated by 1980s sales forces of junk and other bond traders compelling acquirers, both external (raiders) and internal (MBOs) to take on more debt.

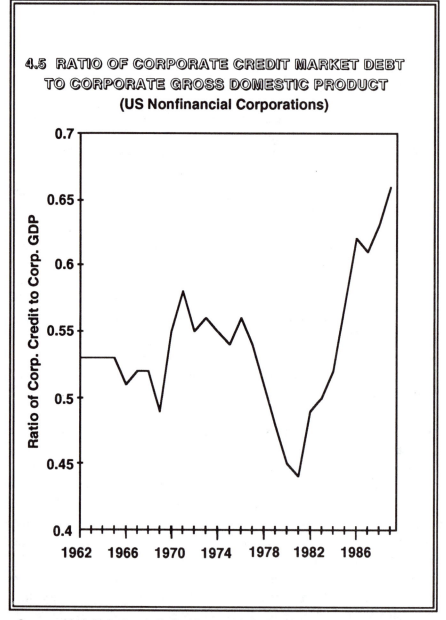

4.5 RATIO OF CORPORATE CREDIT MARKET DEBT TO CORPORATE GROSS DOMESTIC PRODUCT
(US Nonfinancial Corporations)

Source: M.H. Pickering, L.E. Crabbe, and S.D. Prowse, "Recent Developments in Corporate Finance," *Federal Reserve Bulletin*, Aug. 1990.

4.5.2 BANK CONSOLIDATION

In other European countries there are usually no more than a dozen major domestic banks. The United States, in comparison, has over 10,000 banks - a surplus encouraged by the safety net placed under the banking system by the Federal Deposit Insurance Corporation (FDIC). The surplus of financial services occurs in a globally integrating market in which even customers are able to internalize some of the financial functions. Small bank presidents as well as Washington bank reformers agree that "consolidation" within the American banking sector is required. Even the giants are effected; a current wave of mergers and takeovers is underway. Fallen and rejuvenated angels such as Bank of America are merging with the newly fallen such as Security Pacific, only a few years ago an international leader in asset-based financing. Rumors abound about tentative consolidations including Citicorps, Chemical and Manufacturers Hanover. A mergers and acquisitions consultant specialized in the banking sector recently commented that almost the entire UK banking sector is for sale, probably at very interesting multiples. Internal costs savings in this personnel intensive sector have been estimated to be 30%. Consolidation has already occurred in Germany and other European countries by financial integration - or the buying of small prestigious houses by the large commercial banks (also in the USA, e.g., Valley National = Phoenix + Bank One).

In spite of consolidation the US Government has been obliged to bail out several major banks and S&Ls, at least ten of which were substantial holders of junk. The financial risk factor rose with the prime rate. Bankers, accountants and venture capitalists found themselves running the business. When the system faltered as the decade rolled on, banker friend in many but not all instances became foe. Banks creating and encouraging entrepreneurs in the 1980s withdrew their traditional support. For example, as early as 1984—1985, banks required a higher percent payment of principle, even though the ratio of CFEBIT or EBITDA to interest payments didn't deteriorate. As bank lending decreased, junk financing increased, a trend that has repeated in 1991-1992. Concomitant with the increased likelihood of financial distress, bank debt became more seniorized, and the banks not unlike creditors became more likely to prefer liquidation (see Macy's). In addition, as subordinated debt became more public, free-rider problems also augmented.

When banking fingers no longer pulled the financial strings, puppet entrepreneurs collapsed.

Weston maintains that the increase in junk is due to more external financing, interest rate volatility, deregulation, competition amongst financial institutions, and industrial restructuring. Importantly, debt financing increased during the 1980s because of the high levels of liquidity in the 1980s, and the effects of inflation in the 1970s. The change in relative values reached such extremes that Siemens and others found it more lucrative and less risky to invest in the financial markets rather than direct investment in new assets for internal corporate expansion. "Easy" money was repackaged by Drexel Burnham and other financial intermediaries who pursued corporate raiders and management buyout teams, encouraging them to consider high yield bonds for sourcing acquisition finance.

4.5.3 THE ROLE OF LEVERAGED BUYOUTS, OR BANKER AS BUSINESSMAN

In leveraged buyouts investors commit themselves to buy uncollateralized shares prior to the takeover for a small commitment fee (0.5-1.0%). Shares are issued by a shell corporation created specifically to acquire the target's shares. If the bidder gains control, target assets are used as collateral for the additional financing needed to complete the acquisition (B38). *Prior commitment* allows great speed in surprising takeover candidates (B38).

A typical buy-out structure encompasses roughly 60% or more senior debt at a rate typically two points above LIBOR or the prime rate for five to seven years. Senior debt providers also supply overdraft facilities, a maligned but essential source of working capital. It has been said that the senior debt players not only control the deal but also control the company after the buyout, a curious state of affairs when bank expertise in asset-backed evaluation gives way to cash flow analysis and forward projections.

Floored between equity and debt in terms of recourse and subordination is mezzanine finance, or "expensive debt, but very inexpensive equity". Mezzanine is essentially higher-yielding debt, 20—25% or typically four points above LIBOR or prime, with some sort of *equity kicker* attached, usually equity warrants. Mezzanine has prevailed mostly in the USA, constituting only 5% of total MBO funding in the UK, where one-half of Europe's public companies are located. Similar reference shares have been accepted there since the 1940s. Deals are also smaller, and the corporate bond and high-yield markets have only recently begun to cut into the developed equity market. However, in 1986 alone the value of MBOs using mezzanine finance increased by 5 times to just under £1.5 billion.

If the bought-out company fails completely, the equity investor expecting an IRR of 40—60% on the upside, is left without a penny. Only when senior debt and mezzanine strip have been repaid do equity players begin to see returns. However, some equity investors as well as company vendors retain substantial equity stakes even after a buyout or subsequent reflotation.

Shareholders who supported the company as a quoted vehicle are allowed to participate in future success as encouraged by management's conviction in the company's turnaround potential. Sellers are usually prepared to maintain some form of interest after the buy-out, especially if shares are undervalued.

One problem is that the original founder-shareowners anxious to realize firm net worth are frequently reluctant to share power and status. The original owners also obscure closet skeletons such as previous tax evasion or other insider information, to the detriment of new outside interests who will buy up to 51% of the firm, or more. Solutions include the introduction of professional management and international accounting standards.

Early takeover success stories and easy borrowing pushed up corporate debt-ratios. Central figures averaged in the borrowing craze. In spite of new competition in 1986, Drexel Burnham whose Michael Milken largely created the junk bond, still controlled 45 percent of the LBO market in 1988. As a result of legal problems, this share fell to 16 percent by early 1989. In terms of public policy, it is difficult to assess whether the high yield bond market is "good" or "bad" for the economy. One test is a major market correction. From a market peak on 26th August, 1987, through the October crash until November 18th, the S&P 500 index dropped 27%, while the Drexel index fell 40%, even though bond values went up by 2.6% from October 19th to November 18th, with government bond prices up by 13%. In contrast, Taggart asserted in 1986 that junk financing was unlikely to impact the aggregate level of debt or the safety of the financial system, and that M&A and corporate restructuring are determined by more fundamental economic and financial sources.

One special case of the LBO is the management buyout, or MBO. This occurs when management takes over the firm. The MBO vehicle has been prevalent in the UK. From its inception (concurrent with changes in UK company law) in the early eighties, the MBO market grew rapidly until 1989 when activity peaked in terms of both number of transactions and size. During the recession the number of MBOs has tended to drop as well as the size of each transaction. This was probably due to the reduction in available debt funding due to bank loss through bad debts, high interest rates, and the increased prudence of equity providers. Similarly, the "diminishing hoard of family silver" has led to a decline in privatizations. Successful UK buy-outs have good profitability, i.e., strong cash flows (see boom mergers). To the contrary, the supply of companies for sale also increases buy-outs (see recession mergers), and accounts for the continuing streak of British MBO's in the recent recession years. Surprisingly, however, only 18 out of 337 larger buy-outs were from receivership or administration.[31]

4.5.4 LBO RISKS AND PREMIUMS
Opler assesses LBO risk premiums as thus:

> 2.0% = average premium of prime over treasury rate
> 2.5% = average LBO debt costs over prime
> 4.5% = LBO debt costs over treasury - low compared to:
> 8.0% = equity premium, or the differential in stock ROR and bond ROR
>> 10:1 = LBO debt-total equity ratio
>> 20:1 = LBO debt-common equity ratio: (B32)

LBO financing is relatively inexpensive. We assume that capital costs are lower when the target risks are lower as the bank lender is more likely to be repaid. When calculating "deal risk", target stock prices should be included. More difficult to assess are future cash flows, the number of employees that don't leave the firm, the future profitability of the sector, and other future externalities.

---

[31] Chris Beresford, "The maturing MBO market," *Director* (UK), June 1992, pp. 60-66.

The US Savings and Loans Associations (S&Ls) invested up to 11% of their assets in junk bonds. In mid-1985 ten of a total of 3,180 federally insured S&Ls accounted for 77% of total junk bond holdings by S&Ls, or some 10% of total assets (A6). As the American S&Ls have undergone bankruptcy in recent months, suits by them against Drexel Burnham have increased substantially. Properly assessing the risks of leveraged acquisition financing largely remains a *terra incognito*.

4.5.5 REDUCING LBO RISK

In spite of co-called high yields, LBO costs may have been low to the borrower in the 1980s. Moreover, the high yields associated with leveraged buyouts have been estimated as not being high enough. From a 1990s perspective this point is be well justified in view of extraordinary high default rates.

If capital costs are low, then bankruptcy costs are even lower. This is due to several factors including

> 1) the debt workout process;
> 2) sponsor firm strength;
> 3) strip financing by which equity and debt are held by the same parties, or junior debtholders such as insurance companies share in the equity; and
> 4) investor restrictions, or covenants. Amongst firms surveyed by Opler, 97% included covenants in their loan documents that bond the sale of assets; 44% added sinking fund provisions and 30% call provisions, and 13% require certain operating ratios or immediate excess cash flow repayment (see Table 2.2, B32).

4.5.6 OUTCOMES OF DEBT FINANCING IN THE 1990s

In 1990 the most significant sign of the financial squeeze was the large number of deals that failed due to a lack of funding (A5). The seeds of restructuring were sown in the buoyant 1980s world economy by a corporate sector hungry for debt fed by fierce bank competitors. Lending margins sank with the quality of client relationships. High central bank rates and recession lessened bankers' loyalty to company flocks. As one commentator proffered, "the lending bank umbrella has collapsed with the first drops of rain". The demand on internal resources created by financial fire fighting with their bankers hastened rather than curtailed corporate collapse (A15).

Perhaps it is surprising that, even in 1990, sellers (stand-alone businesses and corporate divestors) were reluctant to accept reduced prices for their properties. It is also interesting that the deal failure rate remained about even, with one transaction failing for every 14 completed (A5).

The impact of the famous RJR Nabisco leveraged buyout (B21) on corporate debt raising through the Euromarket is still not fully assessed. When previous RJR chief executive Ross Johnson announced that there would be a RJR management takeover bid primarily financed by debt, RJR's outstanding debt securities plummeted, and bondholders lost approximately $800 million. At one point during the buyout the RJR Nabisco debt/equity ratio was as high as 25:1. At that time the RJR deal was distinguished by two features: its size and the fact that the takeover was initiated by management. Original investors who helped build the company into a market leader felt betrayed. The impact of this one buyout was so vast that confidence in the overall US corporate debt markets diminished.

Growth seeking corporations have increasingly resorted to the stock markets. Initial public offerings have flourished. During the market recession in 1991, US, UK and other companies have requested their shareholders to buy more shares. Investors are not likely to buy US paper on terms so favorable to US corporations again.

Institutional investors (especially pension and insurance funds as well as S&L's) must still recoup losses in the LBO market (C46). With this in mind it is remarkable to note the resilience and short memory of the markets. There are two solutions for restoring the battered relationship between corporate borrowers and investors: (1) clauses in future issues that protect investors against event risk, and (2) poison puts to the bondholder. A round of new equity financing has reduced debt as a percentage of total capitalization. This ratio climbed from 34.2% at the end of 1983 to 46.8% in 1990.

Based on the high correlation between employment and sales, Sheridan Titman and others perceive direct effects of high leveraging on firm behavior. For example, if a firm is highly leveraged, it is more likely to lay off employees in a recession, or whenever sales drop. Reversing the causation, Titman maintains that firms with high costs of changing employment choose lower debt levels. Low-leverage firms are also more likely to lay off because of the saliency for the firm of the socio-political consequences. Firm behavior with regard to employment is viewed once again as a response to the business cycle: fluctuations in labor force adjustment costs lead to changes in the level of debt. Inversely, leveraged firms are more sensitive to employment because these firms are more sensitive to changes in sales levels. Titman goes so far as to claim that in some instances choosing debt is committing to a bankruptcy policy. Thus, as the over-leveraged firm is more exposed to macroeconomic risk, due to increased sensitivity to macroeconomic shocks and financial distress costs.

Gordon Phillips states that an increase in debt leads to a decrease in competitiveness, as debt is essentially a commitment to higher costs. Phillips conditions this assertion with debt asymmetry, or the degree to which the competition is also leveraged. Ease of entry and expansion are also critical. This argument must be qualified further: the *quality* of debt, i.e., the capacity of new investment to realize higher returns, to a major extent determines the competitiveness of the firm, and not debt **per se**.[32]

In general, the impact of debt financing on the firm and the macro-environment will be best understood when there is a clearer definition of debt as well as a full exposition of the bond default rate and the LBO success rate in recent years. This in turn will clarify how junky junk really is.

4.5.7 ARE JUNK BONDS UNDERPRICED?

In spite of a strong market response in terms of pricing efficiency in the early and mid-eighties, takeover junk bonds are reported to be no different than other junk bonds. Is it possible that the overpricing of junk bonds lacks sufficient statistical significance to justify major regulation? If anything, suggest Ma and Weed, low-rated bonds historically produce higher risk-adjusted returns. Junk bonds, then, may have been underpriced, particularly with regard to the collapse of the market starting in 1989 (F9). However this is unlikely.

It is more plausible that junk bonds were overpriced. When confidence collapsed and the junk bond market faltered, especially in 1990, the entire bond

---

[32] Presentations by Sheridan Titman and Gordon Phillips at the American Economic Association Conference, New Orleans, January 1992.

market shuttered. The underlying issue is whether the price collapse is cosmetic, i.e., based on sentimental expectations concerning the market, or is based on real shifts in performance. More recently, in spite of the major payment defaults at the end of the 1980s, Kaplan and Stein have reiterated the argument of Ma and Weed. They suggest that bankers optimistic with earlier success were over-optimistic about prospects for later deals and underpriced LBO loans: "Given the inherent incentive problems associated with deposit insurance, it is possible that an underpricing of risky loans took place (A20)."

Have firms assumed too much debt? The financially cautious might maintain that a business only produces what the business produces: excessive borrowing based on optimistic assumptions about forthcoming "free" cash flows and future growth enhances the likelihood of default and bankruptcy. Not so long ago it seemed that companies owning oil and natural gas could sustain heavy debt loads. But it is tough to service debt, develop reserves and pay dividends all at once. When prices fluctuate, so do cash flows. Asset-rich sectors such as the airlines and department stores clearly have not been able to carry huge debt loads, as witnessed by recent bankruptcies. When times are tough, these companies fall short of the asset coverage required under debt covenants. Notably, many of the branded good companies—and particularly food processors—have successfully managed to cope with heavy post-acquisition debt loads.[33] Henry Kravis' appetite for crackers and Lord Hanson's fancy for branded manufacturers are explained by the success of brand-related takeovers (see 4.4.2).

However, for the most part, the infamous 1980s acquirers in the US, UK and Australia are currently undergoing financial stress. Furthermore, during a corporate auction, a bidder tends to pay *more* than asset values and cash flows warrant. This bidding effect, known as Winner's Curse, is heightened by the fact that there are few longterm rules governing the bidding process, especially with regard to *ending* an auction. Most auctions therefore close when bidding is too high for all but one party (A24).

The coverage ratio is also exogenously effected by what investors choose to hold as securities, and not merely by how the company is internally operated. As the total LBO share of total debt increased, the LBO firm must compete

---

[33] Howard Rudnitsky, "Leverage 101," *Forbes*, Sept. 28, 1992, p. 44.

harder against other borrowers. Tax loopholes then become especially decisive. The press and public opinion become more important in determining final outcomes, as well as the opinion of the independent committee that votes for the takeover or against it.

The impact of economic slowdown—discretionary or spontaneous—on MBOs and mezzanine finance remains to be fully understood. Many businesses are currently under financial stress due to previous assumptions that internal cash flows would substantiate high levels of debt with high interest payments. *Euromoney* states that the guiding principle of equity investment in buy-outs is the internal rate of return - usually between 40% and 60%. A diversifying UK acquirer recently stated that banks currently anticipate a borrower to maintain an IRR of 40%.

The impact of junk bonds can be assessed by the outcomes in the nineties of the 1980s junk wave. The junk bond markets have met public and political resentment: The setback to pension and insurance companies and particularly the American savings and loans associations caused by junk bond failure have cast a shadow on international banks, leverage buyout firms and mergers and acquisitions, in general. Criticism and exposure emerged from within the industry as well as from without. For example, many claim stated that Drexel Burnham Lambert was exposed by major competitors such as Salomon Brothers who didn't like the "smart new kid on the block" who started to challenge their "street cred".

4.5.8 A NEW M CURVE
Using a 1990s perspective it appears that substantial backfiring occurs when capital costs and cash flow projections are overestimated. Then recession cash flows are not enough to sustain the high interest rate burden vestigial of monetary restraint in the previous expansionary and inflationary period. A fatal M curve or "M lag" effect can be defined.[34] The high prices of the preceding growth and maturity periods linger. Most importantly, the interest rate, or the price of money, may remain high for some time, especially if loans were made or junk bonds issued at high fixed rates. The M curve is constituted

---

[34] The term M lag or M curve is chosen for several reasons: "M" indicates that the recessionary effects on the merger curve are monetary, and the analogy with the J-curve effect is brought forth, although the possibility of a bi-modal response is emphasized.

by a series of shifts in coverage ratios due to the income reduction and lower if not deflated asset values in the recession (eg., real estate prices)—*even though* the debt burden remains constant or in some instances increases due to debt refinancing requirements.

The familiar outcomes are restructuring and bankruptcy. Key M&A decision makers may have acquired their golden parachutes, but equity safety nets are torn asunder by heavy leverage ratios.

The parallels between the new M Curve and the old J Curve traditionally cited in international trade are enormous. The J Curve which is constituted by an initial decline in total export income after a home country currency devaluation—without an immediate corresponding or greater increase in export volume—is similar to the M Lag in that both are due to a change in the price of money, i.e., the exchange rate for internationally traded goods and the interest rate for financial instruments. In both instances, buyers don't pick up today's bargains because they still remember or otherwise are still effected by yesterday's high prices. In the case of the M Curve, today's buyer may not be able to buy today because of so much borrowing to buy yesterday. Even though interest rates are uncommonly low at the beginning of the third quarter of 1992, there has been to date only a slender uptake in borrowing, and bankers can't find funds to lend (see the Maschmeier Dilemma).

It is interesting to note that the US merger wave positively correlates in rather rough fashion with US exports as can be seen from a graph elsewhere. More mergers also occur when stock market prices (Tobin's Q) are high, especially relevant to the inflation in asset replacement prices. This implies that mergers increase in the latter boom phases of the GNP when there is more economic activity and still substantial liquidity. Interest rates will tend to rise as money becomes in shorter supply and the government begins to cool down the economy. Finally the M Curve begins visible.

4.6 SUMMARY
Six anomalies can be distinguished that relate to merger finance:

1. Mergers and acquisitions increase in times of growth (boom mergers) but also in times of recession (bust consolidation).

2. Mergers and acquisitions may be positively correlated with low interest rates as well as with high interest rates.

3. An *Icarus Trap* is created by the facile extension of loans to acquirers so that the overall quality of debt is downgraded in such a way that borrowing is more improbable thereafter (i.e., the Debt-Equity Clock is accelerated).

4. Corporate finance as well as business success and failure rates may be object as opposed to subject of a central bank policy cycle. This becomes most clear in relation to inflation and government monetary policy as the *M Curve effect.*

As government debt increases to perilous levels worldwide, one may query whether regulatory heating and dampening of inflation and the economy, particularly with reference to the interest rate, may not cause monetary policy decisions to prevail over corporate planning decisions. Government first. Business second.

Are mergers driven by a "Keynesian dialectic"? Are product, business and merger cycles rebounding in a sinusoidal Keynesian-Friedmanian environment in which government "corrections" draw even deeper economic repercussions? In the case of financial mergers, windows of opportunity created by government policy are arbitraged by correlating strategic financial sourcing with asset accrual and divestment. From this perspective, one might question whether central bank policy achieves its original objective of modulation or suffers from overkill. There are many empirical ways of approaching this issue. One *ceteris paribus* tactic is to conceive of "government-free consolidations" by projecting beyond the Keynesian environment to no inflation controls, and low or no government spending and taxation.

5. Small *private* firms go *public* on the stock exchanges - usually first on one of the smaller exchanges or the OTC before graduating to the American or New York Stock Exchanges. If an acquisition or LBO occurs, *public* firms go *private*, or are reprivatized, or their shares are absorbed by the acquiring firm. After a wave of *going private*, the recent trend is to "deleverage", or make the reprivatized firm (or division) *public*. The grounds for oscillating from private to public at considerable costs to stakeholders is partially revealed by the private returns to the instigators of takeovers, frequently corporate management, that is reviewed in Chapter Five.

Hughes (C46) as well as Lewis (B24) have voiced concern about the social as well as macroeconomic viability for all effected stakeholders of private→public→private→public restructurings. If the often rapid succession of corporate restructurings is deemed undesirable there is at present few legal constraints to modify or prevent this occurrence, at least within the context of a freely operating economy.

Crabbe, Pickering and Prowse (B34) delineate several directly related trends. Due to the extraordinary rise in the 1980s of interest and currency rate swaps (one of the new financial innovations cited in the next chapter) they report a blurring of short, medium and long term interest rates as well as a fading away of the differentiation between domestic and foreign currencies. New financial instruments have also obscured the distinction between debt and equity, as well as between private placements and public issues (B33).

6. The switching from public to private markets is significant within the context of the globalization of market trading as well as the increase in market accessibility to large and small investors via new telecommunications. The computer brings the stock markets everywhere where there is a telephone line or simply remote control. Ironically, having won considerable market power through accessibility, the small investor has tended to relinquish it to large institutions (e.g., mutual, pension and insurance funds) who have gained control over almost half of public issues and debt. There are now more mutual funds than there are stocks in the market.

————— •***• —————

CHAPTER 5
CORPORATE CONTROL AND EXPANSION VIA M&A

"How often do the acquirers know as much about what
makes the enterprise work as the present managers do?
Rarely! What they know is mostly by financial."[35]

PROF. JOE AUERBACH
HARVARD BUSINESS SCHOOL

5.1 A STRATEGY FOR CORPORATE CONTROL: THE BASIC QUESTIONS

What strategic forces lead companies to merge or acquire? M&A is clearly related to expansion, so how do firms expand *without* M&A? Excess inventory leads to the installation of more outlets through direct retailing or concessions. A branch office is then established to manage local and regional sales. A subsidiary or trading company may be formed nearer to market sources or customers. Or a joint venture may be established, relinquishing control and profits in the process but capturing local commitment. So why merge or acquire?

Certain forces trigger concentration and a particular *style* of consolidation—horizontal, vertical and conglomerate. Restructuring becomes

---

[35] In David W. Ewing, *Inside the Harvard Business School,* New York and Toronto, Random House, 1990. Ewing underscores the fact that financial criteria of new owners pay small heed to the need for steady improvements in operations.

prevalent in a particular product *sector*, determining when most mergers happen. Like shifts in the stock and bond markets or relative shifts in capital costs, there are good times for buying companies and bad times. For example, during a recession, companies are more inclined to collapse or divest. From the acquirer's standpoint there are more companies to buy. Diverse profitability paths are thus followed by corporate decision-makers according to business and product cycles. Moreover, certain measures lead to a *successful acquisition strategy*, and others lead to failure. In sum, why do corporate strategists choose M&A as a vehicle for gaining corporate control?

To answer this question we consolidate the checklists in Part Two. Secondly, in the Appendix to this chapter relevant literature that has not been integrated into M&A research conclusively is reassessed. The coherence between merger research and work in other areas provides insights into M&A dynamics which is incorporated here and in Chapter Seven. Literature sources with direct bearing on merger waves include:

> • internalization concepts of the multinational firm and foreign direct investment theories (FDI)
> • strategic aspects of the product cycle
> • technology cycles and long waves, an area where innovation and change have been closely analyze(especially and more recently with regard to the *type* of company that emerges)
> • business cycles
> • new modelling approaches, including the C-Anomaly by A. Post and K. White.[36]

5.2. THE STRATEGY OF MERGER: DATA FROM THE CHECKLISTS

In the preceding chapter the mergers and acquisitions wave was presented as a leading indicator of: stock market rises (by one month), Initial Public Offerings (IPOs), capacity utilization and business failures (three months), and industrial production (5 months). The M&A cycle has also been positively correlated in upswings **and** downswings with the interest rate. Strangely

---

[36]A. Post and K. White have developed the C-Anomaly, a dynamic cyclical model with optional dimensions that has been applied to anomalies in interest and exchange rates.

enough, M&A is negatively correlated with GNP, a matter we will approach once again. The correlations of merger waves with other economic time series will continue to be improved. With certainty it can be said that the number of mergers and acquisitions indicates shifts in macroeconomic variables, but does not appear to alter them directly. Furthermore, the M&A time series is one of the most volatile.

Consolidating the Checklists in Part Two, firms acquire or merge **to accumulate value** in pursuit of the profit motive: **to acquire** technology, R&D, new management teams, and new systems; **to achieve** scale economies in unit costs, operating efficiency, and financing costs; **to maximize** firm size due to enabling changes in technology; **to restructure** and **to modernize**, and **to integrate synergies**, e.g., of central cash flow management (financial), eliminating office and other duplication (savings), and improving distribution (complementary).

Moreover, mergers and acquisitions **increase** when there is economic and industrial growth and stability as well as free trade, a deflationary economy and increases in the US debt.

By far the widest consensus in the literature is that mergers and acquisitions increase due to **international competition** and **corporate globalization** for world sectoral leadership (oligopoly, or "corporate control"). Other companies are also forced to merge ("sink or grow"). Several authors maintain, however, that mergers **do not** cause anticompetitive concentration of power. In fact, they argue, government antitrust law is harmfully reducing efficient allocation without offsetting benefits.

Traditional **supply** reasons that drive companies and governments abroad that also seem to encourage M&A are to take advantage of cheap raw materials and labor (a classic terms-of-trade argument) to capture profits from exchange rates.

More market-oriented **consumer driven** objectives for international M&A are also described. M&A is undertaken to **expand beyond saturated domestic markets** by investing in faster growing economies and to follow clients abroad. A recent example is the rapid and highly competitive expansion of McDonald's, Wendy's and other fast food chains into foreign markets as well as into new markets such as hospitals and schools. It is not disputed that mature industries grow out into new markets although it is curious that the same arguments were used by Lenin to define neo-imperialism and European expansion. Firms expand abroad due to **leads in technology and know-how, reputation and product differentiation**.

Firms also undertake strategic M&A to **decrease export dependence** and to **avoid disfavorable domestic legislation and regulations**.

Business expansion is clearly a major motivating force for M&A and it is not surprising that M&A correlates with economic growth indicators such as rising stock markets and increasing industrial capacity. Companies expand through acquisition to **improve operations and competitiveness** by acquiring new systems, new personnel skills, specific assets (especially technology), or new market position; to restructure, streamline or modernize by internalized investment in the target's product, and by realizing economies of scale for example, by improving **performance** through better management within non-complex, integrated infrastructures.[37]

Firms also expand by acquiring in emerging yet highly competitive industries in order to extend market control, particularly in industries entering the late phase of the product life cycle, or industries with segmented markets, decreasing growth rates, increasing development costs and product demand, rising competition, or industries effected by high taxes and nationalization of highly salient assets. In this sense, acquisitions are undertaken to compensate for instabilities such as wide fluctuations in demand and product mix; excess capacities related to slow sales growth and declining profit margins, and technological shocks. Mergers can improve a company's longterm market position and improve cash flows, although current income is foregone for merger and integration costs.

---

[37] The scale economics argument must be qualified - each restructured deal creates over time either economies or *diseconomies* of scale. The merging of production functions may damage both of them. The benefits of pooled advertising, marketing and control functions must be weighed in against the costs of centralization. The net effect of added benefits vs. added costs is determined mainly by management's integration ability, of management, the changing market environment, and finance costs.

Sectors with high consolidation rates enhance production performance by improved global distribution. The kinds of sectors where this occurs most readily are *mass markets* coupled with *product homogeneity*, so that there is the ability to market through the same market distribution network. An acquirer therefore achieves *marketing economies of scale*.

In sum, *the driving forces of M&A are the basic precepts of firm behaviour: the profit motive and market control through expansion.*[38] Mergers and acquisitions are alternative strategies for financing corporate expansion in specific economic environments. Acquisitions and divestitures are undertaken in order to **enhance returns** to the firm as well as personally to the decision makers most immediately involved in the transaction.

5.2.1 WHY MERGERS SUCCEED

Summarizing the success and failure factors in Chapter 9, successful acquirers buy in the core business line, seek strong local players, focus on the target's competitive edge, realize synergies more by patching than by major upheaval (for example by transferring only a few key executives and systems). Serial acquirers fare better than one-off acquirers. They learn to make accurate valuations, pay the right price for the target firm and tailor earn-outs thereafter, develop and adhere to prior strategic and financial goals, monitor regulatory changes and sustain industrial knowledge.

Those who succeed at LBOs are thorough at pre-acquisition analysis and clear in their goals. They act quickly, correctly, sensitively and with high visibility, keeping top management and key personnel and explaining corporate culture to new employees. Cultural and nostalgic differences are addressed buy developing a new loyalty focus and a sunny vision ahead. After acquisition a firm grip is held on cash flows, overheads, and future earnings through control and reporting systems as well as an integration plan for three or more years.

---

[38]A paper by George Bittlingmayer draws similar conclusions: "Merger as a Form of Investment," Wissenschaftszentrum Berlin für Sozialforschung, IIM/IP 87 13, May 1987. Foundations of the theory of the firm: Ronald H. Coase, "The nature of the firm," first published in 1937 and proceedings of a 1987 conference organized to celebrate the 50th anniversary of the article, in: Oliver E. Williamson and Sidney G. Winter, *The Nature of the Firm; Origins, Evolution and Development*, New York, Oxford UP, 1991.

Synergy potentials are explored and maintained. External changes and relations are monitored, and a unique marketing style maintained.

What **kind of industries** are best to acquire? Basic industries with solid and reliable management, products and earnings are the safest targets. Larger companies can also be acquired easier than small ones, simply because of the larger cash flows involved.

5.2.2 WHY MERGERS FAIL

The most important reasons for acquisition fall-out are 1) the clashing of corporate cultures and 2) acquisition prices that are too high, perhaps because of high price/earnings ratios pushed up by companies from outside the sector, or because of bad timing or unperceived sectoral obsolescence.

Since more complex organizations are created, flexibility and service are lost. Longterm R&D may slow down and logistic strategies are disrupted. Disenchanted by stunted careers, culture shock, inefficiencies, and different corporate focus, staff leave, a critical factor in labor-intensive sectors and the technology sector.

Poor integration, bad management and motivation, stock dilution and other incompatibilities reduce earnouts below expectations in the pre-acquisition analysis. Therefore the target's shareholders are paid less if pro-rated earnout formulae based on future performance were incorporated in the sell price.

Finally, the worst cost of integration may be the high interest payments on takeover debt no longer justified by new cash flows.

5.3 THE STRATEGIC STYLE OF M&A DECISION-MAKING

"Look, for a long time diversification was the magic word. Buying up unrelated companies was supposed to be the secret of success. What happened? Company after company went through humiliating periods of selling off failed acquisitions. Gulf + Western, Borden, Cummions, Scovill, Continental Group—scores of them!

"Why did diversification fail so often? The answer is simple: because it was done in the name of portfolio management. The companies saw their job as allocating capital—lots of money to this division because it's a 'star', not so much to that one because it's a 'cash cow.' Instead of cooperating, business units in diversified firms were often led to compete. Make the most of the links—that's what corporate strategy should be about." [39]

PROF. MICHAEL PORTER

At the 1992 American Economic Association Conference, W. Brian Arthur of Stanford University suggested that there may be no rational behavior, no optimization, no efficiencies - all cornerstones of twentieth century economic theory. Decisions, he postures, are more likely based on anticipation, self-fulfilling prophesies, self-defeating behavior, risk-reward measures, ideological oughts, and jitteriness when informational cues do not make a rational fit.

The role of mood also has played a vital role in determining prevailing mergers style. Think-alike is germane to trend formation. Mood begets mood. How to combine little businesses into huge trusts was a theme at turn-of-the-century dinner tables from New York to Chicago. The Raiding 60s transfigured into the leveraged 1980s, when a central issue was not whether several CEOs dipped into employee pension funds to save the company... we know they did... but *how* so many of them came up with the same idea at the same time. The answer lies beyond the bounds of research, at best in the metaphysical mist of shared intuition. Having leveraged all other available assets, perhaps the large glaring pool of untouched pension monies became an irresistible bull's-eye. In contrast, the early recessionary 1990s are marked by conservatism, no partners;

---

[39] See Ewing, Note 35.

and the preference to have joint ventures or management contracts rather than buy or build. This has been the strategy style of the Westin Hotels and other Japanese groups (Great Britain, in contrast, never had as many MBOs as in 1990/1!).

The mood of the times determines a prevailing strategy style and perception of the optimal strategy mix. Espen Eckbo has touched upon the importance of mood from 1982 onwards with a sort of "leader of the pack" hypothesis that when one firm decides to sell/acquire, the change in that company's stock price will tend to lead the stock prices of other companies in that sector because of expectations of potential similar behavior of other firms in the sector. Following Eckbo, this pull of the pack may constitute a sectoral merger wave. One may in turn inquire what forces led the leader to M&A in the first place and why the pack followed. Shifts in the relative costs of capital in the debt-equity analysis were cited in the previous chapter, as well as the importance of a healthy sectoral coverage ratio as expressed by strong asset values and sustainable and robust cash flows. Structural and strategy causes are also important as well as a prevailing trend towards national and global expansion.

Similar to locational or geographic shifts are corporate structural shifts. For many businesses in the 1990s, scale economies are no longer effective competitive tools. Mass production is giving way to flexible manufacturing systems making smaller batches of a wider array of products such as the Sony Walkmans. The ability to issue (or access) default-free debt has also become relevant, as well as issuing equity (following the Debt-Equity Clock in Chapter Three).

The new organizational think has shifted from invest to divest. Any kind of work to which a company can not bring a special set of skills should be spun off, outsourced, or eliminated. Conversely, divisions sell products and services on the outside market. AMR made more money some years ago selling the by-products of its information systems than it did flying passengers. AT&T. GE, IBM and Shell Oil are in the process of spinning off legal, public relations, billing, payroll and other services. Close-to-the-market units at Bell Atlantic and AT&T buy products and services from the best source, even when the units could have been purchased internally. Opposite to M&A internalization, production and market risks are being *externalized* from under the corporate logo. *Sourcing out* may occur, for example, through *subcontracting* input production, distribution and other functions to outside firms. MCI and Boeing use "systems integration skills" to create operations consisting primarily of subcontractor webs. Multiple profit centers are decentralized, as well as currency exposure in international transactions. Each *component business* acts as an independent entrepreneurial outfit. There is also a delayering of the corporate hierarchy, often with only two to four layers between top executive management and the operative "floor" or line manager.

The "new age" company has a flatter organization structure. AES Corporation, an independent energy producer, holds organizational levels from the CEO to staff to three or four. The Computer Science Laboratory (CSU) at Xerox PARC in Palo Alto is a pioneer in organizational management. CSU has no middle management. Optimal manageability as defined by founder Bob Taylor is 40-50 managers with 20-30 support staff for one CEO. Final responsibility is being "de-centered from headquarters to operating units. Divisions are given true autonomy. Similarly, one of the key success factors in serial acquisitions is letting acquired companies run their own shop. A new horizontal project orientation jams people form disparate functions together on one team, often operating as small profit-and-loss centers.

Conglomerates are out of place in this world of licensing the company's most advanced technology and cannibalizing into several bits for the marketplace the firm's most profitable products. The trend is dying out of fusing one big company from a galaxy of little ones. The new trend is towards small headquarters, little vertical integration, and a focus on key products and customers. The complexity and costs of managing these huge outfits usually far outweigh any benefit to be derived from supposed synergies, and the hope that different cycles will offset one another. The best-performing machine-tool companies in Germany, for example, have small corporate staffs enabling swift responses with minimal vertical integration, saving time and money?

5.3.1 VERTICAL, HORIZONTAL, OR CONGLOMERATE STRUCTURE AND THE VOLATILE FATE OF FIRMS

The normal types of acquisitions are vertical, horizontal, and conglomerate. During the nineteenth century industrial consolidation, growth companies increased market power and economies of scale through "horizontal integration", or buying out other companies producing the same service or product line. Control was also expanded down towards suppliers of inputs and up towards the final consumer market through "vertical integration". Government antitrust or combine legislation was aimed at protecting a competitive environment from collusive business practices. As government regulation cracked down on horizontal and vertical integration, restructuring took the form of diversified conglomerates spreading business risks throughout the economy yet keeping control under the same financial umbrella.

In the mid-twentieth century corporate expansion was dominated by the American multinational company. The multi grew internally via branches and subsidiaries both at home and abroad, and externally by alliances and joint ventures with other concerns. Takeovers by third world country governments in natural resource and other prominent industries was a major force of the 1960s and 1970s. Finally the centrality of the American "multi" was challenged by large European and Asian corporations. In the last decade home governments have looked the other way as corporate assets and revenues grow. Maintaining a competitive foothold in globalizing markets has won priority over allaying the flaws of bigness.

Vertical integration was enshrined in the oil business from pipeline to pump by Rockefeller and shattered by Roosevelt's trust-busting. More recently it is evident in the food processing sector and the financial services. JR Simplot, one of the largest producers of frozen potatoes (for MacDonald's) and other bulk vegetables, has integrated forward into microwaveables and backward into farming, fertilizer production and management, phosphate mining, and R&D. Dhanin Chearavanont who plans to become the world's largest feedstuff, chicken and prawn producer, dominates Thailand's agricultural sector. His company Charoen Pokphand, or the CP Group, joint ventures with Kentucky Fried Chicken and other fast food chains serving chickens. Some inputs are controlled by the company. Outputs right down to the feather and bone are re-integrated into production. Moreover, the CP Group has integrated up into processed foods such as TV dinners and microwaveables. In other sectors the Sears one-stop service center has been emulated by retail banks offering stockbroking, insurance, pensions, credit cards and even travel facilities under one roof.

Pure conglomerate mergers, according to Weston (A6), are more financially motivated than product- or market-extension mergers. Weston attests that conglomerate mergers predominated in the 1960s (culminating in 1968/9) almost half of which were "defensive diversifications" in the defense and aerospace industries seeking participation in a broad spectrum of industries in order to diminish the impact of drastic reductions in the defense budget. The Federal Trade Commission classifies 75% of M&A between the early 1950s and the late 1970s as "conglomerate" (A6). In the 1970s, allegedly undervalued, asset-based natural resource companies were prime targets as hedges against high inflation. Before 1980, most conglomerate mergers may be due to regulation and court verdicts virtually banning horizontal and vertical mergers. In 1981, over 60% of mergers by value were in the natural resources sector, and 24% in the financial services industries, also stimulated by regulation (A6).

The major driving forces for conglomerate-style M&A are to compensate for instabilities of mature industries with wide fluctuations in demand and product mix; excess capacities related to slow sales growth and declining profit margins; the entry of competitive firms; low growth, and major long-term decline in some markets. From a sectoral perspective, Chung (1982) and Weston (1990) observe that pure conglomerates are more heavily levered than manufacturers, or than companies acquiring to expand markets and/or product line.

Horizontal merging is a quick way to expand into new markets. The new and the successful take over the small, the old and the dying. The deregulated American airlines sector in which deregulation exposed excess capacities and inefficiencies is a case in point. Large chemical companies are expanding into niche markets by buying out small specialty chemical companies. Spectrum Signal Processing, Inc, an exponential growth Vancouver firm in the digital signal processing sector, plans to boost expansion by mergers and acquisitions.

Similar to European electronics, a trend toward intra-industry cooperation amongst automobile manufacturers to enhance international competitiveness and rationalization has been consummated by mergers, takeovers, and joint ventures. This is especially evident in Europe, but also in South America. One example is Fiat's purchase of Alfa Romeo. A similar transnational disappearance of an independent manufacturer through outright acquisition is Volkswagen-SEAT. There have been spectacular, but ultimately abortive, attempts at joining forces through direct equity links, such as talks between FIAT and Ford of Europe. Volkswagen and Ford have formed a joint venture, Autolatina thus combining production and sales operations in Brazil and Argentina. However, such horizontal alliances between original equipment manufacturers (OEM) are rare compared to the rash of vertical and horizontal connections that is likely to affect the components industry in Europe and North America (C55).

In contrast, ventures and alliances for even short periods of time are aimed at injecting speed-to-market, energy and novelty, quick problem-solving, and faster improvement. Joint development projects are increasingly conducted with lead customers and vendors, especially in small, specialty markets, to force the market into the firm, and to reduce time-to-market. Outright mergers and acquisitions are becoming less the norm.

Focus is the key: As CD&R Chuck Ames alleges, "In the new era small is not better; focused is better". One sign of the new focus is that the number of corporate spinoffs nearly quadruped in the 1980s. Frank Lichtenberg at Columbia Business School reports that from 1985 to 1989 the proportion of companies that were highly diversified—operating in more than 20 businesses—declined 37%, while the number of corporations operating in only one industry increased 54%. In the 1990s we have already begun to witness *the reorganization of the international company*. Companies are restructuring or divesting ("cannibalizing") divisions unrelated to core activity, even if they are reasonably profitable. Deals are more commercial-strategic than financial because equity still is very expensive. Rates of return and return on equity are still lower. Stressed by an overinflated equity market and heavy debt burdens acquired in the 1980s, Japanese corporations in particular now seek minority participation, joint-ventures, and commercial licensing with a share swap option - a reciprocal way of expanding into new areas.

5.4 STRATEGY MIX

Quality of performance is due to variations in inputs (traditionally known as factors of production) and in the variation (volatility) of the specifications (limits) of the production system.[40]

The same arguments concerning the relative costs factors of production can also be applied to the strategic decision to build or buy, and the relative costs of that factor called capital. One can proceed to investigate factor shifts as well as the recent evolution of the firm.

5.4.1. FACTOR SHIFTS

Critical phase shifts occur in the values of production factors. Keeping up with shifts in relative factor costs is a major function of the foreign investor, and especially the foreign acquirer. Today the global corporate planner must also respond correctly and quickly to international shifts in factor prices. Combining factor costs—locally, regionally and globally—can be termed "strategy mix."[41]

---

[40] A linear black box or cubed matrix approach permits for interaction of each specification or variable with six or more other variables. Other nonlinear functions (eg., the hysteresis, Lorentz attractors, toroids, helices, overlapping vortices) allow for more complex interactions among variables. These functions are more difficult to solve, but almost always offer more degrees of freedom in transmitting, processing and storing information concerning shifts in factor prices as related to output and changing market conditions.

[41] For example, if we take price/volume ratios for land (L), labor or populations (P) and capital (C) as well as other resources, strategic mixing in 3 markets may be expressed thus:

$$(L1 + L2 + L3) + (P1 + P2 + P3) + (C1 + C2 + C3) =$$

total resources TR

TR/ 3 = temporal market equilibrium or market saturation for factors L, P and C

The extent to which a factor cost in any one location varies from the TR/3 value is its comparative advantage (or disadvantage) over other locations. Strategic mixing via foreign investment involves putting comparative advantages to work. For example, a Tobin q value (total asset value/total market capitalization) is a broad indicator of whether acquisition is preferable to investment.

What is a production factor (or a comparative advantage) in a post-agrarian or post-industrial society? Factor values may be described by the fundamental ratio of resources per capita. An extensive natural endowment leads to a high quotient of resources per capita, typical of North America up until the mid-twentieth century. A large population with limited natural resources and small land base, such as Singapore or Japan, has a small share of resources per inhabitant. What have we done with the fundamental factors of land, capital and technology in our ratio? Land is incorporated in available resources, whereas capital and technology provide dynamics to the ratio, i.e, capital and technology exponentiate the value of labor (skill→talent) and of resources (raw material collection and extraction→manufactures→high tech→information services).[42]

Land price differentials have exceptional bearing on production costs. Overcrowding in the UK explains in part why consumer prices (at current exchange rates) are double those in the USA. Similarly, a two-bedroom flat in the outskirts of Tokyo costs the same as the largest residence in the state of Maine. Land price anomalies drive global property acquisition strategies.

Varying rates of capital accumulation and other factors[43] cause perturbations that drive cycles and lead to the accumulation of raw materials and technology. For example, Hewlett Packard bought Apollo in order to obtain work stations technology, expertise, and market position. Acquiring was cheaper than component assembly and new plant construction. Lead times were also less. Acquiring resources meant a cheaper and quicker market debut.

---

[42] If resources (R) per capita of total (P) as R/P. Technology (T) and capital (C) boosters cause multiplier and finally exponential effects, a resource ratio may be described as:

$$\frac{R^{T_R C_R}}{P^{T_P C_P}}$$

See A. Post, *Deepsea Mining and the Law of the Sea*, Martinus Nijhoff, The Hague, 1983.

[43] Interest rates, inflation, level of taxation, employment, money supply and liquidity, equity-debt ratios, and, more traditionally, natural endowments, and current phase of technology and related product cycles.

Demographic or population shifts. Locational population discrepancies arise in terms of numbers and labor wages leading to dynamic geographical shifts such as urbanization, and even war, a substitute for local gang warfare and rioting amongst a core of dispossessed and unemployed youth. There is a qualitative difference between having too much coal and too many people. If the money supply is made to shrink through discretionary policy, a government is not usually deemed genocidal. However, if the average population age is under 15 and the majority of youth are unemployed, underfed and restless (as in Iraq), the choice to achieve national objectives through war becomes a more palatable strategy. War cycles lead to post-war baby booms in affluent economies. As baby booms mature growing living requirements lead to economic prosperity. However, a greying baby boom with basic needs fulfilled may cause a recessionary trend leading to suppressed demand and an oversupply of labor. The recession continues until prices are suppressed to "more affordable" levels. Amongst the employed, housing upgrades and durables replacement begins "no matter what". Consumer demand now enhanced by necessity leads to an economic upswing.

5.4.2 EQUILIBRATION OF PRODUCTION FACTORS

The matter of relative shifts in factor prices is not trivial. Locational factors are no longer equivalent to national aggregates because of the growing importance of regional and global marketing. National policy tools are very much weakened by this anomaly. If production (and services) investment follows cheap labor costs, the government policies of Atlantic Rim countries must seriously confront the problem of out-migration of manufacture to areas of burgeoning population growth, offering labor at prices astronomically lower than domestic wages, to a large extent due to higher standards of living and higher price indices. If labor costs equilibrate internationally, it is likely that living standards will do the same. On a national average, as the poor get richer in poorer countries, the rich get (at least relatively, if not absolutely) poorer in richer nations. This phenomenon is observable in the USA since the end of the 1950s. The recession may also be derivative of factor equalization. As jobs go abroad, so does income. Local consumers consume less, so that even foreign suppliers have smaller markets to supply to. Finally, as rich economies falter, people migrate sectorally and regionally in search of wages. The population bases of North Dakota and other areas, for example, are diminishing. National and regional governments would do well to strip free trade of its ideological rightness or incorrectness, using free trade much like fiscal and monetary policies - beneficial in certain stages of the product, technology and business cycles, and destructive to the domestic economy—and eventually to the global economy—in other stages.

5.4.3 PRODUCT AND TECHNOLOGY SHIFTS

Discussed at length above, product and technology shifts are closely related not only to sector shifts but also to the overall business cycle. Once organic, now highly engineered into four life cycle phases, missing a market window by 3 - 6 months in can mean death to the firm. If the company is of substantial size, the local and in some instances even national economy may be substantially effected. The evolution of the firm is derivative of product and technology phase shifts and related changes in factors values.

5.4.4 SECTORAL SHIFTS

Important phase shifts occur sectorally as well as geographically. Customers and markets induce substantial sectoral changes. In the $16 billion worldwide connector manufacturing market, in which record M&A activity in 1988 doubled in 1989, the number of companies dropped from some 800 to 100. The push towards acquisitions and consolidation was due in part to geographic location, but it was the customers who were finally in command. As connectors account for less that 2% of product value, customers forced consolidation by expecting reduced prices and faster delivery. Sector shifts and subsequent consolidation can thus be market driven.

5.4.5 REGIONAL OR LOCATION SHIFTS

In locational or geospatial terms there is an economic evolution away from traditional "domestic to international" orientation. More and more, demographic, cultural and social factors are decided on a regional level where production is also focused. Macrovariables are increasingly determined from the common market and global levels. Foreign acquisition is thus a part of regional community or global investment strategy.

Research on M&A sectoral and geospatial dynamics should bear in mind Haag's new approaches in locational economics, or economic geography[44]. Haag maintains that the driving mechanisms for long-term economic cycles are unexplained, even though Kondratieff and other cycles have been identified and discerned as real, monetary and institutional (by Delbeke). All three approaches *base the long wave on **capital accumulation**, especially in market-oriented industrial economies*. Haag like others perceives innovative impulses leading to innovation clusters and finally to long waves. Clustering trends are both temporal (1970s and 1980s) and regional (Silicon Valley, Texas' Silicon Gulch, Thames Valley, Cambridge, Edinburgh, Munich). Innovation permeates the local economy, influencing the local labor market, income distribution between wages and profits, residential areas and local service sectors.

As companies ripen with technology product cycles, and as product cycles change from curves to spikes with the shortening of product life, M&A activity has also shifted regionally from the US, UK and other Anglo Saxon countries such as Australia and Canada—first to the European continent; second to emerging economies, and currently to Eastern Europe, particularly the five new lands (NFLs) of Germany under the auspices of the Treuhand.

5.4.5 CORPORATE STRUCTURAL SHIFTS

Phase shifts can also be scrutinized as an *organizational cycle* or clock that relates M&A phase changes to the evolution of company formation as pushed by shifts in technology and product cycles. These changes have paralleled a regional shift in the center of geographical focus from the Anglo Saxon countries towards the western European continent, and now more towards developing economies and eastern Europe. Each M&A sectoral phase has been associated with a different set of technologies and product cycles.

---

[44] A pacesetter in this area is Gunter Haag, *Dynamic Decision Theory: Applications to Urban and Regional Topics*, Dordrecht and Boston, Kluwer Academic Publishers, 1989. Also G. Haag and Wolfgang Weidlich, *Interregional Migration: Dynamic Theory and Comparative Analysis*, Berlin and New York, Springer-Verlag, 1988. Earlier: John H. Dunning, "Factors influencing the location of multinational enterprises," London, Economists Advisory Group, LOB Research Paper, 1979.

These shifts were preceded by other expansion modes. In the earlier centuries of empire building, trade (the buying and selling of inputs and outputs) was undertaken by (Italian and other) ventures and trading companies. This was followed by the opening of internal subsidiaries and branches (typical of American expansion abroad in the 1950s and 1960s) as well as by licensing, and more recently, by concessions or franchises.

M&A phases essentially began in the nineteenth century in the US and the UK, and continued to evolve there and elsewhere. Early forms were horizontal combines, vertical trusts and conglomerated holding companies (Rockefeller) during the 1920s-1930s. Economies of scale and control were won by buying suppliers and eliminating the intermediaries to final consumer. Secondly, corporate raiding—often driven by financial gains as contrasted to strategic placement—typically took the form of conglomerates in the 1960s and 1970s (T. Boone Pickens, Ichan). Thirdly, conglomeration was followed by managerial- and banker-led initiatives in leveraged buyouts during the 1970s and 1980s (Drexel, KKR). Fourthly, a current trend towards asset securitization, IPOs and other forms of second-round equity financing prevails.

All of the above constitute efforts to internalize control. A most recent trend is to get away from mergers and acquisitions altogether, by *externalizing* production and other functions as described elsewhere.

5.4.6 SUMMARY
In short, there are *five simultaneous strategic phase shifts leading to new investment and to M&A*:

1. **Product and technology shifts** the sum of activity of which effects the business (or output) cycle.

2. **Sectoral shifts** described here and in Chapter Two.

3. **Regional shifts** first explored by Dunning and others in terms of location and internalization, but which can be aligned with the business cycle for any given region, such as the nation.

4. **Factor value shifts** of population, land and resources as exponentialized by technology and capital shifts are key drivers of investment and M&A.

5. **Corporate structural shifts** from externalization to internalization via direct investment, including acquisitions. More recently there is a trend back towards externalization with the new focus on core activity, lateralization and out-sourcing.

Phase shift causalities can be schematized:

$$T \rightarrow PG \rightarrow S \rightarrow BC \rightarrow R \text{ transfer} \rightarrow LW + CS \rightarrow M\&A$$

(T) = technology, the sum of the products in a product group

(PG) = products groups, or derivatives of new technologies.

(S) = sector, the sum of product groups

(BC) = the business cycle, the sum of sectors

(R) = resource or production factor values which are eventually affected by the impact of changing technology indirectly causing migration and other locational shifts.

(LW) = long waves stir (CS) corporate strategies/structures to adapt to "chasing" factor value shifts. Companies merge, acquire or divest (M&A), accordingly.

New technologies drive out old—thrusting in new product groups (or "clusters")—begetting and obliterating entire sectors at a time. Factor values adjust accordingly. Labor migrates and resources are transferred, dumped or revalued. Companies change expansion strategies and corporate structure to conform to the forces of technological growth. Firms divest of divisions that have become obsolete, redundant or no longer related to core activity. They acquire companies that lead them more quickly and less dearly down the strategically designated profitability path. If factor shifts include changes in capital costs, then the financial motivations for corporate change are even greater. The phase shifts of these five cyclical groups plus M&A waves are considered further in Chapter Seven.

——————— .***. ———————

APPENDIX TO CHAPTER 5
THEORIES RELATED TO M&A

A1. GROWTH AND INTERNALIZATION THROUGH M&A: THE LESSONS OF FDI (FOREIGN DIRECT INVESTMENT)

Important earlier studies by G. Stigler in 1963 concerning capital and rates of return in the manufacturing industries and by JS Bain concerning threshold values of profitability concentration were culminated in many respects by the notion of internalization of foreign business by investment, including M&A, by J. Dunning. We shall begin with Dunning because of the obvious relevance to M&A, particularly with regard to the potential re-emergence of European monopolies.

In order to improve competition by enhancing firm efficiency and market location, Dunning asserted that companies internalize market imperfections, especially of production and technological sales. Besides referring to earlier theories of international production expansion such as industrial composition and trade or non-trade economic involvement, Dunning adds to Vernon's product cycle model (discussed subsequently) three notions:

A1.1 INTERNALIZATION[45]

By internalizing production maintains through setting up a branch or subsidiary abroad, total control is maintained. Control remains in the firm and not in the marketplace. By strict definition, acquiring a company also constitutes internalization. Although he does not elaborate the relationship between internalization and acquisition, Dunning states "internalization is thus a powerful motive for takeovers or mergers, and a valuable tool in the strategy of oligopolists."[46]

Externalization, or exposing the firm to the market mechanism, occurs through patent selling, franchising, setting up trade, licensing and distribution agreements, in other words, expanding in the market place by releasing control to outside parties.

A Joint venture is observed as joint internalization established by mutual consent. Asking himself why a firm decides to internalize rather than sell or lease its technologies abroad, Dunning concluded that "it does so wherever it is **in the firm's interests** to internalize."[47] Dunning establishes that the decision to buy or build versus lease or franchise has six criteria. Companies make the decision to buy or build and thus keep controls internal in order to:

1. reduce transaction costs
2. avoid insufficient gains from losing control
3. keep control over supply inputs

---

[45] In Dunning: "Whether the enterprises owning the assets are best able to *appropriate their economic rents by selling the right of the use* of the assets to other enterprises, or *by exploiting* the intermediate products themselves, that is, *internalizing their markets*, this choice depends largely on the relative transaction costs and strategic advantages of using external and internal markets; this choice depends largely on the relative transaction costs and strategic advantages of using external and internal markets." John H. Dunning, *Multinationals, Technology, and Competitiveness*, London and Boston: Unwin Hyman, 1988. See also J. H. Dunning, *International Production and the Multinational Enterprise*, London and Boston, George Allen & Unwin, 1981.

[46] John H. Dunning, *International Production and the Multinational Enterprise*, London and Boston, George Allen & Unwin, 1981.

[47] *Ibid.* Chapter Three concludes in a similar fashion that M&A occurs because of the self-interests of the firm and its managers.

4. cope with government intervention

5. protect property rights

6. optimize capacity utilization and overheads, or take advantage of size, join production and integration/diversification (especially true for takeovers and mergers).

Internalization works best in technology intensive sectors and for firms engaged in backward resource integration. Telesio in Dunning concludes that firms with more R&D investment license. They invest more when firm size is greater as well as experience.

A1.2 LOCATION

Location is a central thesis in Dunning, Vernon, Bergsten and more recently Haag.

The **location functions** of the multinational enterprise are central management, design, R&D and accounting and other controls which remain at headquarters in the hands of nationals under domestic law. Even when companies such as Nestlé have 95% of total corporate activity located outside Switzerland, the corporate culture and operating mode remain national. Dunning also observed that investment flows out from countries with:

- 10% educated and trained workers in the population
- R&D spending 6% or more
- industrialized rather than resource-rich countries
- higher earnings

He also maintains there is no correlation between population size and foreign investment.[48] Therefore, it is likely that industrialized countries with higher earnings as well as more R&D, education and training will tend to acquire abroad more, although without respect to the size of the home population base.

Dunning asserts that foreign investment tends to be in low or mature technologies (more relevant to later phases of the product cycle). A first phase of foreign investment is simple import substitution. This constitutes the

---

[48] Ibid.

allocation of resources for rationalized specialization 1) in similar end products, or 2) through vertical or process specialization.

Dunning dealt with locational issues in the context of the growth of multinational enterprises (MNEs). He perceives that the significance of value-adding and transaction-cost determinants in turn vary according to country-, industry- and firm-specific factors.[49] The multinational enterprise finds much of its justification in the **diffusion** or transfer of technology. This process begins with innovation, continues through technological interdependence and finalizes in integrated technological systems (one could call them "beginning-to-end" systems), eg., the linking of imports to diffusion. One example is import-hungry Japan's reliance for 85% of its raw materials from abroad. Japan's global expansion are linked to securing an import base. This leads to MNE hierarchies with asymmetrical vertical interdependence (recall Forrester's bootstrap theory whereby a part of company output is re-diverted as a corporate production factor or input). Regional integration may build up that are based on *intra-firm transactions between international oligopolists*. Dunning asserts that the multinational firm (created by mergers and acquisitions as well as by internal growth and external marketing) makes business more efficient. However, he claims, governments limit this global efficiency by controls on the transfer of technology and antitrust action.

A1.3 OWNERSHIP-SPECIFIC ADVANTAGES

Ownership advantages compel firms to go abroad. These include patents and trademarks, management and organizational skills, preferential access to inputs and markets, and economies of size and scope. FDI arguments are asset-based and ressemble Tobin's Q. Expansion depends on having a special asset. If foreign transaction costs are high and property rights are difficult to protect, a firm will tend to invest (buy or build) rather than license. Acquiring companies can be expected to own or control special assets, even if these assets are only financial clout.

---

[49]John H. Dunning, *Multinationals, Technology, and Competitiveness*, London, Boston: Unwin Hyman, 1988.

A2. MERGER WAVES AND THE PRODUCT CYCLE

> *"Some of the cycles companies ride in the process of becoming successful are getting shorter: Product cycles, changes in technologies or industrial structures, performance cycles...Success breeds the causes of failure. Failure breeds the new stimulus towards success."*

DAVID MITCHELL, MAKING ACQUISITIONS WORK
LONDON: BUSINESS INTERNATIONAL, 1988

How does M&A and foreign investment relate to the product cycle? Let us start with Dunning observations, then historically revert to Vernon's,[50] concluding in main part of Chapter Seven with a new approach. Dunning delineates the product cycle by stating that because of high transaction costs, the young firm will be sited near innovating activities. In the first phase of its technology cycle the firm is unlikely to be internationally involved. Later, however, the firm looks beyond the local market for *additional sales* of at least some of production.

In phase two of the product cycle, locational advantages shift away from the innovating to a foreign country, spurred by competition. Standardization and codification allow copying and assimilation by other firms. Not only FDI and acquisitions may occur abroad, but also arm's length selling of technology through licensing or co-operative agreements. In any instance, sunk costs are best covered in phase two and afterwards in new markets at home and abroad (see Wendy's). The strategic causes of mergers and acquisitions are also those that drive multinational (foreign direct) investment as spelled out in the 1970s and thereafter by Fred Bergsten and others.[51]

---

[50] Raymond Vernon, "International investment and international trade in the product cycle," *Quarterly Journal of Economics, 80, 190-217; and "The product cycle hypothesis in the new international environment," Oxford Bulletin of Economics and Statistics*, 41, 255-67.

[51] C. Fred Bergsten, Thomas Horst, Theodore H. Moran, *American Multinationals and American Interests*, Washington, Brookings Institution, 1978. Also Raymond Vernon, *Sovereignty at Bay; the Multinational Spread of U.S. Enterprises*, 1971; and R. Vernon, *Exploring the Global Economy: Emerging Issues in Trade and Investment*, Lanham, MD, University Press of America, 1985. With regard to comparative advantages in developing countries see Louis T. Wells, *Third World Multinationals*, Cambridge, MA, Massachusetts Institute of Technology, 1983.

In phase three of the product cycle, Dunning perceives exports from the foreign affiliate, even back into the home market. In phase four, the original ownership advantage may completely erode in *all* markets, much like asset depreciation, as the technological gap narrows.

Locational advantages have also shifted with time from early resource-based investment (typical of empires) to market-oriented FDI. In the 1970s government learned to attract foreign investment through favorable foreign investment packages. Internalization works best in countries where governments support mergers and industrial concentration, and where the probability of general market failure is less.

The relative weight and importance of M&A as a major expansion mode for FDI and all new investment need to be established by further empirical work. For instance, of 521 foreign-owned companies surveyed by the State of Washington, acquisition was the vehicle for entry of 29% of all companies surveyed. Expansion was planned by almost half of all respondents. Proximity to key industries, markets or suppliers was indicated by respondents as the prime factor for locating there.

In this light, further research may also identify M&A **not** related to growth and market upswings. For example, M&A has been successful in high-performance and high-growth sectors. But so have licensing, joint ventures, corporate venturing, tactical marketing and production alliances (collusion), notably in the European electronics sector.

A2.1 FOREIGN DIRECT INVESTMENT

During the 1960s and 1970s a great preoccupation of economists, especially economists in business schools, was explaining the expansion of US foreign direct investment, or "FDI", in Europe and elsewhere. In his famous 1966 article on the product cycle, while coming to grips with shifts in international trade and investment (of which M&A is a part) Raymond Vernon decried the "inadequacy of the available analytical tools."[52] Vernon de-emphasized classic comparative advantage arguments as well as the international equilibrating mechanism. Instead he stagelit innovation timing, scale economies, and the role

---

[52]R. Vernon, "International investment and international trade in the product cycle," *Quarterly Journal of Economics*, 80, 190-217.

of ignorance and uncertainty. At the same time Vernon confronted the popular maxim of information equally accessible to all (similar to the faulty twin notion of perfectly clearing markets). He emphasized instead the centrality of geographic location and entrepreneurial access to communication. Vernon pointed out that just because the innovator has the scientific principles doesn't mean the product will "take" in the market. "Take factors" cited by Vernon are: 1) higher income and high labor costs combined with poorly distributed capital and 2) new wants. In brief, Vernon states that the higher wages demanded by laundresses precipitated the drip-dry shirt and the home washing machine.

Vernon highlights the following factors while exploring the product cycle and its relationship to new international investment (including M&A):

A2.2 START-UP

• **Early unstandardized design** (e.g., the great variety of automobiles before 1910, radio designs in the 1920s, and of notebook computers in the 1990s); unstandardized inputs, processing and final specifications.

• **Early monopolies** and **low price elasticities** of demand. Vernon attributes these factors to a high degree of production differentiation, which we find largely contradicts the point above. We would attribute early monopolies to zero or low price elasticities of supply as high transaction costs appear fixed—until scale economies come into force and production is streamlined by modular molding for a variety of products (Sony now produces over 40 types of Walkmans based on two or three basic models with slightly varying feature arrays).

• **Early need for swift communication** and **flexibility.** Easy and low-cost communication throughout the United States that can be expected to migrate elsewhere should provide extraordinary headway for start-up firms.

A2.3 MATURATION

• **General product standards** are required to achieve economies of scale, lower production costs, expand locally and abroad, and encourage long-term commitments, especially through lower prices.

• **Mature product variety or product mix** - or product risk-spreading by diversification of product line, and as a result of specialization. Vernon doesn't refer to the search for "new locations" in terms of internal market "niches" in ever more competitive markets by branching or articulation in Phase III which we build into the merger wave model in Chapter 7.

• **Entry barriers** - Bain devised a list of barriers to entry in American industry, de-emphasizing price collusion while underscoring the ability of new companies to enter the market and undercut prices.[53] In other words, oligopolies keep the little guy out with scale economies, absolute cost advantages, and product differentiation. Hymer, finding entry barriers an insufficient argument, noted that foreign investing is *not* a common practice, but highly concentrated amongst a few large firms (the Seven Sisters in petroleum), which in turn are centered in a few, oligopolistic industries. The recent exhaustive Brookings study by Blair, Lane and Schary arrives at similar results for mergers and acquisitions. They witness bubbles of acquisition activity in lead sectors by a few large serial acquirers. They also note that in some sectors there is virtually no M&A. Technologies where there are no acquisitions tend to be smaller, "mom and pop" operations, such as leather. This suggests that *M&A occurs in a certain phase of the technology cycle*, an issue we explore below. Furthermore, small networks acquire their way into becoming larger networks: vivid examples are offered in the food, radio and tv, and pr/advertising sectors.

For example, an extraordinary number of takeovers by serial acquirers occurred in the 1980s in the global advertising and public relations sector, particularly in Britain. Success ratios have been diverse. In contrast to the early high profitability on the acquisitions trail of Shandwick PLC, Saatchi and Saatchi Co PLC and the WPP Group tread deep and uncertain waters. Having acquired the giant American J. Walter Thompson (JWT) and many others, WPP severely suffers from indebtedness and other current problems concerning intragroup synergies.

The Saatchi brothers floated their stock in the 1980s, making paper fortunes in the process. The firm also indebted itself in order to create a global network of regional offices in order to offer international clients cross-referrals, or

---

[53] Joe S. Bain, *Barriers to New Competition*, Harvard University Press, 1956.

worldwide marketing services (the "follow client" motive for M&A). Ambitious attempts to expand in the United States brought the company close to failure by running up too much debt. Shares in Saatchi and Saatchi dropped by 67% in 1990.

Aggressive purchase by WPP's Martin Sorrel of JWT and other companies during the 1980s turned WPP into the world's largest marketing services group. WPP debt rose to $550 million. The WPP Group became subject to split-offs by regional offices due to client conflicts. J. Walter Thompson was subjected to client defections because competitors held accounts at the other firm. Key executives subsequently resigned. In its first three years as part of the WPP Group, JWT lost $450 million. A warning of decline in profitability by Mr Sorrell in 1990 wiped 70 per cent off the value of WPP shares. As restructuring in 1991 was followed by further problems in 1992 when Sorrell revealed a 38 per cent fall in profits. A series of disposals to reduce borrowings have been slow to materialize. Banks are now reviewing a debt-for-equity swap.

Niche expansion typically occurs through franchising in the pattern established by Anita Roddick of the Body Shop. However, a recent trend—reaching even towards the legal and medical professions traditionally dominated by stand-alone partnerships—is to build up franchise-like agency networks via acquisition such as Joe Foster's US firm In Speech specializing in speech therapy. Finally, asset undervaluation—a key for Tobin's Q to come into effect—tends to occur in mature, oligopolistic sectors such as oil.

Vernon also noted that the degree of *world concentration* in several US-dominated, mature oligopolies (aluminum smelting, automobiles, copper, petroleum production/refining, pulp and paper, zinc) declined from 1950 - 1970, mainly because of the rapid growth of European and Japanese firms. Argentina, Brazil and other newly industrialized countries are also taking a bite of the oligopolistic cake in steel and similar mature industries.

A2.4 CAUTIOUS INTERNATIONAL DIVERSIFICATION
Vernon's expanding entrepreneur is faced with the choice to *trade or invest* abroad by setting up a local production facility. Strangely enough, trade and joint ventures have dropped out of M&A and related research. The only choices of today's entrepreneurs, as covered in recent literature, are to buy assets (M&A), or to build them.

The decision to build or buy is predicated on the "Q Factor", based on Tobin's Q theory. The corporate acquirer will buy a firm when stock prices are low, finance cheap, interest rates while paying down debt are low, and when current or previous high inflation rates have raised the prices of finished fixed assets. The expanding corporate executive builds when assets are cheap not relative to previous time periods, but to other locations or markets, and low inflation has held target asset prices down. Assets are cheap locally when the local economy has lost its buying power and there is very low capital accumulation and a dim perception of growth in demand.

A risk to the outward-bound entrepreneur (say to Asia) is not the "take" market risks inferred by Vernon, but rather the risk that local competitors in their own markets may copy and produce the product before the home producer has an opportunity to properly assess the risks of international expansion. Vernon suggests that the main criteria for producing abroad is low labor costs, an assertion substantiated by the 1980s migration of production from Japan to Hong Kong, Singapore, Taiwan and Korea; and then broadly westward to Macao, Thailand, Indonesia and India. The new wave of European and American investment in PR China and Southeast Asia confirm this trend.

A3. MERGER WAVES, TECHNOLOGY CYCLES AND LONG WAVES

> *"The world economy is now in its seventh year of growth, with few signs of a real recession ahead. Is the business cycle dead?"*

THE ECONOMIST, AUGUST 5, 1989, P. 57.

To fully understand how merger waves subscribe to the economy as a whole, it is useful to revert to the lengthy literature on so-called technology cycles, the prolonged ones of which are referred to as long waves.[54] The expression

---

[54] J. D. Dunning and J. A. Cantwell, "The changing role of the MNE in the creation and diffusion of technology" and other articles in Fabio Arcangeli, P.A. David, and Giovanni Dosi, Eds., *The Diffusion of New Technology*, Oxford University Press, 1988; Christopher Freeman and Luc Soete, *New Explorations in the Economics of Technical Change*, London and New York,

(continued ...)

technology cycle is similar to product cycle when there is a predominant standard bearer with related products being subsidiary such as components. Business cycles are essentially output waves. They are closely related to technology and product cycles because they provide the dynamic limits or external (independent) variables to technological and product fluctuations. Technology, product and business cycles provide the dynamic economic climate within which merger fluctuations occur. It is therefore important to understand their behavior.

There are many elegant theories on technology and business cycles. Each tends to address one initiating cause of wave-like behavior. Rather than dwelling on one theory we briefly present leading theories to form a composite view of factor interaction and economic wave causation. Theoretical assertions are criticized as required to fine tune the whole picture as relevant to M&A.

A3.1 THE LONG WAVE PIONEERS: 1920S AND EARLIER

Parvus, Van Gelderen, and **S. de Wolff** attributed waves to *business replacement reinvestment.* Cycles are thus caused by product life. Most notably in this group is **Kondratieff** who extensively analyzed investment in new technologies by studying commodity prices over 100-plus years up to the 1920s. Kondratieff proposed the famous *long wave,* or an expansion period for a major new technology of some 24 years, followed by a decline period of years. Comparing the M&A waves cited in Chapter Two with the Kondratieff long

Pinter Publishers, 1990; and Giovanni Dosi, Keith Pavitt, and Luc Soete, *The Economics of Technical Change and International Trade*, New York, Harvester Wheatsheaf, 1990. Also see earlier works of Joseph A. Schumpeter, *The Theory of Economic Development; an Inquiry into Profits, Capital, Credit, Interest and the Business Cycle*, 1934; N. D. Kondratieff, *The Long Wave Cycle*, Translation by J. M. Snyder, New York, Richardson & Snyder, 1984; Colin Clark, *Conditions of Economic Progress*, 1957; and Gerhard Mensch, *Stalemate in Technology*, Cambridge, MA, Ballinger Pub Co, 1979. Others contributing to this area are also schematized below.

5.A.1 M&A AND KONDRATIEFF CYCLES AND THEIR DIRECTION

M&A WAVES	KONDRATIEFF LONG WAVE	SECTORS
	1. 1789-1814 - UP 1815-1849 - DOWN	riverboats & canals
	2. 1850-1873 - UP 1874-1896 - DOWN	railroads
1898-1902 UP	3. 1897-1920 - UP 1921-1940 - DOWN	automobiles, petroleum, & construction
1920-1929 DOWN		
1940-1947 UP	4. 1941-1965 UP 1966-89/91 - DOWN	chemistry, transport, air & construction
1960s UP		
1980s DOWN		

waves, one can expect lags and M&A consolidation occuring at the end of new technologies.

But our assumption does not hold true! Merger waves do not occur mainly at the end of technologies in the maturation and consolidation phases. In fact, if Kondratieff waves and merger waves represent true time series, *merger waves occur more frequently during periods of technology growth and less during periods of decline. The main point is that mergers increase in both periods of expansion and contraction.*

Recently, **A. Gary Shilling**, a Kondratieff disciple, suggests that expansions occur during popular wars and declines during popular wars. Declines, he suggests, are due to too much capital investment, debt kill, overbuilding, and overproduction.[55] Recently **Nigel Atkinson,** an insolvency specialist at Touche Ross UK, has similarly observed the "one project too far" syndrome: Growth undertaken for growth's sake leads to over-extension—including ambitious programs of acquisition and other expansion on a weak financial base. Key factors for failure, he notices, include technological obsolescence, problems with one customer, encroaching competitors, undue reliance on key suppliers, loss of permits or licenses, overtrading, and domineering chief executives unable to respond to change.[56]

Cringely has remarked that it takes society roughly thirty years to *absorb a new information technology into daily life.* It took about that long to turn movable type into books in the fifteenth century. Telephones were invented in the 1870s but did not change our lives until the 1900s. Motion pictures were born in the 1890s but became an important industry in the 1920s. Television, invented in the mid-1920s, became mainstream only in the mid-1950s. The personal computer emerged in the early 1970s and is halfway down the road to being a part of most people's everyday lives.[57]

---

[55] A. Gary Shilling, "This could be the eve of a false recovery," *Forbes*, Mar. 18, 1991, 74-75.

[56] Nigel Atkinson, "The Facts of Life," *Director* (UK), May 1992, pp. 89-90.

[57] Robert X. Cringely, *"Accidental Empires. How the Boys of Silicon Valley Make Their Millions, Battle Foreign Competition, and Still Can't Get a Date,"* Addison-Wesley Publishing Company, Inc., Reading, Mass., 1992, p. 44.

A3.2 THEORIES OF ECONOMIC FLUCTUATIONS: SCHUMPETER AND THE 1930s

Another Kondratieff disciple and leading cycles theorist is Joseph Schumpeter. He identified "*creative destruction* whereby new technology clusters emerge during depressions, driving out the old. This cycle is led by innovative entrepreneurs. Economic upswings correspond with the introduction of new technologies. Schumpeter argued that capitalist business cycles are a summation of:

1. a 40-month Kitchin inventory adjustment cycle[58]
2. a 9-year Juglar cycle major capital investments
3. a 56-year + Kondratieff cycle - new technology investments

Phases One and Two are monopolistic. The turning point is a shift towards competition. In Phases Three and Four there is a tendency towards convergence between monopolized and de-entrepreneurialized corporations, on the one hand, and bureaucratically planned socialist organizations, on the other (Schumpeter in Galbraith 1967). At the end of Phase Four new consumer goods (each with its own product cycle) as well as new methods of production and transport appear and new markets are created.

A3.3 GROWTH AND CAPITAL MODELS: 1950s - 1970s

Mensch asserted that new clusters of *basic innovations* and *improvement innovations* create new markets. *Monopolized concentration* results, which is followed by new competition. Older companies (Sony) bring in rationalizing or *pseudo-innovations* (44 types of Walkmans). The new capacity is too great for the domestic market. *credit-financed export markets* become vital. New competition is coupled with growing saturation. However, LDC and other new consumers soon reach their credit limits. Demand becomes saturated. The government can not offer fundamental solutions, and a recession sets in. Finally, however, a new upswing is started by "Sachzwang"—rather like demand-pull.

---

[58] Kitchin maintained that the "limit" of each major cycle is 1) a peak of exceptional height, 2) a high bank rate and 3) panic.

Kalecki (1970) and **Goldmann** (1975): maintained that *investment cycles* exist *without generating output cycles* due to a the lack of multiplier effects.

Bauer (1978): identified four *investment phases:*
> • First phase "Bauer investment run-up" - many investment projects go through
> •Second phase "Bauer rush" - investment activity accelerates
> •Third phase "Bauer halt" - decline in approval rate of new projects
> •Fourth phase "Bauer slowdown" - investment declines

Rostow (1975) also proposed that there are *energy and raw material long wave cycles* that determine stages of growth.

A3.4 ACCELERATOR AND CYCLICAL DYNAMIC MODELS: 1930s TO PRESENT

Samuelson (1939), **Hicks** (1950), **Goodwin** (1951), **Rosser and Rosser** (1991), **Puu** (1990, 1991) each contributed to the notion of one- and two-stage *accelerators* with possible *nonlinear outcomes.* Sterman added that both cycle and chaotic dynamics are due to lags **Sterman** (1985); shorter lags lead to shorter cycles. Rosser and Rosser explore the concept that investment in the capital goods sector is dependent on the growth rate, or *capital self-ordering*, a factor in macroeconomic fluctuations recognized as early as 1933 by Frisch.

Nonlinearity is required by most continuous and self-regenerating systems. Yet western science has been dominated by linear applications in engineering, large because of the awkwardness and complexity of multidimensional nonlinear formulae before the advent of computer solving. Currently the term nonlinearity is loosely exchanged with the term chaos or chaotic approaches.[59] However, nonlinearity also refers to recurring behavior, or cyclicity.[60]

---

[59] See recent works of Norman Packard, Richard Dawkins, Edgar Peters, G.L. Baker, J.P. Gollub, Buzz Brock, Gunter Haag, Jerry Silverberg.

[60] See note 2 in Chapter Five.

A3.5 CAPITAL THEORIES

Mandel (1980) purported an *industrial cycle* defined by the acceleration (upswing) and deceleration (downswing) of *capital accumulation*. At the peak, it is impossible to invest the total mass of accumulated capital at an adequate rate of profit (compare 1992 when mutual funds and low interest rates are coupled with oversold stock markets). In the trough, underinvested capital reserves are put to use.

Colin Clark (1960) asserted that during the 1960s the world economy will transfer from a capital-hungry phase to a capital-sated phase.

Jay Forrester proposed an *investment multiplier accelerator* coupled with *rational behavior* effecting *capital consumption* and *saturation. Bootstraps* occur when a sector uses part of its own output for production (vertical integration).

A3.6 HUMAN FACTOR THEORIES

Trotsky (1923), **Mandel** (1980) defined a long cycle based on *class struggle.*

Chris Freeman, John Clark and **Luc Soete** (1982) described a *labor shortage* long wave theory whereby innovation has employment generating effects.

Post describes below a *population-war cycle* related to general factor shifts.

Braudel (1949) outlined a multi-century geographical cycle of *demographic-ecological actions,* an approach pursued by **Haag** et al.

Day and **Walter** (1989) define *epoch cycles* of the hunter-gatherer, village-agriculture, urban-trading, and the industrial era.

A3.7 BUSINESS CYCLE THEORIES AND LONG WAVES[61]

Since World War II early classification-by-statistics studies of the business cycle were pioneered by Burns and Mitchell,[62] who not only statistically confirmed the work to date by Kondratieff, Kitchin, Juglar, Schumpeter and others, but also laid the foundations for business cycle measurement in general.[63] Interesting enough, based on their early empirical attempts, Burns and Mitchell put forth quite conclusively that the results of various business and long cycle theories give widely diverging results. Business cycles and long waves do not seem to demonstrate covariance. Only Juglar cycles correspond roughly to the trough dates of sever business depressions.

Since Robert Lucas, business cycle research has been dominated by regression techniques, on the one hand, and by Barro *et al* who maintain that "real" business cycles that are not driven by monetary policy.

There are important incongruities in the technology wave and business cycle theories to consider before proceeding to an integrated merger wave model in Chapter Seven.

---

[61] See Ronald H. Coase, "The nature of the firm," first published in 1937 and as proceedings of a 1987 conference organized to celebrate the 50th anniversary of the article, in: Oliver E. Williamson and Sidney G. Winter, *The Nature of the Firm: Origins, Evolution and Development*, New York, Oxford UP, 1991. More recently: Robert J. Barro, *Modern Business Cycle Theory*, Cambridge, MA, Harvard University Press, 1989; or: Gunter Gabisch and Hans-Walter Lorentz, *Business Cycle Theory: A Survey of Methods and Concepts*, Berlin and New York, Springer-Verlag, 1987. Concern with business cycles dates back; for example, see Robert E. Lucas, *Studies in Business-Cycle Theory*, Cambridge, MA, MIT Press, 1981; Arthur Frank Burns, *The Business Cycle in a Changing World*, 1969; Paul A. Volcker, *The Rediscovery of the Business Cycle*, New York, Free Press, 1978; Ludwig Von Mises, *On the Manipulation of Money and Credit*, Dobbs Ferry, NY, Free Market Books, 1978; Friederich A. von Hayek, *Monetary Theory and the Trade Cycle*, A.M. Kelley, 1966.

[62] See Arthur F. Burns and Wesley C. Mitchell, *Measuring Business Cycles. Studies in Business Cycles No. 2*, National Bureau of Economic Research, New York, 1947.

[63] From 1854 - 1932 they observed that full cycles last from 3 1/3 years up until almost 8 years. Expansions last 21 - 46 months, and contractions from 16 - 47 months.

A4. APPRAISAL OF LONG WAVE AND TECHNOLOGY APPROACHES

A4.1 THE MYTH OF THE INNOVATOR-TURNED-ENTREPRENEUR

Schumpeter and others conceptualize waves of inventor innovation as a response to economic shifts. Inventors are apparently considered to be in short supply until a golden age of depression draws out clusters of innovators responding, for example, to increased demand for products with lower costs and higher efficiencies, perhaps due to a need to replace worn-out assets under the severe restraints of reduced capital spending at the end of a recession.

However, the contrary is true today. Innovations are, if anything, in oversupply; the critical product decision is choosing which technology will be developed into a market product. One IBM official maintains that his company alone has a backlog of technologies ready to be developed that far surpass the general market's ability to absorb and pay for new products. Markets are more finite than ideas. Furthermore, only technologies that take off count. A big pool of potential technologies in an old and/or poor culture may not elicit a market response.

The notion of product and business cycles being pumped by depression-inspired innovators deserves several qualifications.

As Dosi points out, innovation waves do not necessarily occur with depressions. Peaks in new ideas—part of Dosi's "technological paradigms"—can not be defined solely by economic factors.

There is a lingering implausibility to the notion of a depressed folk and a depressed economy vaulting great new ideas riding sufficient financial wherewithal to leap over the normal 95% failure rate in order to deliver a brilliant new technology to market. Savings don't necessarily increase in a depression. There may be net transfers to consumers, as in a socialist economy where more wages are generated than products. As we now can witness, in a downturn consumers as well as lenders are overstretched. Today it is underinvestment by pension and mutual funds and by smaller capitalists that contributes to the piling up of reserves.

These reserves of depression-skeptical investors are drawn back to the investment market when durables—refrigerators, roads and must bridges—absolutely be replaced, and/or by generated demand (the opposite of generated obsolescence), say by new technological developments.

However, most attempts at product launch fail, even in abundant periods. In a deep recession, development to market launch is dependent on sufficient finance, say from venture capitalists, or early investors in fixed assets, or owners of positive cash flows from food and other basic needs seeking to diversify. Furthermore, the *propensity to innovate - to undertake basic research and R&D - may not vary much in stable societies,* rich ones or poor ones. In contrast *the propensity to market launch, which in many instances is engineered, or discretely managed, may be stronger in a recession towards the end of an earlier product cycle.*

Large corporations manufacture innovation in a systematic way at what may be termed "virtual idea factories". In face of markets with limited generation product life, basic research and R&D are undertaken as survival insurance. The process of invention, technology or product development, marketing, and product life management has become a **science** for large corporations with enormous development budgets sometimes surpassing the government budgets of many countries. Moreover, products are often conceptualized, developed and marketed as part of product groups.

There are two kinds of research: basic research, and research and development. Basic research—the search of knowledge for its own sake—provides the scientific knowledge upon which R&D is later based. If a product ever emerges from basic research, it is usually fifteen to twenty years later. That is, there is a 20-year time lag from basic research via R&D to production.

Basic research is undertaken by governments, and is usually war-related. University research is either government funded or theoretical. Only a few companies do basic research, and they normally have at least a 50 per cent market share due to the large resources required. As much as 1 percent of annual sales will be devoted to insuring a technological lead in the future.

Research and development, or R&D, invents and develops a product for sale. New technologies are developed to be used in a specific product, based on existing scientific knowledge. The development part of R&D designs and builds a product using those technologies. Development can occur with research, requiring licensing, borrowing or stealing research from somewhere else.

Furthermore, *the time lag between the start of basic research and market launch can be assumed to accelerate or dampen technology trends.* During the deepest part of the recession in 1991, for example, this author observed 14 new products in USA markets. Most important is the fact that the development and marketing of new ideas depends on product management, capital availability and market receptivity, or finding solutions to customer needs. Innovations do not suddenly "happen". They are given sufficient selection and support to make them marketable. For every one hundred ideas there is one market product, or maybe less. Only 5% of new high tech start-ups succeed. Unusual circumstances are necessary for ANY entrepreneur to "make it", as the cutting edge of technology is ridden with risk and failure. Innovation and new product development are low probability numbers games. Successful Silicon Valley entrepreneurs refer to success factors such as timely production and market arrival in very short time windows of perhaps only five to twelve months.

In this context Kleinknecht's "diffusion swarms" seem less swarmy. We suggest that *innovations "cluster" locationally more than in time.* Silicon Valley in California has been a breeding ground for new technologies since World War II through booms and busts.

A Hewlett Packard representative responsible for taking new products from the R&D phase to the market phase assesses that in the electronic testing and measurement equipment market, ten new innovations were brought out during the slow 1970s, while only one or two innovations occurred during the booming 1980s. This assessment[64] suggests that *innovation waves, if they occur at all, may be linked to the final stages of earlier business booms (not recessions) when competitive forces led to research and development for new leading edge products.*

Time lags explain the illusory appearance of innovations in slump periods. Basic research in the computer sector consumes about five years, during which problem identification in response to consumer needs is just as important as finding a solution. Research absorbs another four to five years. The most critical point on the product cycle curve is *emergence from the three-year + development phase.* If the product comes out of the development phase six months late, 30 - 50 % of profits may be lost to competition. If the product comes out too early, requisite market and technical infrastructure for product support may not be in place. A premature market arrival is especially critical as marketing is very expensive.

An important point here is that *the early "ramp up" phase of the product cycle is about all the launch company can effectively control.* The start-up or growth part of the curve must be engineered to be as steep as possible. This is achieved by ensuring that:

> 1. The message is delivered to market, and the idea and its design serve together as a *solution* to customer needs.

> 2. Distribution is effective. Production is managed so that there is an ability get to market in a timely manner.

> 3. The necessary infrastructure is in place to coordinate timely production with delivery. is available, including education and pretraining; planning tools and delivery systems; control systems; and a trained and disciplined labor force.

> 4. The ratio time/costs is tightly controlled.

---

[64] . . .which deserves empirical consideration along with market launch cycles in general. . .

In sum, the evolution in operations management parallels the evolution in technology. *There is not one cycle and one cycle alone that devolves along the evolutionary path, i.e., technology.* There is also evolution in the handling of credit and methods of payment, production methods, transport/delivery systems, and marketing systems, subsidiary support, and in related technologies.

UK booms tend to be consumer driven, suggesting the force of the market in driving product cycles. One interesting fact emerges from the computer sector concerning the *importance of the consumer market to product and technology cycles. If the mainstream market phase is much longer than three years, then a components problem is created. Keeping up a constant component flow is complicated thereafter. This suggests that the technology cycle is in large part component driven.* The apex of the market phase - the middle part of a typically flattened bell-shaped curve - is determined by market size. The onset of the decline is fixed and beyond the control of the launch company, as it is determined primarily by the competition and new market developments. The launch company's only real chance is thus controlling the ramp-up, or the steepness of the start-up curve.

We thus find it more likely that innovation clusters and emerging technological waves are outcomes of market booms and component cycles rather than depressions.

A4.2 THE MYTH OF NEWNESS AND ONE GRAND CYCLE

The technology literature tends to treat innovation the same as time clusters of ideas that flourish into new successful industries. Too much emphasis is given to technology, information and "newness" as the midpoint of the pinwheel of change. Further, the leading edge with its high risk/reward rates and high failure rates is only one phase of the industrial life or technology cycle. To understand the product, technology and business cycles and their bearing on merger cycles it is important to delineate the importance of each phase of the product cycle. Indeed, it is important to understand the nature of cyclicity itself. A further definition of the fluctuation aspects of cycles is required. This task is addressed in Chapter Seven.

Most important is the change that occurs in the relation of production factor prices - change providing a locational focus and leading to serial overshooting, asymmetries and perturbation, and inevitably to industrial reorganization. Relative shifts in factor costs lead to symmetry breaking in the cycle of development: both internal and external. M&A is an important form of industrial re-organization, and is inherent to the product cycle.

There is an interorganizational multiplier to cycles. For example, one can define four organizational stages in the technical development phase in the computer sector, driven by four different personality types. In the first development phase designers and foundry factory developers gain satisfaction from creation and realization of their ideas. They may not have the time nor patience to see the product through to market as they move on to other concepts. Therefore, the second phase falls in the domain of scale-up engineers. The third phase is largely engineered by market launch executives whose main concern in matching changing consumer needs in a competitive environment new technologies. In the fourth phase, mature market managers ensure sound production and market delivery.

When times are tough the market managers, normally more concerned with ensuring stability, predictability and security for themselves and the firm, will listen more than ever to the designers and developers, who may have found their hands tied and voices silenced during the later growth intervals. There is thus an intra-bureaucratic aspect to cyclical behavior. With cutbacks due to recession, unemployed engineers will tend to launch the consultancies and businesses they were already planning based on new technological configurations.

Of equal importance to innovation and technology waves are:

• the availability of risk-taking venture capitalists or investors with capital or credit willing to invest in new businesses rather than mutual funds and other safer havens.

• *ample spare time* for the new technology cult to toy with their hobby. Describing technological innovation in the computer sector. Cringely observes:

" Programming is very much a religious experience for a lot of
people. . . . They can become almost evangelistic about the
language. They form a tight-knit community, hold to certain
beliefs, and follow certain rules in their programming. It's
like a church with a programming language for a bible."[65]

To recap, innovation and technological change depend on capital availability;
the right concept and design as a response to market needs; the right
infrastructure; the right managers and management systems - not one bright
idea from a depression-aroused inventor.

A4.3 THE MYTH OF THE INDEPENDENT CYCLE OF RELATIVELY FIXED DURATION

The notion of cluster can be redefined while examining the notion of fixed
cyclical duration. Another myth promotes a time series of relatively
independent technologies regularly recurring in time. How can this notion be
qualified?

• Firstly, the notion of a standard life for product and technology
cycles such as a 50-year long wave plus replacement investment cycles—in turn
perhaps based on sun spot cyclicity leading to crop and finally price cyclicity
(and reserve cyclicity to replace equipment according to de Wolff)—is hard to
grasp in a non-agrarian global economy. Moreover, products don't have the
same life. In many instances *product life is shortening*. The high technology
sector verifies shortening product span most vividly: Mainframe life used to be
around twenty years. The current life of a personal computer is eighteen
months, or less. In general, the shortening of the product cycle life is also
accelerating. The notion of a specific product or technology life is obstructed
by socio-economic anachronisms. For example, one major lag effect in the
British economy is the lasting durability of Victorian capital equipment and
infrastructure - much of which is still used today, rather than replaced.

• Dosi suggests that the shape of the technological trajectory is not
particularly defined -although once a path has been selected in terms of a
preferred and marketed technology, it sticks. This is an *exclusion effect*. The

---

[65] Gary Kildall of Digital Research.

first phase of a prototype product or technology wave is steep with an incipient outlyer, the middle phase is flat during the second and third phases of standardization and commodization, with potholes of market failure or decline, and the fourth phase gradually declines. This matter is explored in Chapter Seven.

• The final breakthrough to market is indirect:

"Nearly everything in computing, both inside and outside the box, is derived from earlier work . . . All these technologies found their greatest success being used in ways other than were originally expected. [66]

Thus there are *overlapping generations of technologies*, the old spawning the new, the new taking the place of the old. Major and minor technologies are exposed to the same processes of start-up, growth, maturity and obsolescence as products and product groups. Toasters evolve as well as automobiles, although without the same accelerator and decelerator effects on the economy at large.

• Furthermore, not all technologies that succeed in the market have equal market weight or industrial strength. As Bill Gates of Microsoft noted, money is made by being *the standard bearer* of a major new technology. The de facto industry standard is set by market share. For one standard-bearing technology there often arises "a number two spot."[67] A natural relationship seems to exist between *primary and secondary standards* marketed in a manner that make them complementary. A primary product fills the market

---

[66] See Note 12, p. 75 and p. 45.

[67] "When Lotus 1-2-3 appeared, running on the IBM, and only on the IBM, the PC's role as the technical standard setter was guaranteed not just for this particular generation of hardware but for several generations of hardware. The IBM PC defined what it meant to be a personal computer, and all these other computers that were sorta like the IBM PC, *kinda* like it, were doomed to eventual failure . . . *They* weren't different enough to qualify for the number two spot . . . IBM compatibility quickly became the key, and the level to which a computer was IBM compatible determined its success . . . Big Blue's share of the personal computer market peaked above 40 percent in the early 1980s. In 1983, IBM sold 538,000 personal computers. In 1984, it sold 1,375,000 . . . By riding IBM's tail while being even better than IBM, Compaq sold 47,000 computers worth $111 million in its first year—a start-up record." Cringely, Note 12.

requirement for standardization. In this regard it is component driven. The more or less 15 per cent of the consumer market that is ready for something new - due to expansion, replacement requirements, or a natural proclivity towards change, tends toward the product bearing the secondary standard. As the standards become commodities in the third mature market phase, reverse engineering ensures that clones abound. Commoditization thus drives prices down and forces standard setters to innovate. As the "t-shirts" or nerd cult discover a new professionalism, IBM and Motorola are co-designing a chip which is also being defined in conjunction with Apple that is to be the basis of IBM and Apple's next generation of computers. A fresh strategic mood and style are born.

———— .***. ————

CHAPTER 6
TAXATION, DEREGULATION
AND ANTITRUST LEGISLATION

The impact of government on corporate restructuring is more difficult to assess. Can laws create what Alan Clarke calls "vacuums of growth opportunity"? Deregulation, especially of the financial services, is often specified as a cause of M&A.[68]

Some contend that state takeover regulations raise expected takeover costs. State antitakeover laws are said to erect regulatory barriers, thus benefiting incumbent managers of target firms at the expense of shareholders.[69] Perhaps based on these arguments, the US Justice Department is now preparing new merger guidelines to determine if a proposed merger encourages anti-competitive practices. Department officials state that the proposed changes clarify guidelines but do not challenge the legality of takeovers. The guidelines are aimed at concentration, entry, efficiency gains, and insolvency.

Following this reasoning, if finance is available, say as retained earnings or in the capital markets, corporate managers will "play the law" to gain comparative advantages. They expand through external acquisition, as

---

[68] See Checklists, especially Chapter 7, Part 3 and B24.

[69] David I. Kass, "State and Federal Regulation in the Market for Corporate Control: A Comment," *The Antitrust Bulletin* XXXII/3, Fall 1987. Also compare Bain's barriers to entry in Chapter Five.

Following this reasoning, if finance is available, say as retained earnings or in the capital markets, corporate managers will "play the law" to gain comparative advantages. They expand through external acquisition, as opposed to internal growth, if it is less costly to buy out existing assets rather accumulate new ones.

6.1 TAXATION AS A CAUSE OF MERGER

In 1981 Peter Drucker pointed out that the current merger movement in the United States paralleled the tremendous wave of acquisitions in Germany from 1920 to 1922. During this period of *chronic inflation,* fixed assets were purchased by buying companies at market prices well below book values, and even further below replacement costs. *The low stock market valuations of companies over the past decade is due in large part to sustained under-depreciation of assets because of tax regulations.*[70]

Tax legislation is often cited as a primary cause for M&A.[71] Some officials at the US Department of Justice maintain that taxation law is the *exclusive* cause of mergers and acquisitions.

Advocates of merger-for-tax-benefits argue that mergers occur because:

1. *Inheritance taxes are avoided by selling* the company. Rather than face stiff inheritance taxes which can reach 70% or more of total assets, the founder-owner sells the company, which is usually private. Children are able to participate in the benefits of selling the company via stock ownership, often through a trust with favorable tax status.

2. *Interest payments on loans are tax deductible,* whereas stock dividends are taxable. Leveraged buyouts increased during the 1980s in order to reduce taxes (although some maintain that acquiring firms do not borrow more). Mergers are induced by shifting levels of equity trapped within firms by the adverse tax treatment of dividends (the "trapped equity" argument B10).

---

[70] Peter F. Drucker, "The Five Rules of Successful Acquisition" *The Wall Street Journal,* October 15, 1981.

[71] There are 14 citations of tax causes in the checklist of causes of M&A in Part Two.

3. *Accelerated appreciation* of old assets is possible with acquisitions, but not if assets are purchased new.

4. *Recapitalizations* allow taxation benefits. An intermediary in the 1982 Allied takeover of Bendix informed the author that the $32 million deal was largely motivated by the creation of $25 million in tax credits. After Allied bought Bendix, the acquiror was able to take advantage of Bendix' three years carry back of tax credits. The credits helped to finance the takeover. Tax credit availability as a motivation for M&A has been disputed for 94% of all mergers and acquisitions (D6). In any case, today companies with available tax credits are hard to find.

5. *Tax-loss carryovers* are captured by mergers and acquisitions.

6. Paying for new companies by *stock-for-stock exchanges* avoids taxes altogether.

Little comprehensive work has been undertaken on the effects of different tax regimes, either between periods in one country (for example, see Bittlingmayer's work on United States antitrust legislation[72]), or amongst countries. The effects on mergers of limited tax regimes versus high tax regimes can then be properly assessed and compared to the effects of changes in monetary policy.

6.2. DEREGULATION AS A CAUSE OF MERGER

Whether regulation plays a predominant force in mergers and acquisitions is more difficult to measure. The Part Two Checklists contain almost twenty references to deregulation as a cause of M&A. The enormous impact of changes in government policy towards business become clear if we consider recent developments in the US airline and banking sectors as well as the UK airline, financial services, telecommunications and electricity industries. Needless to say, the sell-off of over two thousand companies by Germany's Treuhand will have a great influence on domestic economy. The tremendous bearing of government monetary policy has already been discussed.

---

[72] G1 in bibliography and Note 74.

One of the best examples of the deregulatory effects is the American airlines industry. The American commercial airlines industry expanded with the return of pilots and airplanes to the USA after World War II. Aided by government subsidies for flying airmail, new companies including American, Braniff, Continental, Delta, Eastern, Northwest, Pan American, TWA and United Airlines flourished. Overstacked bureaucracy and government supervision may also be a legacy from the US Air Force. The Civil Aviation Board (CAB) controlled all domestic routes and fares, allowing regional airline monopolies to develop. One of the outcomes of monopoly is that union demands for wage increases and other concessions for airline employees were met; in the regulated environment as costs to the company were passed along to the customer through higher fares.

At the end of the 1970s during the Carter Administration, Alfred Kahn, head of the CAB, totally deregulated the airlines. Competition opened up on all domestic US routes. Fare controls were also abandoned. Under the solid management of Bob Crandall at American Airlines and Steve Wolf at United Airlines the strong became stronger as the weaker failed. In somewhat more than ten years Eastern, Midway, Pan Am, TWA, America West, and Continental underwent major structural changes, or disappeared.

In short, deregulation of the US airlines industry led ultimately to bankruptcies and acquisitions. Likewise in Britain changes in government regulatory policy have led to the consolidation of BOAC, BEA, British Caledonian, and British Airways.

In 1980 US President Jimmy Carter signed a law allowing savings and loan associations to pay market interest rates on deposits. The act was part of a radical deregulation of the banking and S&L industries, increasing competition. One outcome (see Chapter Two) was that S&Ls became more inclined to make high-interest loans to real estate developers and buyout managers. As the developers and MBOs failed, the S&Ls went down with them. Secondly, US laws are easing on interstate banking. The enormous proliferation of American banks generated by old laws is thus subject to massive failures and subsequent consolidation. Stigler and Peltzman argue that government intervention provides a mechanism to transfer wealth from one group to another.[73] Ironically, the US Federal Government will spend $300 billion of taxpayers' money in the 1990s to pay off depositors at failed S&Ls. Further tax funds will be allocated by the hard pressured Federal Deposit Insurance Corporation (FDIC) to pay off depositors at failed banks. Massive wealth transfer due to government regulation is certainly evident at the end of the twentieth century.

Deregulation of the UK banking sector during the 1980s led to massive takeovers amongst discount houses, stockbrokerage firms and major banks to provide a full range of financial services under one roof. The increased costs caused by expansion have seriously threatened almost the entire British banking sector. Many banks are now for sale. Costs have also been raised by the necessity of meeting the stringent and lengthy filing requirements of five or more British financial regulatory agencies.

The exclusive control of British telecommunications by British Telecom has devolved by privatization, through the sale of BT shares to the general public. Furthermore, the British telecommunications sector has become a duopoly with further competition in sight. Mercury Telecommunications now competes directly with British Telecom as a principal carrier and a host of other companies provide increasing services. Germany is following suit. Although the pandemonium of US free market telecommunications has not yet been met in Britain, the costs of telephone calls and other services are two to five times above the US.

The UK Central Electricity Board has also been privatized. A large number of bidders have competed to acquire individual water authorities, and the overall performance of decentralization and privatization have yet to be discerned.

6.3 ANTITRUST LEGISLATION AS A CAUSE OF MERGER
The current merger talks between Air Canada and Canadian Airlines demonstrate the duopoly and monopoly effects of M&A. Consolidation may enhance efficiencies, especially in mature markets with surplus capacities, yet at the same time the collusive nature of mergers is undeniable.

---

[73] Kass, op. cit.

Concerned with the influence of politics and business regulation on the general level of stock prices, Bittlingmayer regressed quarterly returns on concurrent changes in industrial production and wholesale prices and on current and leading case filings (based on earlier work by Fama and Schwert). He thus develops a measure of the impact of legislation on merger and acquisitions activity. By comparing the (expectation of) filing of antitrust cases to merger waves, Bittlingmayer reveals that *an increase in (expected) case filings by the US Department of Justice and the Federal Trade Commission significantly precedes a decrease in merger activity in all instances.*[74] Swings in antitrust case filings, he maintains, *explain between 6—32 percent of the observed variation in annual stock returns for 1904—45 and major sub-periods after changes in real output are taken into account.* Each case filed is associated with a 0.5 to 1.9 percent drop of the DJIA. Furthermore, aggressive antitrust crusades under Presidents Theodore Roosevelt, William Howard Taft, Herbert Hoover, and Richard Nixon led to economic slumps in 1907, after 1910, 1929, and 1969. Hoover's Attorney General William Mitchell announced on October 25, 1929 that he would vigorously oppose antitrust violation, and that the administration had not given clearance to a single proposed merger. Most remarkably, the stock market dropped 25% on the two business days thereafter. In contrast, under the more restrained administrations of Presidents McKinley, Coolidge and Reagan, antitrust enforcement reached low-water marks three times in the hundred years since the Sherman Act was signed in 1890. During those 19 years, inflation-adjusted per-capita GNP grew at 2.5%, as compared to an average of 1.8% in the other 81 years of the century.[75]

In general, Bittlingmayer remarkably concludes that *"between 5 and 30 percent of the total variation in the Dow is directly attributable to antitrust filings."* However, since production may itself have been affected by antitrust agitation, these results are conservative estimates of the total effect of case filings on the trust issue such as policy pronouncements, legislation and political posturing."[76]

---

[74]See George Bittlingmayer, "Republican Trustbusting Leads to Disaster," *Wall Street Journal*, July 8, 1991; and G. Bittlingmayer, "The Stock Market and Early Antitrust Enforcement," September 16, 1991, and "Stock Returns, Real Activity and the Trust Question," October 27, 1991 (Working Papers at the Graduate School of Management, University of California at Davis).

[75] *Ibid.*

[76]Ibid., "Stock Returns ... ".

Bittlingmayer's startling and convincing arguments assign credibility to the advocates of legislation as a major cause of shifts in mergers and economic activity in general. Further empirical work is required to assess the relative weight of taxation causes as opposed to financial and corporate strategic causes of mergers and acquisitions. If it is true that mergers lead fixed investment as from 1968—1973,[77] and that both merger activity as well as investment activity are pro-cyclical, then regulatory flaring and cooling of the economy would directly bear on the number of mergers as well as the level of investment. The effect of antitrust regulation is heightened by government measures that effect stock prices and interest rates which are positively correlated to mergers and acquisitions.[78]

Similarly, the impact of antitrust legislation on corporate restructuring and business performance can be further understood by crossborder comparisons.

It is important to recall, however, that antitrust laws were originally aimed, not at acquisitions *per se* but at corporate *size*. The purpose of antitrust is to prevent price setting and other monopolistic malpractices that prevent competition. Although few would dispute the price advantages offered by the economies and technologies of scale offered at McDonald's and Wendy's the belief that large companies are inherently "bad" still persists, even in a world where the ability to compete globally is central to domestic welfare. Mergers and acquisitions lead to consolidation, not necessarily to monopoly. In most instances, the rationalization of assets and the elimination of overcompetition by M&A serve to *improve* competition, rather than impede it.

Large corporations dominate in mainstream business, with newer and smaller businesses located in "feeder" industries that service the larger groups, or otherwise perform niche functions. Large firms provide standardization and market muscle; small firms offer innovation, flexibility, maneuverability and smaller production lot sizes. In recent years close cooperation between large and small has taken the form of outsourcing, subcontracting, and joint venturing, and financial support.

---

[77] See George Bittlingmayer, "Merger as a Form of Investment," Wissenschaftszentrum Berlin für Sozialforschung, Berlin, May 1987, Discussion Paper IIM/IP 87-13.

[78] Ibid.

6.4 DISTINGUISHING FAIR RETURN FROM MALPRACTICE

The ethics of mergers and acquisitions are reaching center stage. Who and what are the foundations of corporate law meant to protect, and for what reasons? What practices are inherent to sound business, and which are not?

These philosophical and practical questions challenge the fundaments of the regulated market economy. They were pivotal in the 1985 US Congressional Hearings and to reviews by the UK Mergers and Monopolies Commission and Takeover Panel, as well as the UK Office of Fair Trade.

New laws tailgate change. Yesterday's innovation can be today's malpractice. Unfortunately, public ethical disclosures succeed the event, and leading edge innovators who "got in wrong" can end up in jail. Innovators always stand the risk of being tomorrow's criminals due to the retroactive nature of new laws. The CEO, the CFO, as well as major shareholders support mergers when corporate restructuring via the M&A entry and exit route is perceived as the optimal way to enhance economic returns—both to the firm and to the core decision-makers themselves. Some of the new methods for undertaking takeovers in the 1970s and 1980s have retroactively come under severe attack.

Even though it is a part of the longterm pattern of corporate expansion and international economic involvement, 1980s M&A constitutes a major departure in corporate finance and performance. Subtle departures, however, give extraordinary power to large corporations with strong acquisition teams enabling massive crossproduct and crossborder market penetration. This has been especially true for new market entrants from Japan, Hong Kong, Taiwan, and more recently from Singapore, Korea, Indonesia and Thailand.

The fundamental question of malpractice is clouded by the lack of measurable indices concerning the "fairness" of mergers and acquisitions, even though antitrust legislation has been extant for over 100 years. To make matters worse, segregating right from wrong is complicated by dispute. For example, Rohaytn attacks corporate restructuring for generating too much debt (F13). The validity of this argument depends on the ability to assess how much debt is correct for a given economy. In contrast, Michael Jensen argues that mergers are a valuable vehicle in an economy for consolidation and rationalization—for the periodic self-cleansing necessary for a thriving economy.

Is M&A good or bad? Most societies do not prosecute citizens for being poor businessmen. Inversely, societies tend to discount *successful* mergers and acquisitions. In contrast, leaders of *unsuccessful* mergers, acquisitions and buyouts are denigrated, if not prosecuted.

How does one properly assess the impact of bad legislation on good mergers and acquisitions? Much of the pioneer work in venture capital and takeovers during the 1980s in Britain has been wiped out by irresponsible government interest rate policy that in 1991 alone forced large sections of the British economy into bankruptcy—throwing even staunch mainline industries into economic turmoil.

The question that legislators must resolve is what regulatory and tax laws magnify contributions by mergers and acquisitions to the general economy, and what laws are necessary to discourage malpractice. Unless a set of benchmarks are established for judging acquisition performance, this task will never be performed with any degree of success. We hope that this book is an preliminary contribution in establishing indices for assessing M&A behavior.

———— •***• ————

CHAPTER 7
MERGER WAVES—
A CYCLICAL DYNAMIC APPROACH

"With the possible exception of Bittlingmayer's (1987) 'merger as investment'
view, no theory to date has been found which can account for the historical
record with more than a modicum of explanatory power."

T.C. OPLER AND J.F. WESTON (UCLA)
"THE IMPACT OF MERGERS ON OPERATING PERFORMANCE,"
PAPER, AEA CONFERENCE, WASHINGTON DC, DEC. 1990

7.1 INTRODUCTION: THE EVOLUTIONARY DYNAMICS OF PRODUCT AND MERGER CYCLES

To our knowledge to date there has been no general theory for the merger
wave.[79] In this chapter a general approach to merger waves is presented based
on cyclical dynamics. A general equation for merger waves is also presented as
well as an interpretation of the cyclical dynamics of merger waves. Those
concerned more with practical outcomes than with theory would do well to
disregard this chapter and proceed to the Checklists in Part Two where M&A
causes and effects are reviewed.

---

[79] Although Eckbo has investigated the possibility of sectoral wave behavior as mentioned in
Chapter 5.

7.1 MERGER CYCLE PHASE ONE: START UP

PHASE ATTRIBUTES	PHASE CHARACTERISTICS
NAMES	trough, start-up, pioneering
DIRECTION	down - up (coordinate at bottom = - -)
TYPE OF INVESTMENT	core restoration, growth inflation of previous 2 phases leads to buying of second hand (Q) assets at low interest rates, incipient implementation of innovations from basic research and R&D in capital-rich phases.
TYPICAL SECTORS	food, banking, chemicals
FACTORS	abundant inventories, mass formation, value-shedding, technological retrenching, inelastic demand causes anomalies
TYPE OF FINANCE	cashless alliances as well as joint ventures for risk-sharing rather than competitive incremental risk seeking; more equity and initial public offerings, barter
TYPE OF M&A	M&A as seed investment, core/horizontal, market alliances/joint ventures
GEOGRAPHIC SPREAD	isolation, locational comparative advantages develop, outmigration by strong and fit
TYPICAL BUSINESS CYCLE PHASE	bottom of the recession and pull-out
LARGE OR SMALL	smaller targets
PRIVATE OR PUBLIC	private
HOSTILE OR FRIENDLY	friendly

7.1 MERGER CYCLE PHASE ONE: START UP
(continued)

TYPE OF GOVERN-MENT POLICY	low interest rates, tendency towards leftist politics toward end of phase (government spending), subsidization and takeover of industries that are labor intensive and suffering
SHORT/LONG TERM	longterm integration

DEMONSTRATION OF PHASE CHANGE ATTRIBUTES:	**PHASE CHARACTERISTICS**
SEEK	focus on expansion in core activity
ROTATION	augmenting, incipient heating up, capital-hungry inventor/entrepreneur amasses value and seeks scarce investment monies
SYNCHRONIZATION	GNP flat, borrowing flat, M&A lessens but continues because prices attractive to buyers with recession survival strength
AC/DECELERATORS	initial conditions of demand inelasticity and accumulation, unemployment, assets wear out, underproduction
SPECIALIZATION	local niche comparative advantages including price/e.o.s.
ANOMALIES OR TRIGGERS	underemployment of assets and production factors, tendency towards liquidity traps, monetary (IR) stimulus and govt. spending, assets wear out, asset rationalization, restoration and replacement
PHASE SHIFT	war, economic integration, opening of new markets

Recent studies on mergers and acquisitions are aimed at the justification of quantitative techniques and less at the exploration of basic concepts. The results are often technically sound but narrow in scope with limited applicability. In this chapter basic concepts some of which have been explored in econometrics, statistics, physics and engineering are integrated in the appendix to expose the centrality of cyclical behavior. The body of Chapter Seven applies the concepts to merger waves. More empirical work should follow.

Comparing merger waves with product, sector cycles and aggregate business cycles enables the evolutionary aspects of cyclical change to be observed. By taking financial, strategic and legal causes as major value drivers for M&A, the cyclicity of merger activity can be attributed to phase-shift overshooting leading to perturbations or anomalies.[80] Product and business cycles are rich soils for the perturbations required to generate major changes in macrovariables.

M&A waves can be understood from the standpoint of cyclical evolution, emphasizing search through specialization or complexity-building; and the generation of "possibilities" and functions through perturbations ("anomalies"). Stability is achieved by *synchronization forces in oscillating flow regimes*. The approach may be summarized as yield surface modelling and synchronization for optimal parametric yield with minimization of random defectivity.

The basic model[81] is premised on expansion and contraction (a volatility distribution) around a central time-dependent axis, the axis itself constituting a moving average, a reflection of the total sum of continuous systemic equilibria. The highest probability of occurrence, is not "at equilibrium", i.e., not on the axis itself. Occurrence of the number of mergers and acquisitions at any one time can be viewed as the sum of polar coordinates most readily expressed by the radius, or in radians. Variation in this cyclical system is

---

[80]Also asymmetries, disequilibria, symmetry-breaking, random defectivity, kinking in the causality chain, or simple variation of specification limits. In all cases the function remains the same, i.e., synchronized equilibrium or "status quo" is disturbed.

[81]Based on the C-anomaly developed by K. White and A. Post for determining IR and XR changes in the capital markets.

dependent on 1) the number of variables and co-determinative axes with constant time (defined by periodicity and system specificity); 2) the presence of lags that effect, for example, production and marketing and 3) perturbations caused by lags and specification variations. The buildup of simple (angular) momentum during contracting or expanding phases can also pull the cycle away from its "center of gravity", or initial conditions, setting off *search* for a new equilibrium.

Energy, technology, productivity and price shocks have traditionally arisen from harvest variation in agro-economic societies, more recently from changes in government behavior. A familiar example of anomaly perturbation is the change in capital accumulation and total liquidity leading central banks to lower or raise interest rates. M&A is directly effected. If a government lowers interest rates to increase liquidity and stimulate the economy, the stickiness of low asset prices (due to tax reporting and carried book values as well as other accounting methods) compared to the high market costs of replacing assets induced by earlier inflation causes two time lags to coincide that will encourage acquisition as the chosen form of expansion. The analysis of this behavior is a relatively straightforward empirical exercise.

Simple new information may also be sufficient perturbation to cause great change. Adverse and sudden stock price reaction to bad news is one example. For example, the negative vote of 50,000 Danes on European Economic integration in the summer of 1992 was enough to send global bond markets spinning. A weak approval of 51% by France in the autumn had the same effect.

The cyclical behavior of merger waves may act as an "M&A barometer" of product and sector phase shifts amplified by changes in the GNP (business) cycle. Like changes in the global debt/equity ratio to which it is closely related, the M&A indicator signals sectoral change like a cyclical *economic clock*.

To observe the relationship of merger waves with product, sector and technology cycles as well as macro-productivity (business or GNP) and

7.2 MERGER CYCLE PHASE TWO: GROWTH

PHASE ATTRIBUTES	PHASE CHARACTERISTICS
NAMES	growth, uptrend
DIRECTION	up - up (coordinate = - +)
TYPE OF INVESTMENT	acquistions of new assets and know how through direct investment and takeover, technological inculcation, and related take-off R&D
TYPICAL SECTORS	leading-edge technologies in mass markets, components and related services, computer systems technologies requiring large capital infusions and offering skilled engineering
FACTORS	tooled components in small design batches are expensive, but relative infrastructural and labor costs low
TYPE OF FINANCE	venture equity, high-cost relative to prevailing low interest rates
TYPE OF M&A	M&A as growth and control investment by vertical acquistion of suppliers, intermediaries to customer markets, or horizontal acquistion into new locations or highly related product with same or similar distribution channels
GEOGRAPHIC SPREAD	local production, markets expanding geographically, mature industries with excess capacity and debt seek to service large, low-income markets in other locations
TYPICAL BUSINESS CYCLE PHASE	boom mergers
LARGE OR SMALL	many small, but growing larger
PRIVATE OR PUBLIC	private, some public
HOSTILE OR FRIENDLY	friendly

7.2 MERGER CYCLE PHASE TWO: GROWTH   (cont'd)

TYPE OF GOVERN-MENT POLICY	free trade, liberal subsidization
SHORT/LONG TERM	longterm acquistion of specific technology and short-term turnaround or selling off of the rest of the target
DEMSTR. OF PH. CHANGE ATTRIB.:	**PHASE CHARACTERISTICS**
SEEK	market survival through advertising, product differentiation, new locations, customer servicing
ROTATION	heating up, expanding cyclical phase, higher income per quarterly cycle
SYNCHRONIZATION	high risk, high reward, stock market up, debt up, GNP increasing, economic activity and expansion increasing, exports and export dependence increasing, exchange rate increasing, inflation and replacement costs increasing, increases in costs of capital, interest rates, and junk bonds, M&A increasing
ACCELERATORS	profit motive, capital availability, low interest rates, expanding market demand pull, product and corporate adaptation to market; if cycle non-sinusoidal, this phase and decline are periods of highest acceleration
SPECIALIZATION	from low product articulation in first-to-market phase with relatively long run lengths because of significant applications required as well as customer education and support; towards special-feature niche specialization
ANOMALIES OR TRIGGERS	earlier ph. 4 heating-up and discontinuities: uneven economic development (nonlinear attractors), production breaks, variable duration of fixed assets, rents/prices cheap ("one-month's free rent for new tenant"), but property, luxury and "dispensable" sectors suffer while cash cow (basic foods) sectors watch. The anomaly of high growth is the high failure rate, *even amongst winners*, and thus high differentiation.
PHASE SHIFT	discretionary product cycle manipulation from flat or clamped to spiky peaks through speeding up of ramp-up phase, overlapping new product generation, thereby lessening component supply dependence in the maturity phase.

investment/financial cost cycles, the concept of life cycle[82] with evolutionary complexity can be introduced. To simply we choose a growth sector with seasonality or cyclicity highly correlated to the GNP. This assumption is qualified for downtrend mergers.

A standard, four-phase model is constructed. Each phase has value drivers, critical mass levels *and characteristic corporate restructuring*. The phase space in the model is the product life cycle, which is equated with sector. Acceleration and deceleration occur in each phase, for example as measured by productivity, liquidity, or shifts in the relative costs of capital. The four phases are the normal life cycle phases of birth or start-up, growth, maturity and decline.

What is the difference between phase change and phase shift? The former denotes evolution or movement *along* the life cycle curve. The latter involves a realignment or shoving of the entire cycle, best portrayed by a technology leap or jump which constitutes a shift of the whole technological paradigm. A technology shift, for example, may lead to a total cyclical realignment or resynchronizing of the economy (sail vessels → steamboats → railroads → cars → airplanes). After adjustment, economic indicators once again exhibit covariance, or oscillating co-movement along the cyclical trajectory. Some technologies are more germane than others. Most "drive" or key frequency technologies are related to transport, communication and war. . .and more recently to health. The application begins with start-up activity in the trough of a recession;[83] however, start-ups are not precluded from other phases. For purposes of clarity it is easiest to use this association established by Schumpeter, C. Clark and others, recalling that the leading edge with its high risk and failure rates is only one phase of the life cycle.

---

[82] Phase cycle analysis can be applied to a wide variety of economic events such as stock price evolution, foreign investment expansion, retail market price formation and clearing, business trends, and so on. Life phases are also familiar in cellular or biological systems as well as inanimate systems such as the life cycles of stars. For example, Having passed through protostar stellar formation, the sun of our solar system, for example, is well into the long mainstream phase of a stable stellar life, before continuing along into radical super novae decay or white dwarf senescence. However, life cycles are not by any means everywhere. They act as descriptors of continuing systems, and are observable at what can be termed "*the significant level of reference", which is that level where systems recur.*

[83] . . .although there is no deterministic reason for doing so. As already stated, evolution is intrinsic to all four phases.

7.2 THE PHASE DYNAMICS OF MERGER WAVES

The trough or depression is characterized by accumulation (clustering aggregation, overcrowding) resource abundance, and value shedding. Inventories increase. Real estate prices drop. The price multiples for target companies fall. Wages fall or remain static. Even the price of money, or the interest rate, goes down, and Keynesian liquidity traps may occur. High volatility may be experienced in the money markets as capital unemployed in production seeks preservation elsewhere. Since resource values accordingly drop, *the laws of locational comparative advantage* take hold. Required locational isolation surprisingly occurs at the center; the more that unused resources accumulate as the economy "spins up tight" due to loss of momentum, the more it pays off the business to rationalize or "focus" activity on key areas and to arbitrage depressed yet better values "at home" with relatively higher values "elsewhere": either at different geographical locations, in the future, or with value-added through manufacture or servicing. With reference to money accelerators, it takes less time for one dollar to circulate "once" through the economy. Although perhaps not yet physically manifested, the economy "heats up", developing the momentum required to break out of depression and proceed to the growth ramp-up period when "heating up" actually becomes manifest. M&A in this period is undertaken for either "seed investment" acquisition of required assets and know-how at rock bottom prices; asset replacement or upgrading, and consolidation (merging) of faltering sectors and excess capacity. Banking and the airlines industries, for example, are currently undergoing major consolidation.

The growth phase—*la vie en rose* of free-market politicians—begins. It is a golden era of uncertain length leading to propagation and expansion, widening of the competitive base; product commoditization, and a heightening of angular momentum as the system expands. It is often faster and cheaper for new and growing firms to gain assets, technology and qualified management by acquiring other companies than building up the firm. Control is also gained by vertical acquisition of suppliers and of operations intermediary to final consumers. Horizontal and quasi-horizontal acquisitions are also made to expand rapidly into new geographic markets and to make a new distribution network worthwhile by offering many products in a related line. Boom mergers are smaller, but tend to become larger as the acquirer grows. Typical sectors

7.3 MERGER CYCLE PHASE THREE: MATURITY

PHASE ATTRIBUTES	PHASE CHARACTERISTICS
NAMES	maturity, prosperity, golden era, renaissance
DIRECTION	up - down (peak = + + coordinate)
TYPE OF INVESTMENT	for shorter run lengths and well managed distribution systems
TYPICAL SECTORS	canals, railroads, automobile, chemicals, transport
FACTORS	commoditization (i.e. high volume, low price, mature technology and advanced production controls {e.g. just-in-time planning}, high competition), expensive assets, high property values, high wages and employment levels (e.g. featherbedding)
TYPE OF FINANCE	cash from cash cows; cash and stock; cash, stock and debt packages based on strong creditworthiness; debt-like equity and equity-like debt
TYPE OF M&A	M&A as mature consolidations investment, aggressive financial, vertical and conglomerate diversification for additional rent capture and risk spreading, aggressive strategic entry to new (global) markets and currency zones
GEOGRAPHIC SPREAD	growing, international dispersion
TYPICAL BUSINESS CYCLE PHASE	prosperity mergers
LARGE OR SMALL	large, or small by large
PRIVATE OR PUBLIC	public, private, LBOs, MBOs
HOSTILE OR FRIENDLY	hostile and friendly

7.3 MERGER CYCLE PHASE THREE: MATURITY   (cont'd)

SHORT/LONG TERM	financial turnaround and asset stripping, long term diversification
TYPE OF GOVERN-MENT POLICY	growth inflation fighting by higher interest rates, antitrust; high taxation, previously govt (LDC) takeover of proven technologies (with declining profit margins and market control)
DEMONSTRATION OF PHASE CHANGE ATTRIBUTES:	**PHASE CHARACTERISTICS**
SEEK	profit preservation, continuity
ROTATION	low r.p.s. (r.p.y.) due to expansion
SYNCHRONIZATION	GNP peaks, end of prosperous era, expansion peaks, bank lending and bridge lending capacity peaks, M&A grows and peaks as sellers willing to sell; this third period can be long and prolonged (golden era), unless discretionary measures are taken by manufactures to shorten it(product cycle management) to reduce dependence on component suppliers
DECELERATORS	overshooting, or momentum disequilibrium form engineer and market gluts, "everybody's already got one", although competition still keeps trying to jump on the bandwagon
SPECIALIZATION	exclusion effect of new technology in this monopolization or commoditization phase, social articulation (cultural "blossoming"), local buy-outs for regional or national expansion by professional "boutique franchising", e.g. therapy, medical, law, and tax preparation chains
ANOMALIES OR TRIGGERS	overextension, huge centralized overheads (e.g. R& D and basic research with returns 5-15 year away) overspending, overinvestment, extensive borrowing, loss of momentum (cycle stretched out at 'large orbit', "it takes longer to get things done")
PHASE SHIFT	boom profits entice investors to bust-overcapitalization and overproduction just when overcompetition and price dumping already threaten the firm

competition increases. More and more profits are committed to R&D, basic research, public relations and corporate identity.

In the third phase of maturity, large corporations with tremendous asset bases and extensive creditworthiness use strong cash flows and debt to buy out other firms. Financial maneuvers are rampant. M&A is undertaken to acquire earnings, asset strip, to diversify cash flows, and to expand into new markets. A recent trend is for professionals—lawyers, medical practitioners, therapists to buy out other professionals in different locations.

Good news does not go on forever. The crest (apex, peak) of maturity or prosperity is actually a "cooling off" period of extreme isolation which has been reached by hierarchy-building of large organizations as well as specialization (articulation, scaling, enslaving). It takes longer to get things done because it is more complex to send the inter-office message through the bureaucracy and receive a response. It takes more time to do the same thing. Dispersion and dissemination problems annoy distribution. Middle management controls the designers as well as the CEOs. The system is "overstretched". It is all "spun out". Investment capital is "hard to land", and debt financing costs reach all time highs along with interest rates. Momentum is lost.

Due to sudden angular displacement combined with the high degree of articulation (bifurcation or branching at the event frontier), the times are ripe for anomalies (perturbations). As failure and bankruptcy rates suddenly skyrocket, panic sets in. Big projects and new promotions are abandoned as a search for survival solutions on a personal as well as institutional level ensue. Perturbation anomalies (essentially arbitrage opportunities due to added value) are given serious consideration. *Open-window anomalies* are given the utmost of consideration. The old Kuhnian paradigm is broken. The onset of a new-era technology will ripen, fruitioning after the rapid descent to the trough.

A rich man—poorer man syndrome prevails: firms with steady cash flows and cash reserves that can survive lingering high interest rates, e.g., suppliers of basic commodities, take over companies that collapse under the weight of debt-servicing and dwindling demand. Highly relevant is the general significance of trough and crest events to what we term *payoff cycles*, or what happens to value-added residuals or profits with a basic shift of paradigm (mean, boundary, parameter). Payoff is profit, income, or *Mehrwert* (in both the traditional and modern sense). The payoff (income or profit) cycle exhibits four phases with reference to the firm: in the trough[84] or at the beginning, the new firm has negative income. As the successful firm expands in the ramp-up or growth phase, debt write-off occurs and profits are generated. In the third phase of maturity, profitability is anticipated to reward earlier indebtedness. Towards the middle and end of the maturity phase, the company becomes susceptible to takeover as a perceived "cash cow". This is particularly true of brand-name products. The anticipation of high growth rates and a long and successful maturity and prosperity phase must have been the driving force that led managers and bankers alike to allow takeovers based on heavy leveraging in the 1980s. Now corporate buyers (often national governments) of other companies often buy doom: the decline phase of the previously new or improved product, the forces of overcompetition, and declining profit margins are close at hand. The smile of success conceals the portents of decline and failure.

Boom profits also entice investor towards bust overcapitalization and overproduction. . .or the excessive payment of dividends. This also occurs more in the mature phase when overcompetition and price changes already threaten firm survival . In the later part of the phase there are also price wars and shifts in monopolies over the product cycle (e.g., the current gluts in the laptop computer industry coupled with discretionary market price ("yield") management are driving down laptop prices). A "recap shock" also occurs with the slowdown in variables/sales due to market saturation and overcompetition.

These firm level observations are adaptable to the macroeconomic level via product, business and technology cycles. An alarming shortening of the product cycle has occurred since World War II. Firm and sector performance are stymied by rapid technology generations, overcompetition, saturation, obsolescence and bankruptcy. This frustration is common in the computer industry and frontier technologies where megaconsolidations and spot takeovers abound. A rapid global transition from the new laptop computer industry to the still newer notebook personal computers is taking its toll. In the UK, information technology (computer) mergers slackened by 32% to £1.6

---

[84] for the business firm at hand, which in this model parallels economic trough, thus remaining true to the Schumpeterian tradition.

7.4 MERGER CYCLE PHASE FOUR: DECLINE

PHASE ATTRIBUTES	PHASE CHARACTERISTICS
NAMES	decline, down turn, cooling off
DIRECTION	down - down (quadrant = + -, bottom = - -)
TYPE OF INVESTMENT	distress borrowing or firm sell-offs to service and working capital
TYPICAL SECTORS	high tech, real estate, transport, sports and leisure, luxury goods, prepared frozen foods, industries affected by major technological shifts (horses, rail-roads, autos and highways, hotel/motels, adding machines, typewriters)
FACTORS	steep drop in asset values, labor and resource unemployment
TYPE OF FINANCE	equity rights and buy-back, IPOs, recaps
TYPE OF M&A	M&A as clean-up and asset re-allocation, thus investment consolidation, MBOs, consolidation of basic industries, less activity
GEOGRAPHIC SPREAD	corporate dismemberment and focus on core
TYPICAL BUSINESS CYCLE PHASE	bust
LARGE OR SMALL	smaller
PRIVATE OR PUBLIC	both drop off
HOSTILE OR FRIENDLY	benevolent

7.4 MERGER CYCLE PHASE FOUR: DECLINE
(continued)

TYPE OF GOVERN-MENT POLICY	contradictory maladjustment; interest rates still held high, accelerating recession and price deflation
SHORT/LONG TERM	cancellation of takeover plans by buyers

DEMONSTRATION OF PHASE CHANGE ATTRIBUTES:	PHASE CHARACTERISTICS
SEEK	survival by downsizing
ROTATION	acceleration of the downward spiral
SYNCHRONIZATION	GNP drops, low interest rates, management failure, recession stock market boom possible due to low bond rates, M&A increases because prices attractive to buyers with survival strength
AC/DECELERATORS	market demand slackens, costs of indebtedness prevails
SPECIALIZATION	turnaround consultancies and insovency law firms take the place of market makers
ANOMALIES OR TRIGGERS	rich-man, poorer-man, or interest rate segregation of good and bad debt, "recap shock" as onset or recession causes slowdown in sales
PHASE SHIFT	price wars and monopoly shifts (e.g., the PC markets)

billion (roughly US$ 3 billion) in the first three quarters of 1991. This happened in spite of energetic rationalization in recent years, especially in core hardware and support services sectors, including distributors, dealerships and maintenance companies. Nonetheless, software houses specializing in particular market sectors still command premium prices. In general, smaller firms absorbed by acquisitions are expected by acquirers to provide regional markets, proprietary information (patents, know-how), and/or distribution channels.

M&A increases in the *mature phases* of an industry (currently, airlines and finance houses in which global services exceed demand). Another common motivation for acquisition is rich asset turnaround, i.e., asset stripping for re-sale. However, in the case of state takeovers of "third world" mining companies, the perceived revenues of a firm and its economic visibility in the local economy are often the first signs of maturity, senescence and demise. In the past, governments have tended to nationalize companies into state-owned enterprises just when they have reached the declining phase of the product cycle.

In general, based on a study of 1,117 manufacturing companies with sales over $10 million, it seems that big companies are more profitable than small ones and natural game for hungry acquiring predators. However, when an outfit reaches around $2 billion in annual sales, complexity increases, profits taper off, and divestment becomes a theme. Corporate spinoffs slowed slightly in 1991, although in the longterm divestment remains strong[85].

Preserving the competitive edge is one of the most common reasons why mergers and acquisitions happen. Staying competitive is important domestically and internationally, particularly within the context of European market integration. Comparative advantages gained include circumvention of trade barriers; growth beyond saturated domestic markets; use of cheap productive labor and other favorable factor prices abroad, or avoidance of environmental and other governmental regulations. Acquiring companies also migrate towards politically and economically stable economies. Money is attracted towards stable, deflationary, growing economies where (debt)

---

[85] John Labate for *Fortune*, "Competition," April 20, 1992, p. 53.

financing is available. Mergers are also highly sensitive to favorable and disfavorable tax and antitakeover legislation.

The phenomenon of what may be termed *rich man-poorer man* comes particularly in play. For example, Eastern Airlines and other airlines were bought out in part or whole by stronger partners of the moment (Eastern's acquiror Continental subsequently went bankrupt). UK NatWest's Malcolm Cameron, a senior executive for acquisition finance states,

> "Between 1981 and 1985 the buy-outs were from children-of-the-recession companies. Alot of loss-making subsidiaries were sold at steep discounts to net asset value as an *option to closure.* Now, when virtually any company comes up for sale, a management buy-out is considered. Triggered by a period of takeovers, profitable subsidiaries are now sold at *substantial premia.*"

Mergers increase when the general risk of bankruptcy appears greater, maintains Weston. Recent conglomerate bankruptcies and setbacks (Bond, Maxwell, Trump, Campeau, Belzberg, the Reichmann Brothers, Skasey) would suggest a contrary trend that is more in line with the Icarian Trap described in the Appendix. In any case, the risk premium on low-grade corporate securities and bonds is higher, eg., when the interest rate spread between high- and low-quality bonds is greatest. Thus there may be more bankruptcies when junk financing is more expensive, i.e., before interest rates are lowered due to post-prosperity recession, and access to refinancing becomes critical.

Strategic motivations and product cyclicity may bow to financial cyclicity: MBOs dropped off with the 1987 stock market crash with the parallel rise in interest rates. Takeover finance became more expensive (except in those instances where bidders' stock prices increased relative to sellers').

Yet failure has always been a great force behind M&A, particularly in sectors that are cutting back or shifting to new geographic areas such as steel and other raw materials sectors. The recent round of mergers and acquisitions in the airline and banking sectors also demonstrates that M&A occurs in sectors where there is an overabundance of competitors. Other sectors particularly prone to M&A have been discussed in Chapter Two.

7.3 THE MERGER WAVE: DISCUSSION

7.3.1 MARKET FOCUS AND THE SECTORAL CYCLE

Mergers and acquisitions are more effective if there is a close fit between corporate investment strategy for optimizing the profitability path and the core production activity. It is impossible to have an effective core focus without taking technology, product, and sectoral changes into account.

Three types of sectors are particularly vulnerable to M&A: highly differentiable product sectors; cyclicals and large capitalization sectors, consumer growth sectors.

Products with high differentiability such as exotic microwaveables usually are easier to market and lead to higher profits. Products with low differentiability such as vegetable crops are tough to market and lead to lower profits. One way to cope with this difference is to emphasize that the product itself is only one of the things that the company sells: reliability, delivery, service, and perceptions of status are as important. A company with undifferentiated products is led to diversify by acquiring companies offering these services.

Another technique for marketing low differentiated goods is to assess which buyer group is the best target and then to produce, price, promote and distribute the product or service so that it appeals strongly to that group. Important factors are the industry of the target group, the best location from which to service them, and their overall market status. Obviously buying near or into the customer base through acquisition is also a success strategy.

7.3.2 A MERGER WAVE EQUATION

It is possible to think of the merger wave as a sort of clean-up squad of the business and product cycles. If successful, mergers cause rationalization, expansion and control. Unsuccessful destroys corporate ethic and throws the firm in debt, if not bankruptcy. The risk factor in M&A is as high or low as the enormous potential rewards, which is in keeping with the mercurial variability of the merger wave.

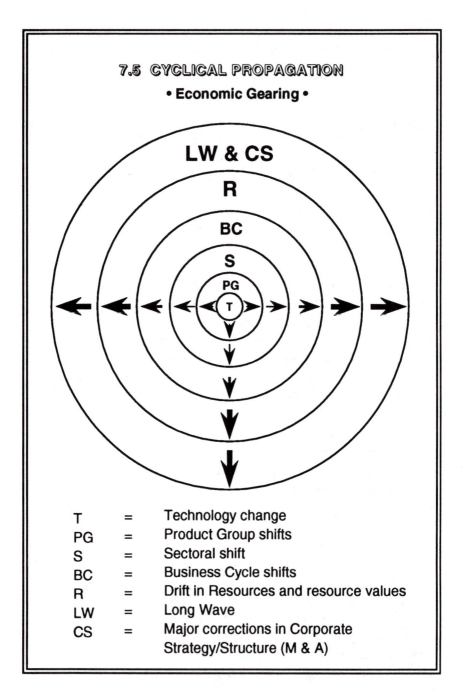

7.5 CYCLICAL PROPAGATION

• Economic Gearing •

LW & CS

R

BC

S

PG

T

T	=	Technology change
PG	=	Product Group shifts
S	=	Sectoral shift
BC	=	Business Cycle shifts
R	=	Drift in Resources and resource values
LW	=	Long Wave
CS	=	Major corrections in Corporate Strategy/Structure (M & A)

The major factors of the merger wave can be presented as such:

$$F + S + G + P = MW$$

where F represents financial factors (capital cost and debt-equity phase shifts in Chapter 4), S the strategic components for growth, control and survival (as the response of corporate strategies and corporate structures to phase shifts in technology, product groups, sectors, business cycles, resource values, and long waves in Chapter 5), G is government (out-of-phase control by monetary, fiscal and regulative measures in Chapter 6), and P accounts for prevailing psychographics, or current mood and strategies concerning proper and profitable forms of investment via mergers and acquisitions (in Chapters 2, 3 and 5).

An extensive elaboration of the components of each factor of the equation can be found in Part II, or by referring back to corresponding chapters.

Some kind of multiplier can be placed in front of each factor, depending on which of those factors is highly sinusoidal and which are more volatile. Volatile factors weight and distort sinusoidal ones. The relative weight and shifting of factors determines whether the M&A cycle goes up or down. In other words, the weighting of each of these factors determines the functional or cyclical characteristics of the merger wave, as well as their synchronization, or co-movement.

Co-movement in oscillating wave regimes instills mutual re-enforcement, if not amplification. Losing phase coherency causes distortion (noise), or 180-degree cancellation.[86]

The M&A wave is a very pointed or spiky one, a result of the lack of phase alignment amongst the five factors of the merger wave equation. Governments do not seem to be performing a contrarian   (out-of-phase) cancellation function very well. Or it may be interpreted that M&A as a sort of last resort

---

[86] Compare in the appendix disruption, disaster, catastrophe and chaos. Another view of entropy is also provided by this phenomenon.

---

for economic alignment acts as a residual power and thereby exhibits lumpy behavior.

7.3.3 EFFECTS OF GOVERNMENTS ON MERGER WAVES

Planning and government intervention can accelerate phase changes or phase shift the business cycle or merger wave, causing substantial reallocation of resources.

In fact, the government *may even act as the principal cause of cyclical change* through changing policies on the interest rate, money supply, government spending (most in war [2/3 of all investment] health [1/3] and universities in the US), taxation and regulation. Furthermore, up until recently and particularly in developing countries, governments have tended to take over industries that are perceived as keys to the economy (rail roads, mines) or faltering employers. These industries are usually already in late Phases III or IV and past the peak in rates of return.

Do governments target systemic maximum-efficiency load, i.e., optimal cyclical behavior, or overload? Free trade, free investment regimes and uncontrolled mergers and acquisitions are sometimes constructive to the national economy—and eventually to regional market and global economies—at other times devastating. When is more entrepreneurial and market latitude, on the one hand, or more regulation, on the other, required? The answer to this fundamental question is ruled by synchronization and anomaly perturbations of the four phase cycle.

7.3.4 CONCLUSION: FROM SINGLE-FACTOR TO MULTIFACTOR CAUSATION: ASK NOT WHAT CAUSES MERGER WAVES BUT HOW

Monocausality as an approach to merger waves and cycles (or technology and business cycles) is ruled out by the notion of the relative degree of synchronization or co-movement of many variables in oscillating flow regimes (similar to cyclical or seasonal covariance). Multipliers assigned to factors and sub-factors determine the significance to merger waves of debt-equity ratios, direct investment, capital hunger, growth in output relative to capital stock, the profit rate, the income distribution between labor and capital, and all the other factors contributing to merger waves delineated in this book.

Similarly, the long debate about the long wave—which Burns statistically could not identify for the business cycle[87]—remains vague, as the phase length has never been reasonably established (somewhere between 45 to 60 years in no particular pattern). What is feasible is to pin down the drive mechanisms of the mergers and acquisition cycle, meanwhile observing the gradual shifts in the *shape* of the wave. Speculation about the principal causes and effects of M&A is reduced by gauging the multifactorial dynamics of the M&A phase environment which is essentially driven by cyclical behavior itself.

———— .***. ————

[87] Arthur F. Burns and Wesley C. Mitchell, *Measuring Business Cycles*, New York, NBER, 1946.

APPENDIX TO CHAPTER 7
MODELLING THE EVOLUTIONARY DYNAMICS
OF PRODUCT AND MERGER CYCLES:
SOME BASIC PRINCIPLES

"Begin by characterizing the defining properties of evolutionary process. One is an increase in complexity; another is an increase in information processing capability. Still another is the constant ability to generate new possibilities, which then come to have a function or purpose."

NORMAN PACKARD, THE UNIVERSITY OF ILLINOIS CENTER FOR COMPLEX SYSTEMS.
(ON FORMULATING MODELS OF EVOLUTIONARY PROCESSES)

OMNI, JANUARY 1992

A1. MERGER WAVES: ADVANTAGES OF USING A CYCLICAL DYNAMIC APPROACH

Some of the major principles of cyclical dynamics are identified below. Cyclical dynamics are usually prevalent wherever there is growth and evolutionary replication. This approach thus provides an explanation for inherent change and adaptation. Because of space and contextual limitations, its broad implications are only initially explored.[88] The mechanism of cyclical change is the focal point of the chapter and not any one economic event. This is a viable approach because of the universality of cyclical models.[89]

---

[88] English is chosen over mathematics which has become sectoralized.

[89] Cyclical dynamics and rotation incorporate elements of both wave and particle theory.

The value of a life cycle approach compared to a linear or chaotic one is the possibility of endogenous replication and continuity while accounting for responses to parametric changes.[90] Although many of its principles are already recognized in other economic terms, its importance to economics lies in its integrative and explanatory powers.[91] For example, the question is answered why innovation occurs at the borders; in fact, borders both external and internal are more closely defined. Cutting through the variegated levels of evolutionary complexity, the reasons for growth and adaptation are also granted causation by the cyclical model.

At certain times the economy is *more volatile* during which Peters suggests **an increase in economic activity is more likely to occur**. A certain level of volatility generates perturbations or anomalies. What are other inherent benefits of cyclical dynamics? One major advantage of a recurring cyclical trajectory are the functions of seek, selection and integration from a wider range of exogenous probabilities, along with *replicating, endogenous and self-modulating trajectories*, or functions. References to self-regulation, self-organization and auto-adjustment indicate that cyclical dynamics are in force. A cyclical as opposed to linear path is more robust, shock-resistant, and efficient. That is, in physical terms a curved trajectory covers the largest number of points in any given space the fastest, substituting deflection behavior for collusion. A further advantage to a cyclical dynamics approach is that learning, persistence and variability are allowed to coincide. The helical or cyclical structure is also distinguished for replication.[92]

Germane is the recurring nature of the cycle in a continuing system with stability features.[93] In fact, a system is constituted by the whole of all cycles

---

[90] In chaotic terms, drips may be re-created, but the probability of re-creating drips depends not only on the water flow but importantly on the fortuitous availability of another faucet. It is a one-time-only deal. Furthermore, initial conditions describe origin (water flow source) only insofar as how the initial conditions are themselves articulated.

[91] The postulates are also highly observable in fields as diverse as plasma physics, fluid dynamics, sociobiology, stellar dynamics, and recent nonlinear analysis.

[92] For example, in DNA-RNA creation or oscillating flow regimes.

[93] . . .never truly recurring due to the impossibility of returning to a single moment.

hierarchically scaled within it.[94] The seasonality of cycles is not absolutely but relatively stable; if subcycles deviate beyond the system's boundary conditions (or parameters), a new set of locii or initial conditions[95] eventually through the revolutions of time defines a new system. Otherwise, the so-called system attractors—which can be thought of as a set of exogenous *and* endogenous origin rules—may be sufficiently destroyed to end the system, or its "life cycle".

The hierarchy-scaling of cycles occurs in a general system of *oscillating flow regimes*. In-phase crests and troughs reinforce each other. Out-of-phase peaks cancel each other out.[96] For example, a money accelerator and multiplier are dampened by changes in the interest rate and money supply. *Key frequencies* provide for *regulated switching* at sub- and supra-critical *turning points* (e.g., peaks and troughs). At these critical junctures, the system either auto-corrects or "comes back" to the systemic mean, or "goes far out" into the zones of anomalies if not chaotic systemic dissimulation. Although co-movement of cyclical variables has been observed and measured for some time,[97] determination of the key frequency or variable continues to baffle business cycle empiricists.[98] Synchronization occurs at the lowest energy path: it takes

---

[94] Compare Mandelbrot's fractals and Hermann Haken's enslaving principle.

[95] Either extraneous conditions with stronger field forces or endogenous recapitulated conditions. The system's initial conditions—especially if the system is chaotic—are deterministic only for a period of limited duration.

[96] It is interesting to note that there are only two opportunities for co-evolution in cyclical regimes: 1) cogging, or inverse rotation of two proximate rotating systems, and 2) intertwining, or double helical behavior. Otherwise, proximate systems can not spin in the same direction (unless both are enslaved in a larger system). Herein lies the determinative characteristics of the cycle.

[97] See Chapter Five.

[98] Recent econometric measuring of particular note includes Andrew J. Filardo's work on time-varying transition probabilities in "Business Cycle Phases and Their Transitions," Working Paper at U of Chicago, Nov. 1991, based on Hamilton's 1989 work using quarterly real GNP data from 1952 to 1984 documenting that both the timing and duration of contractions and expansions can be accounted for in a fixed transition probability Markov switching model. According to Filadro, Hamilton's work goes a long way to demonstrate that univariate modeling can capture business cycle phases that correspond to periods of expansions and recessions. James Hamilton, U of Virginia, "A New Approach to the Economic Analysis of Non-stationary Time Series and the Business Cycle," *Econometrica*, Vol 57, Mar, 357-384.

less energy to go with the flow, especially during fast growth, than it does to break out of it[99].

A2. EVOLUTION, PHASE-CHANGE, SEEK AND SPIN: THE CYCLICAL TRAJECTORY OF CHANGE

Growth evolution is constituted by relative shifts in the value statespace of the macro-environment, i.e., a shift in the relative total values of stocks, bonds, and other financial instruments as well as in economic variables (inflation, liquidity, and measures of productivity), and in the number and form of companies in the pool of firms. This is a dynamic, evolutionary multi-equilibria model as opposed to the static equilibrium model of the efficient market hypothesis (EMH) in traditional economics. The new system is evolutionary in the sense that responses occur to perturbations or anomalies at critical points, i.e., at the boundary conditions, particularly (but not exclusively) in the peaks and troughs. These responses are "remembered" in the cyclical trajectory. The cyclical system is dynamic because there is self-correction according to internal and parametric changes as time goes on[100]. The path of growth is one of intergenerational contraction and expansion. The level of significance is the generation, not the individual.

---

[99] In this context, entropy may be considered as a lessening of oscillating co-movement, or systemic despair or collapse.

[100] Cyclicity must be considered a subset of nonlinearity. A non-linear curve may be continuous (endless). But is it systemic (coherent and orderly), or is it noise? One may argue that noise is a misunderstood trajectory, but we find cyclicity to offer more positive and predictable outcomes, thus its importance. Explosions and dissimilation are interesting in many instances, but the attributes of cyclicity such as recurrence, continuity and a phase transition of observable states or phases make cyclicity particularly appealing for understanding evolutionary behavior. The problem with cyclicity is that it is usually approached two-dimensionally with little respect for multidimensional space and multiple trajectories occurring dynamically in specific sets. These areas are being explored by the author in more depth elsewhere.

Phase changes and *phase shifts* are based on the *four-phase growth engine* of start-up (s), growth (g), maturity (m) and decline (d).[101] A system is evolutionary once the "key is switched on". Before that, in the sub-critical phase, no growth occurs because there are not sufficient savings and income to drive the increased demand for output. Therefore accelerators and multipliers are not triggered and do not come into effect. For example, many of the African economies still in the pre-growth phase have actually fallen into per capita output decline.

The subcritical phase of no/low growth and low diversity is overcome by what may be termed "pest economics". A pest can be defined as: 1) something that thrives in today's (initial) conditions; 2) something that destroys the status quo in such a way that status quo economics are impaired or destroyed, and 3) something that may destroy current economic diversity.[102] Pests require enough "trash" or other forms of accumulated resources in order "to make a living". Not surprising, the wastes of previous periods, especially if related to energy production and transport, provide the reserves that trigger growth today when coupled with a "pest" or a systemic thriver that exploits those new reserves. The subcritical boundary threshold or "trough parameter" is surpassed when the pest takes hold of the new resource base and thrives. The pest anomaly boosted by accelerators and multipliers can develop explosively into a new mainstream status quo. The period of growth may stabilize as a period of maturity, depending on the level of statistical symmetry (clearly expressed, for example, by sinusoidality). Finally, a supra-critical boundary condition or "peak" pressures the pest resource base with overexploitation and depletion. The pattern of growth is broken as wave symmetry-breaking occurs. New perturbations or anomalies appear as the old wave order breaks down. This is the greatest hour: At this point the system auto-adjusts to new (initial) conditions, or declines in phase four.

---

[101] Phase change or transition refers to evolution *along* the cyclical trend line (e.g., from growth to maturity). Phase shift indicates that *the whole wave has moved* in terms of degrees of position in the time reference; the whole functional relationship is moved forwards (earlier) or backwards (later) in time.

[102] Similarly, pests that attack humans and human food sources will determine future evolution to the degree that neither discretionary evolutionary engineering nor supracritical desertification come into effect.

Four basic modes of change can be identified:

1) Simple aggregation (agglomeration), or "piling up" of resources (asset accumulation) with low systemic articulation.

2) Simple random occurrence. Economic windows of opportunity are created by "bumping and mixing" in a rudimentary formative phase, or after a chaotic event such as a market crash or extraneous (social or political) event. This category has the lowest probability for stability, continuity and recurrence.

3) Linear change. This mode is useful for stability-seeking, fixed-location engineered growth or development, but less useful for describing change at system boundaries or parameters, even if those parameters (e.g., as in a phase-locked loop model) contain self-adjustment mechanisms. Linear systems tend to impose stability but do not readily adjust to change. Under duress they break instead.

4) Cyclical incremental change. Cyclical dynamics provide the highest probability for continuous dynamic systemic evolution because of continuing reiteration and adjustment. This is the mode of phase growth models.

Seek is a primary attribute of the imperfectly stable cyclical system. Continuous systems by nature seek survival and self-regeneration, or else they collapse in a crowded universe with competing dominions[103] of limited resources.[104] The Post Probability Function states that the possibilities of

---

[103] Crowding is not unique to economics markets. In general, overcrowding at the core is an initial condition for causing sinusoidal expansion and subsequent contraction.

[104] This is also due to the fact that the probabilities of occurrence (the number of apple seeds) are vastly greater than actual occurrence and replication (the apple tree). Although a seeking function by necessity is intrinsic to evolutionary systems, the reason may not be obvious. Does this mean there is some sort of omniscient arbitrator in a deterministic or teleological environment? Does seeking give purpose and meaning? The notion of an allocative hand distributing production functions and rewards throughout the system ("justly", if the notion of perfectly clearing markets is assumed) has been central in the science of economics since Adam Smith. More recently, Fabio

(continued...)

occurrence are much greater than the actual *Erscheinung,* or final occurrence.[105] For example, a London-based venture capitalist estimates that for every 100 company proposals reviewed, ten are selected for financing by the firm, five break-even, and one succeeds, an *Erscheinung* or success ratio of only one percent. Seek is a process of searching for economic or other equilibria, followed by auto-adjustment to new equilibria due to the input of new information. Overshooting and undershooting are examples of seek around a reference point or dynamic target. Seek may be regarded as a continuous series of static Marshallian snapshots.

Seeking occurs in a profit and loss (or phase-shift) economy by overshooting at momentary market equilibrium, then dampening (or decaying) towards the current market clearing point. As the product cycle matures, firms grow and expand to survive in an increasingly competitive environment. Mergers and acquisitions are ways of seeking survival through expansion. Firms without n-drive that cease to seek are put up for sale or dissolved. Thus the number of firms available for acquisition increases. Although the average moves forward, equilibrium may never be reached. Therefore, it is critical how the moving average is defined.

Dosi points out that there is a process of search along a cylindrical technology trajectory for new technologies (one can think of technological push interacting

---

Archangeli and others have applied the notion of an uncertain *trembling hand,* thereby introducing uncertainty principles and, by inference, risk-reward structures. We would add to this notion a trembling, *seeking* hand—searching the hidden nooks and crannies of the markets for crystallizing anomalies, or windows of opportunity created by uneven development and success/failure event-screening by boundary conditions at the peak or at the foot of the trough.

But why does the hand seek and tremble? What drives the system? The answer is simple yet non-trivial: If seeking is not indigenous to the evolutionary path, there is *no* evolution, ecomomics, no world, nor universe. If there is not an internal drive for self-perpetuation and self-replication in a dynamic and competing environment, the system will not perpetuate itself. It will cease to be.

[105] The effects are not trivial. The result is leaf-like bifurcation with acceleration effects along a deterministic evolutionary path departing from the initial conditions. Occurrence probabilities are system-specific with evolutionary features. Isolation provided by boundaries changes probability structure, e.g., the high-numbers game of exogenous dissemination vs the low-numbers game of the womb.

with demand pull). Organic technological **paradigm shifts** follow.[106] Dosi brings out the importance of sociopolitical or techno-economic time lags. One can also think of the role of cycles in shifting between monopoly equilibria.

Spin is essential as the probability of systemic continuity is enhanced by rotation, or system spin. When orbital systems stop spinning they collapse. A cyclical system makes available the recurring dynamics of rotation. If the system is perfectly sinusoidal, these characteristics include double reflection plus inversion symmetries[107] (see (5) below).

Furthermore, rotation causes systems to "wind up", eventually allowing them to speed up: the frequency of an alternating electric current increases with the increased rotation of the solid conductive slip ring (frequency also increases with the addition of extra poles). Interestingly and importantly, *as the diameter of the rotating system decreases more revolutions occur in the same amount of time if the velocity is constant. Conversely, expanding systems have less revolutions for every time period, as it takes longer to go around once.* The importance of this simple factor in determining recession and the height of economic activity can not be overestimated. Note that economic activity is demarcated in rotational time units: seconds minutes, hours, days, weeks and years are derivatives of the earth's rotation around the sun. Rotation and spin demonstrate cyclical behavior along the time trajectory. Two dimensional wave rotation exhibits sinusoidal behavior. Spherical rotation constitutes orbiticity. Cylindrical or helical rotation importantly provide vortical perturbations and lags (see below).

The comparative advantages of cyclical change include:

(1) Learning, persistence and variability as well as replication coincide.

(2) The system may be tightly closed or open at different intervals along its time trajectory, that is, the probabilities of occurrence at the front-end time frontier are constantly encaptured in historically persistent structures. A

---

[106] ...similar to Kuhn's paradigm shifts in science. See Dosi in Chapter Five.

[107] I.e., they appear the same upside down and/or backwards.

cyclical system may "spin up tight" or "wind down" (see (5) and (6)), i.e., overall velocity (the rate of change) is adjustable.

(3) The time axis may be viewed either at the origin of a circular polar coordinate system, or at the circumference measured in revolutions around this "moving average".

(4) A cycle has high descriptive value. A cyclical system can be delineated clearly by dimension and by axis. A one-dimensional system is a point which is also the origin and axis of the system. A two-dimensional system—the traditional perspective of economics—characteristically displays the time trajectory along the horizontal x-axis. Even though the related mathematical modelling may be profound, the common "mental picture" of the 2-D chart with linear approximations—almost always in the first (northeast) quadrant of the cartesian coordinate system where outward movement along the axes is always positively correlated—has led to what may be termed *chalkboard myopia in finance and economics.* New computer software allows easy manipulation of many dimensions and differential movement along the axes, providing opportunity for new, multidimensional and multi-axial approaches. The 3-D view permits evolution from Euclidean to spherical dynamics. A 4-D perspective (e.g., bipolar) can describe spherical evolution along a cylindrical path where vorticity patterns are evident.

(5) Whilst much time has been spent measuring cyclical watersheds or turning points, little effort has been made to explain their intrinsic behavior. Intrinsic cyclical behavior needs to be described qualitatively before it can be measured. The cycle itself in manifesting crest and trough dynamics as well as growth and maturity phases accounts for the turning point. Apex and trough events are significant and well-demonstrated by locational shifts in resource values (refer to discussions in Chapter Seven).

A3. ACCELERATION

Cyclical dynamics adequately explain accelerators and decelerators as well as stability and instability characteristics (e.g., once the system is going up/down, the likelihood of continuing to go up/down increases). Varying degrees of acceleration are closely linked to synchronization. The explanation for this universal behavior is more evident in physics than it is in economics, and applies to "on-off" probability ranges and the electro-magnetic principles of single or multipolar environments which provide for switching as well as the build-up in angular momentum.[108]

Sinusoidality and oscillating flow regimes—with speed along the trajectory equal at all points—equate well with perfect markets and perfect competitors of equal size.

But this is not the way the world works. Big, small and lumpy prevail. For example, before World War II, business cycles were skewed in such a way that booms (ramp up) were short and quick, and recessions long and drawn out. Since World War II, the business cycle has been more optimistic: Growth phases have been longer and corrections quick and steep. The business cycle—which is really a cam-shaped ellipsoid as opposed to a sinusoidally derived sphere with acceleration probabilities equally distributed—is lumpy, itself acting as a perturbation or accelerator with built-in, sling-shot angular momentum.

---

[108] There are several possible approaches here, but the important point which is usually overlooked is the principle of rotation. One is the continuous switching from input to output models due to vortical momentum on a seasonal basis which is most approachable in the seasonal agricultural sector. Secondly, in multisectoral environments switching becomes more complex, less predictable, and more overlapping as the forces of synchronization become more difficult. Thirdly, in multiaxial environments refining the laws of expansion and contraction are fundamented on continuous endogenous synchronization to ensure systemic survival. Fourthly, a Markov chain as well as STAR and other econometric models allow digitizing, building symmetry in asymmetry by coping with noise: if there is a one-order increase, does this increase the probability of a one order decrease? Are there recurring "word strings" or "heart beats" in the alphabet dynamics of volatility? Fifthly, we might question what is the e-m field or synchronization of a spinning body? An electric field is based on what may be termed "open-ended ying yang", i.e., if the northwest quadrant rotates clockwise, by necessity gearing requires that the northeast and southwest quadrants will rotate anticlockwise, and consequentially the southeast quadrant *ipso facto will rotate clockwise*. *Stability is locked in.* One example is a tennis ball with top spin. There is changing relative velocity around the ball; the ball is boosted at the top of its rotation due to the direction of its spin, and is dragged in the bottom quartiles of its spin. Consequently the ball drops more remarkably in its flight.

The roaring mouse sometimes controls the lion. The higher rotational spin of small gears can control large gears, primarily due to enhanced efficiency and torque per cycle of ripple effects and interlocking cycle regimes.

The merger cycle is influenced by what may be termed a *domino capital liquidity effect* as conditioned by inflation, liquidity lags and time variability of the interest rate. The number and types of mergers are most influenced by *capital availability* as reflected in changes in debt and equity costs to the firm. As might be expected, **inflation** provides a superior example of acceleration dynamics. Some of the functional characteristics of inflation can be described as thus:

A3.1 THE INFLATION SAFETY VALVE

As clearly exhibited by Tobin's Q, the inflation/deflation of fixed assets and other factor values clearly causes dynamic realignment of factor values to new *factor equilibria*. The resource ratio is affected accordingly. The impulse towards M&A is stimulated as a consequence.

A3.2 THE VON MISES PRINCIPLE

"Going up is coming down and coming down is going up": Each phase of the life cycle contains the seeds of the next phase. The causes of recession are inherent to the growth period. As firms grow, replicate and consolidate, simple seed rules and anomalies (perturbations) determine the height and amplitude of the current and subsequent product cycle and related merger wave. Poincarian "initial conditions" are endogenous and "self-contained". Auto-adjustment or cybernation by cyclical modulation of the initial conditions, according to "changed circumstances", describes endogenous "stability."[109] Volatility or cyclicity allows for change as well as its subsequent resolution. Thus, memory (of past cyclical phases) and information processing are implicit to the system, not only at the state-space locus of initial conditions, but at each phase of the evolutionary cyclical path.

For example, the raw materials for the next merger boom, an overconcentration of cheap assets with lagged capital availability and interest rates held low to stimulate investment, occurs in the trough phase (Tobin's Q). The normal view of recession is slow. However, in the trough the cycle is "all

---

[109] I.e., the degree of sinusoidality or volatility, or, in other words, the continuity of evolution.

spun up" and torque is high.[110] The cycle will burst out into a growth phase. In 1989, merger and other investment activity reached a peak. According to a Steve Marsh, a Seattle-based M&A specialist at KPMG, an international accounting firm, "the buck is passed on to the next fool" during this phase . Based on prolonged and accelerated price inflation for target firms, assets and real estate in general, the speculator is able to sell on the inflated asset at a handsomely taller price. Overall indebtedness also increases. Angular momentum reaches its peak and the system reaches out even further from normal equilibrium. The system is abnormally susceptible in this overheated state. The crest or upper parameter can be viewed as a temperature watershed followed by a cooling or winding down period of recession.

A3.3 THE ROLLER COASTER PRINCIPLE

What goes up, must come down. . . *faster*, at least since World War II when global expansions and stock market booms have tended to have long growth periods and relatively brief periods of declines. *Duration dependence* is also visible in shake-outs and corrections which have become more short-lived, if not more violent. The rapid and discretionary shortening of product and technology cycles (laptop to notebook computers) makes them spiked and even more subject to perturbations.

INFLATION ACCELERATION

Coterminant with the above is the amplification effect of inflation. As inflation accelerates with growth due to spending and a previous eased monetary policy (time lag anomalies), the tendency to expand by asset acquisition as opposed to new investment is amplified. Likewise, as inflation decelerates, e.g., due to previous market and capital saturation and stringent monetary policy to contain the earlier inflation, asset acquisition through M&A decreases correspondingly.[111]

---

[110] Inversely, "you don't get something for nothing," especially a lot of it. There must be sufficient heating up, concentration of energy and resources to build up the tension required for economic expansion. It is not probable that all begins with a big bang, preceded by less than a small whimper!

[111] For example, Securities Data Co. reports that the value of mergers in the USA dropped 32% with 4,407 deals worth $143.6 billion in 1991, compared to 5,150 deals valued at $211.9 billion in

(continued...)

A4. GROWTH EVOLUTION VIA SPECIALIZATION: COMPLEXITY AND BOUNDARY DETERMINANCY

One method of growth and survival is niche specialization or *added complexity.* 1) to structure; 2) to the mathematics of structure and information processing, and 3) to operations and production functions.[112] The march towards differentiation—or succession in specialization—is especially relevant to merger waves as related to product and technology cycles; in this instance evolution is more of a moving average of phase changes as opposed to a series of (market clearing) equilibria. Phase changes are also evident in corporate restructuring.

Specialization relies on different tools. *Surface* or *interface dynamics* drive border differentiation (or parameterization).[113] The probability of differentiation of exogenous from endogenous factors is enhanced by provision of border screens or filters, and by aggregation and articulation at the border. "Sticky surfaces" provide horizons" where "things happen"[114] and events are controlled by "triggers" and "switches". *Homogeneity* is thus differentiated by the new possibility of discrete zones. For example, as regional markets have been invaded by corporate raiders, M&A and other cross-border transactions have been gaining in frequency (Chapter Two). Bifurcation or branching -

---

1990. Likewise, global merger value plunged by 39%, largely because of the European recession, from 9273, worth \$498.4 billion in 1990 to 8,193 deals worth \$303.7 billion this year (Source: *USA Today,* Dec. 30, 1991, B1.)

[112] There is a current trend in nonlinear analysis to consider *patterns* of complexity before the basic *functions* of complexity are fully understood. Basic forms may be based on the four modes of change described above, the cyclical mode always being the most critical. Linear geometric forms as derivatives of branching provide articulation of limited duration or tertiary importance. (Spin-offs are derivatives of larger cycles, and one can conceive of a fern-like cycle tree with nonlinear and linear characteristics, but this form is probably rare and primordial.)

[113] In physical terms we might think of barriers, walls, event horizons, crusts, and even skin. Simple surface dynamics are created by diverging vectors, say of thermal pressure zones or water. Different force vectors are created by two bodies spinning in opposite directions, a comparative advantage of cyclical dynamics. Vortical and other time lags also provide effective parameterization or the perturbations, triggers and differentiation necessary for active surface dynamics.

[114] Simply note the high degree of articulation at the earth's surface.

similar to boutique franchising or special service companies - also permits niche specialization - just as horizontal acquiring in specialty chemicals or public relations.[115] Similar is hierarchical complexity, or pyramid building. Some of the Canadian interlocked holding companies are based on this principle. Much of franchise expansion is based on *specialization in simplicity*. To illustrate, by providing the basic building blocks, shoe repair and key cutting franchises speedily provide repetitive functions.

However, the Post Paradox states that growth specialization via complexity may lead to doom: When the 1980s economic boom in Great Britain grinded to a halt in late 1989, the first company sectors to suffer profoundly were niche specialization companies such as corporate identity and p.r. firms, companies providing identity products such as labelled silver balloons and large, fashionable events; sports and entertainment; the leisure, hotel and restaurant industries; and luxury items such as gourmet foods. Large-scale debt financing, the hallmark of the 1980s, may be considered a sort of niche financing that led to bankruptcy.

A5. THE CENTRAL ROLE OF PERTURBATIONS OR ANOMALIES

An *anomaly* is a window of opportunity created by uneven sectoral development (perturbations or vortical time lags) as accompanied by shifts in the relative costs of production factors that entrepreneurs harness to enhance profits. Anomalies are similar to Packard's possibilities, which when selected for survival, become system functions. We choose to call this process *success screening* at critical points, or at the parametric boundary conditions.[116] These anomalies are stirred and configured further in the growth and maturation phases by 1) continuous incremental change, 2) by steep discontinuous change or 3) by radical collapse of the *origin-rules cycle* and its replacement (based on current probabilities) with something else. In cyclical

---

[115] Similarly, Steve Hawking has noted that, in general, there is a trend from uniformity to uniform disparity via original perturbations.

[116] In fluid- or aerodynamic physical systems we may refer to similar events as part of surface dynamics.

dynamics time is the independent variable.[117] The time trajectory invariably moves forward. Time may be measured along the central cylindrical or spherical axis, or as a moving point along the circumference. Changes along the time trajectory lead to the cyclical behavior. In other words, the overall shape of the time-strung cyclical trajectory is highly relevant to the types of events and structures that occur along its path.

Perturbations have many names: Anomalies, symmetry-breaking, phase-kick transitions, discontinuity, sub- and supra-critical turning points, boundary break-through or the breaking of perfect sinusoidality or regular dampening is caused by 1) stability, or the stagnation of variables, 2) exponentiality, 3) lags, and 4) perturbations[118] and its extreme form chaos, both often caused by lags.

The function of perturbation is to provide open-window anomalies which constitute new opportunities, if integrated, or catastrophes, if not. Perturbations are due to endogenous deviancy, exogenous new information, and success selection.

One can distinguish between period and duration dependence as opposed to perturbation dependence. One example is regular lamina expansion with intermittent contractions, which can be one of four sorts: 1) disturbance (everything is o.k. but only up to a certain point); 2) disaster (mild, reversible, shocks, but don't push your luck); 3) catastrophe (irreversible shock: luck pushed), or chaos (once it's bad it can only get worse).[119] These varying degrees of discontinuity are potential *boundary breakthroughs,* depending on the amount of induced volatility, the level of departure from initial conditions,

---

[117]This does not imply that time is unidirectional; since time is system specific, like a clock, it may loop back on itself, for example in a phase-locked or spherical structure.

[118]Current popular forms are burst and bubble generation, morphological accidents, and the work of discretionary "shock masters" in high technology, retail, and bio- and medical technology.

[119]The literature and terminology of chaotic dynamics including attractors and other nonlinear phenomenon is now fully developed. As an introduction see G.L. Baker and J.P. Gollub, *Chaotic Dynamics. An Introduction,* Cambridge, UK: Cambridge University Press, 1990; or Edgar E. Peters, *Chaos and Order in the Capital Markets. A New View of Cycles, Prices and Market Volatility,* New York: John Wiley & Sons, 1991.

and the presence of the necessary degree of coherence to ensure systemic survival.

Perturbations in M&A are expressed by market windows for rapid growth caused by new technologies or by trade links with new markets during the growth phase, by sectoral congestion and depression in the mature and decline phase, and capital cost anomalies in all phases. Dosi identifies a discontinuity in technological change and socio-economic transformation. This anomaly expresses the role of sociopolitical and techno-economic time lags, or the role of merger and other cycles in shifting between monopolistic equilibria essentially external to the market system and price mechanism.

A6. VORTICITY DYNAMICS AND ECONOMIC LAGGING THROUGH PERTURBATIONS

Volatility dynamics characterizes relative volatility and economic outcomes in different sectors. For example, supply shocks lead to price surprises requiring dynamic adjustment. This is how firms respond to individual prices, depending upon the covariance between output and inflation. Cyclical volatility is the course of change and systemic adjustment to change.

Vorticity dynamics become obvious in a multidimensional environment. For example, the total GNP for the business cycle, or the total volume of M&A for one merger wave may be viewed as the volume of two contiguous vortex cones. Every year GNP changes, and according to the degree that ARIMA and other regressive models hold true and today's outcome is derivative of all earlier outcomes, shifts in the GNP are described by the evolving vortical trajectory. If the vortical axis is taken as the mean, then the GNP polar coordinate system delineates a profit and loss economy. Boom periods are described in quadrant two (northwest). For example, recessionary periods are described by quadrant four (southeast), and so on.

The vortex cone is inherent to all growth models, pumping or oscillating from expansionary peak to recessionary trough. Rotation and momentum acceleration/deceleration effects are allowed to come fully into force.

The production of lags or perturbations required for evolution are inherent to vortices due to the time shifts involved in perimeter or circumference changes.

If time and speed are constant (recall that both are defined in terms of the system's revolution or some external reference system), then changes in the size of the circumference (amplitude or radius) of the vortex cone is enough to change rpm's. Simple changes in circumference size cause accelerating and decelerating effects for the system. In economic terms there are many ways to define circumference, such as the speed it takes for one dollar to flow through the economy, or company attainment of payback.

Adding vorticity lagging (overlapping) enhances the probabilities of surface dynamics; indeed, surfaces are to a certain extent internalized by sheath coiling. To envisualize overlapping think of a surfboarder shooting the pipeline of a wave. The replicative functions of vortices are strong: If a barrier is introduced into a homogeneous flow regime, the flow is divided into right- and left-handed "owl eyes" through vortex pairing or shedding. This rotational dichotomy, essential for a.c. electric current generation, is also essential for cyclical gearing, or synchroni zation.

A7. SYNCHRONIZATION: THE KEY TO SURVIVAL

How are phase-change factors synchronized? What allows for the co-movement of economic indicators? What accelerates or decelerates/dampens the economy? Why is economic change sometimes smooth, at other times abrupt? The answers lie in how the economic system is geared or synchronized, and how the system alternates from plus to negative states by changes in polarity.

Maximizing economic behavior involves correct gearing of firm activity to the given parameters of technology and product change. What wins the competitive race is the ability to synchronize firm behavior to specific parameters while predicting and correcting for both endogenous and exogenous perturbations. For example, during the mature and declining phases of a business sector, consolidation and focus on core activity gear the firm with changes in the product cycle.

The ideal gear has no moment of inertia, no stored energy, no friction, and perfect meshing. If the cycle is sinusoidal, its radius and angular displacement are the same at all points, and the sine wave changes polarity at its zero value, alternating between positive and negative values. This is the world of perfect competition with frictionless market clearing. The relative size of two gears results in a proportionality constant for the angular displacements, angular velocities and transmitted torques of the shafts, or poles. Similarly, the relative size of gears determines the *degree of co-movement of economic indicators* in oscillating (cash and other) flow regimes. Oscillating flow regimes are created by the addition of additional rotating systems. Keynesian economics essentially involves cancelling out forms of economic behavior (recession) by phase-out, or the introduction of waves of opposite forces (acceleration via government spending and monetary stimulus). If phase-out is out-of-line, then noise is created (eg., stagflation), and the economy becomes "harder to read". What drives the business cycle are key frequencies, acting as triggers or switches for the economy as a whole. But as Arthur Burns stated, in spite of many attempts to assess what *is* the key frequency, no one has assessed the major variable in the set of indicators for the business cycle.

How does the economy begin the long ascent from deep recession to the crest of the boom period? Small gears of increasing revolutions are used like those on a bike more for work on steep slopes because less force is required to overcome inertia. As velocity increases, so does the GNP.[120] Large gears with close meshing are used for going faster on the flatter, smooth-sailing terrain of the mature phase of the cycle, and with tailwind multiplier-accelerators on the downhill descent, Although larger gears are tougher to turn, it is possible to develop more momentum and challenge the parameterization of the system's initial conditions. However, the higher you go, the farther you fall.

Why don't chaotic discontinuities and other perturbations take over more often? Why doesn't the famous flapping of the butterfly wing lead to hurricanes more frequently? In a highly synchronized environment, it takes **more** energy to arrive at discontinuity. The price of discontinuity, or creative perturbation, is the energy consumed in achieving it.

The debt/equity ratio can be regarded a gearing ratio that adjusts with time according to phase changes and phase shifts in the economy. Interest rates rise

---

[120] GNP mass = momentum/velocity

with economic velocity. For example, junk bond lending increased in the 1980s as people earned more money, there was more money to be lent. As pointed out as early as Kitchin, the economic peak is associated with high bank rates. Wealthy, successful societies tend to have high interest rates in the mature phase of the wealth cycle. Overleveraging tends to ensue. As banks reach the limits of lending capacity, governments may also be overstretched due to extended public borrowing.

A wealthy and prosperous country trades extensively. Another example is provided by the interaction of the trade cycle with exchange and IR cycles. As a substantial amount of total purchasing is abroad, a secondary market in the country's currency commences, and offshore transactions occur between third party non-nationals. The power of using the discount window to control the interest rate is thus degraded. Arbitrage opportunities between the spot, futures and options markets may also substantially reduce the economic efficacy of the discount rate. The dollar is traded amongst third parties with other power market currencies in the future and options markets in London, Paris, Frankfurt, and elsewhere. As now observable, as investment and mergers increase, the debt market slows down and the economy becomes recessionary. Some of the lending that now occurs is used for working capital and debt servicing of previous loans. If the desirable debt service charge is 1½ times cashflows, then as cashflows decline radically due to recessionary gearing, funds for debt servicing must be raised externally. Private source funding also declines. Thus a tendency to raise new funds through new offerings in the public stock market.

——————— .***. ———————

193

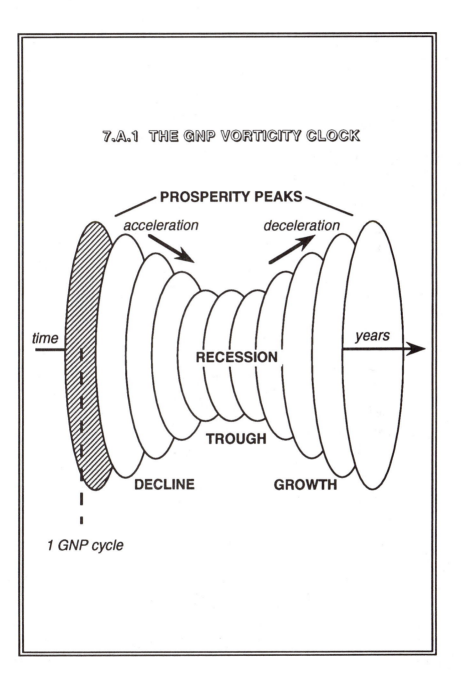

7.A.1 THE GNP VORTICITY CLOCK

PROSPERITY PEAKS

acceleration   *deceleration*

time

years

RECESSION

TROUGH

DECLINE   GROWTH

1 GNP cycle

CHAPTER 8
A CHECKLIST OF CAUSES:
WHY FIRMS MERGE

8.1 FINANCIAL

8.1.1 CAPITAL MARKET LIQUIDITY

Costs

of

Capital

• Capital market conditions and their underlying causes pilot periods of high merger activity: I30

• Saliency of capital costs in periods of high merger activity: I31

• Past values for the 500 stock index, capacity utilization rate, and for domestic debt are positively correlated with current merger activity, while past values of the T-bill rate and GNP are negatively correlated with current mergers; thus, interest rate changes affect costs of mergers; short-term increases in the capacity utilization rate leads to increases in mergers, and the stocks of debt and money have no consistent effect on mergers: F3

• Funds can now be sourced at lower costs: D1

• M&A increases with high costs of capital as firms with poor access to capital merge with firms with better access: D22,I8

• When costs of capital are reduced by a decrease in earnings variability, then falling risk premiums on securities and rising investment opportunities increase conglomerate mergers by enhancing financial synergies: I8.

• Financial variables (relative costs of capital, monetary stringency, risk premiums) are more important for pure conglomerate mergers than for product or market extension merger: B39. (By inference, pure conglomerate mergers increase with cheaper and more readily available finance).

rest

es

• Real interest rates (a proxy for capital costs) and the general size of the economy effect merger activity: D21

• M&A increases when interest rates rise: B30

• A decline in mergers follows an increase in interest rates: B39

• Low interest rates increase M&A's: F17

• Lower interest rates lead to more acquisitions by acquiring firms relying heavily on borrowed funds and bond sales: F3, I26

• Macroeconomic conditions cause about 1/3 of merger variation, and real interest rates appear to have the greatest influence: F3

rage

• In 1980s abundant leverage was available at attractive terms so capital costs very low (450 points over Treasury rate: B31), especially given high-risk beta: C46

• An increase in high-yield (junk bond) market activity parallels an increase in M&A activity: C44, C68

• S&L's have increased their holding of junk bonds (thus increasing finance available for M&A'S): C35

• Statistically, firms that merge do not borrow more: there is actually a decline in the debt-equity ratio: D6

• Acquiring firms have higher-than-average leverage ratios and acquired the opposite; leverage increases even more after takeover, suggesting that less risky firms can employ more leverage to acquire more risky firms: B39

• Like Third World loans, real estate and energy-related loans, banks have encouraged acquisitions to bolster bank fee income as other revenue sources diminished: D37

• Availability of bridging finance increases M&A: C41

Inflation • 1970s inflation increased asset values creating opportunities to acquire and depreciate - at the same time reducing real corporate debt, especially of highly levered acquirers who acquire more by debt financing (also see Taxation): B24

Currency • Weak domestic currency increases foreign M&As: C16, C86, D44

• Currency fluctuations encourage M&A: G7

8.1.2 STOCK MARKET PRICES AND VOLUME
• Increases in stock prices increase M&A's: F17, I14

• Decreases in stock prices decrease M&A's: I14

• M&A is procyclical and grows more rapidly during expansions and more slowly during recessions: F3

• If interest rates are expected to drop and stock prices to rise, firms merge now: B39

• An increase (decrease) in stock prices is followed in a quarter by an increase (decrease) in merger activity: I26

• Recession and depressed stock markets offer buyout situations at attractive prices: B3

• When general stock market indices are high, and the sectoral index is low, owners in the latter sector will tend to sell - for a premium: C1

• Before 1980 M&A increased with bull markets; the 1987 crash did not slow merger activity: D16

• In mid-1991 tight credit and an uneasy economy caused a divergence between low prices in the M&A market and near record high stock prices due to : A20

• LBOs increased with the stock market crash: D28

• High stock prices decrease LBOs: F16

• Stockholders' confidence increases in managers' growth objectives during a market upswing: E15

• Increased volume in stock market is correlated with more M&A's: C51, C63

• More mutual-to-stock conversions increase M&A: D32

• Share ownership concentration facilitates takeovers as small shareholders may hold onto shares irregardless of price : C30

• 20% of the variation in the merger series is accounted by variation in stock market trading volume, although merger activity may cause flux in trading volume, or both respond to a 3rd variable: B30

• Merger activity is closely related to stock trading, stock prices, and business incorporations; a merger peak is reached one month earlier than stock market peak, but its trough lags by three months: I34

• Restructurings act as vehicles to transfer wealth from bondholders, workers, and other corporate stakeholders to shareholders: C37

• A company with depressed stock prices has an increased probability of being taken over: D17

8.1.3 FIRM PROFITABILITY AND SPECULATION
• Investment is superior for building up the firm: C14

• Capacity utilization affects M&A in the short run, i.e., firms acquire when delays occur in obtaining delivery of new capital goods: F3

• Alternative investment opportunities are less attractive: B38

• The company has excess cash: D3, D4, F17

• Cheaper to acquire growth (or buy back own stocks) rather than start a business from scratch (see q-ratio below): C92, F4

• To strip assets, i.e., to buy a company target at a discount for further sale of currently undervalued assets, say because of current inefficient management or suboptimal capital structure: C84, D4, F4, F14

• To arbitrage between stock price and asset value, as expressed by Tobin's q-ratio (market value of debt and equity + asset replacement costs); high interest rates and inflation drive up asset replacement costs so it is cheaper to buy assets by takeover than buy new ones: C83

• Asset values after 1970s and early 1980s inflation were higher than equity values: B33

• [MBO] Managers acquire undervalued assets and earnings at a discount: F4

• Debt co-insurance: dual-firm cash flows spread insolvency risk: F4

8.2 STRATEGIC

8.2.1 GROWTH: VALUE GAINS TO ENHANCE FIRM PERFORMANCE
• To acquire technology:
C70,C93,D37,D51,E17,E2,F12,G5,G7

• To realize economies of scale:
C19,C55,C70,C91,C92,C93,D37,F12

- by lower unit costs, specialization, operating efficiencies in horizontal mergers, by the financing of larger lump sums in conglomerates: F4

- when minimum efficient firm size increases due to technology, etc, takeovers occur: B30

• To gain a specific asset (technology, r & d, management team): F4

• To capture profits by transferring general and specific management functions (production, marketing): B38

• To acquire new systems (i.e., not products or markets) C35

• To acquire faster and at lower risk than developing internally: B38

• To restructure: C6, C43

• To streamline: C43

• To modernize: C43

• To grow by internalizing investment in target's product: B38

• To correct for management failure: B13

• To correct for overcompetition (eg, Japanese & US banking):A3

• To realize synergies by integration: C39,C18,D27,D37,E17,E10, F4,G2,H2[121]

---

[121] Compare: "Synergy was the holy grail of conglomerates in the 1970s looking for a raison d'être where none in fact exists. . .or 2 + 2 = 5. We define it here as doing more with the same resources, or the same with fewer": C46

. **Financial**: central cash flow management, amalgamation of tax set-offs, more efficient accounting methods, use of pension fund surpluses, opportunities of automation due to larger scale

. **Savings**: eliminating duplication or overlaps, more use of expensive front office and other facilities, cash from the sale of old facilities in expensive areas

. **Complementary**: increasing market share and product line, geographic coverage, market force, distributors; rationalizing staff, distribution, service and back-office facilities, product range, advertising, R&D, technology, backup services, increasing control of suppliers and advertisers: D37

8.2.2 BUSINESS CYCLES
• Mergers lead industrial production by more than 5 months: B38, I29

• Merger waves more closely correlated to stock prices than to industrial production, except in periods of low merger activity: I24, I34

• Merger activity peaks usually precede apogees of the business cycle, with irregular time sequence in troughs: I34

• Mergers peak before overall economic activity, suggesting the pool of firms suitable for acquisitions has diminished as merger activity returns to a low: I29

• Merger activity precedes business failures by one quarter and the relationship is negative: I26

• New investment opportunities are due to GNP growth: B38, C35

8.2.3   ECONOMIC AND POLITICAL ENVIRONMENT
M&A increases with:

• Economic and industrial growth: C44

• To create cost advantages due to economies of scale and exchange rate: **B39**

• To enhance repatriated profits by exchange rates: **B39**

• To sell to avoid disfavorable (foreign) legislation: **B39**

• To acquire cheap productive labour: **B39**

• To follow clients (especially banks): **B39**

• To assure a source of raw materials: **B39**

8.2.4.2 INTEGRATION OF EUROPEAN COMMON MARKET

• 1992 European unification increases M & A: C8,C16,C32,C48, C55,C58,C59,C70,C76,C78,C87,D9,D23,D30,D45,D51

   † open borders will end protected markets

   † companies are forced to go international

   † financial markets are being deregulated

   † foreigners invest to avoid being blocked out of the EC market

8.2.5 STAFF (no observations at time of survey)

8.2.6 MANAGEMENT MOTIVES

• The businessperson is more expansive during economic prosperity: F14

• M&A increases management status, higher salaries and perks: E20, F4

• M&A serves managerial motives that do not maximize shareholder returns, e.g., sales-maximizing teams prefer to acquire, even at high prices: I28

• Managerial objectives may drive acquisitions that reduce the bidding firms' values: B29

8.2.7 DEFENSE AGAINST ACQUISITION

• Firms acquire to avoid being taken over: G7

• A significant number of MBOs are initiated only after a hostile threat: D49

• Companies restructure to thwart takeover: B28

• Acquiring firms that become takeover targets made acquisitions that significantly reduce their equity value; firms that do **not** become takeover targets make acquisitions that raise their equity value: B28

• Three studies show an overall average premium of 53-56 % after a hostile threat over the day earlier share price: D49

8.3 LEGISLATION, REGULATION AND TAXATION

• Deregulation (in the financial sector) increases M&A: B25,B33,C8,C11,C45,C50,C74,D7,D24,D32,E4, F5,F6,F7,F8,F12,G3,G8,G1

• Legislation effects M&A activity both positively & negatively: E19

• Tax legislation effects the number of M&A's: B33,C21,C53,C58,C77,C88,C89,D16,D21,D39,E13,F16,F17,G6

8.1 TAXATION BENEFITS ARE NOT A MAJOR MERGER MOTIVE

Potential Gains to the Acquirer from the Transfer of Tax Gains and Losses of the Target (as a % of target firm's market value)

No. of Mergers with Potential Gain from: (by size of gain)	Target	Parent	Total
No gain	277	293	570
Below 5%	20	8	28
5 - 10 %	7	5	12
10 - 25%	11	6	17
Above 25%	3	6	9

	Average Gain (of those with positive gain)		
Unweighted	12.7	15.4	13.7
Weighted	5.5	14.3	9.0

Source: A.J. Auerbach, and D. Reishus, "The Impact of Taxation on Mergers and Acquisitions", in A.J. Auerbach, ED., Mergers and Acquisitions (NBER Project Report), Chicago: The University of Chicago Press, 1988, 77.

Furthermore, from a series of logit regressions, the authors also conclude that "there is little evidence ... that the corporate tax effects we have identified are important in determining the form of the merger transaction".

• Changes in the US Internal Revenue code making interest
payments, not stock dividends, taxable, triggered the 1980s
takeover boom: B24

• The US Economic Recovery Tax Act (ERTA) of 1981 allowed for
accelerated depreciation of newly purchased **old** assets as well as
completely **new** assets - encouraging "churning transactions", or
buying used assets to depreciate them from scratch on a step-up
basis: D49

• The US ERTA raised the capacity of Employee Stock Ownership
Plans to borrow money from a bank, buy the firm's shares and then
deduct both interest **and** principal payments on the loan, thus
allowing for value gains: D49

• Since bidders can write up assets to recover a higher amount of
depreciation under tax shelter, the bidder may consent to pay a
higher premium for target: B39

• Mergers may bring tax benefits, and sometimes these are large,
but there is a lack of convincing evidence that taxes are an
important determinant of overall merger activity: D6

• Tax benefits from higher leverage as well as the capture of tax-loss
carryovers, and an increase in the asset basis used for depreciation
allowances: B33

• Benefits from the increased use of tax losses and unused credits
have shown to be insignificant 94% of the time: D6

• Statistical analysis fails to support that basis step-up is a typically
important in larger mergers: D6

• Surprisingly, tax deductibility of interest rate payments is not an
incentive to merge: (statistically, firms that merge do not borrow
more: there is actually a decline in the debt-equity ratio): D6

• Tax deferral benefits: Stock-for-stock exchanges avoid taxes; (but capital gains tax due when equity sold): B39

• Expanding by leveraged take-overs allows interest deduction (instead of costs incurred by e.g., stock issuance) and enhances the ability to use tax shields - as inflation reduces the amount of outstanding debt: D6

• To avoid capital gains taxes on shareholders, a (US) corporation must qualify as being absorbed into the parent in a reorganization, the stock must be voting stock, and the corporation's tax aspects must be taken over intact. This severely restricts the ability to acquire with cash or to have the tax advantages of stepping up assets. However, the bidder gains any unused tax credits or tax losses that the target has carried forward, plus "built-in" future tax losses: D6

• Merger waves are due to changing levels of equity trapped within firms by adverse tax treatment of dividends: E13

• New antitakeover law decreases M&A's: C28, F10

• M&A increases if antitrust bills are being reviewed: C28, E1

• Legislation (Warn Act-USA) obliges firms to give employees notice when they will be fired: C80, C90

• Legislation that creates trade barriers increases M&A: D17

• Court decisions effect M&A's: C2

• To avoid environmental and other governmental regulations by acquiring old plant rather than creating new: B39

——————— .***. ———————

CHAPTER 9

A CHECKLIST OF EFFECTS: POST-ACQUISITION OUTCOMES

9.1 FINANCIAL EFFECTS OF MERGERS AND ACQUISITIONS

9.1.1 CAPITAL MARKET LIQUIDITY

Cash flows

• M&A's drain firms cash flows: C3, C94

• Cash flows decrease about 5% one year out, and almost 50% four years afterwards. Cash flow to assets falls slightly before industry adjustment and falls 20 % after 1 year, after 4 years rising to 6.2% : B32

• Financing with cash signals the bidder's ability to sustain substantial future cash flows from its existing assets and indicates bidders' private information on the profitability of the takeover: B39

• Capital outlays historically have increased following M&As: B39

• After several inflation years, firms operate below their debt capacities; free cash flows may grow if revenues keep up with inflation while interest payments do not; managers use money more freely and less efficiently (making them takeover candidates): D49

• Mergers lead to decreasing returns on assets and on equity caused by capital requirements growing faster than profits: B6

• Declines in capital expenditures and R&D follow M&A: B32

• New capial outlays in acquired companies' operations increase significantly over premerger outlays: B39

• The rise of bankruptcy and costs may be reduced by mergers; thus, M&A may cause the cost of capital in the resulting firm to be lower than in the component firms: B39

Equity
• Bidder takeover financing with equity signals that the ability of the combined firm to internalize the investment opportunities is not great with respect to internal financing: B39

• In a new professionalized "Casino Society", M&A strips away equity, replaces it with shaky high-cost debt, and destabilizes markets: F13

Leverage

• A positive correlation exists between net borrowing and M&As: G7

• Leverage generally increases following M&A: B39

• M&A leads to higher leveraging (as a means of payment), which causes:

          † rising debt ratios
          † a downrating of (16%) corporate debt
          † a decrease in bond values

† restructuring, which is associated with 38% of downgrades

† poison puts, or exchanging bonds at cost, or exchanging bonds for stock at change of management: B39

† tax and agency benefits: B30

• Mergers increase leverage due to increased debt capacity rather than utilization of latent debt capacity: B39

• M&A creates over-leveraging: D31

• Leverage grows by 10% one year out: B32

• Speculative activity in M&A increases debt unduly and erodes equity resulting in an economy highly vulnerable to economic instability: F13

• Acquiring firms generally have higher-than-average leverage ratios and acquired firms lower: B39

• Leverage and debt-to-equity ratios generally increase substantially - especially for conglomerates - following M&As: B39 et al

• Diversified conglomerates use more leverage than nondiversified firms and increase ROE by over 1% even though return on total assets is lower: B39

• Studies suggest a bias toward overstating the impact of mergers on leverage: B39

Junk   • Returns on high yield securities too low: B20

• Externally induced financial dilution is bad for shareholders: B39

• Mergers respond inversely to prior changes in bond yields (e.g., junk bond financing), although this relation is weaker than to stock prices: I26

• Assets are saddled with debt with no chance of being repaid; in a recession this load is unsustainable: B24

• Cheap junk bond financing of acquisitions drives up the prices of takeover targets: B24

• Interest payments increase after the merger, implying higher leveraging: I23

• M&A's do not cause higher interest rates: G9

• Diversified conglomerates improve their rate of return on shareholders' equity by 1.3 % more than nondiversifed manufacturing firms by using greater leverage, although return on total assets is lower: I7 in B39

• Firms wasted funds in the merger boom and left the economy heavily burdened with debt: D47

• Latest trend towards de-levering through restructuring due to banks tightening up on the credit availability and other difficulties for firms raising debt, and the relatively favorable costs of equity financing: B4

• In 1990 there was a trend away from highly leveraged financial takeovers to all-cash strategic acquisitions of small to medium-sized growth niche firms: B39

9.1.2 GENERAL EFFECTS OF MERGERS ON STOCK MARKET PRICES

• Value is created by mergers and takeovers; target firm shareholders gain 15-20% and acquiring firm shareholders on average do not lose: B39

• At least in the short-term, takeovers do not significantly improve stock prices of acquirer, and may even lower them: B11,C29,C30,C37

• On average, takeovers increase value of target shares: B14,C29,C37,I2. However, this reflects market assessment of undervaluation, rather than altered cash flows and increased wealth: B32

• Changes in merger activity and changes in stock prices both lead changes in industrial production: I26

• Empirical studies suggest there are negative returns to shareholders when new outside financing is used, whether in the form of debt or equity: B39

• The sale price of divested units is 90% of the purchase price, and 143% of the target's pre-takeover market value. 1980s targets appear worth less than bidders paid, but more than the target is worth before takeover. This is consistent with event-study findings of small negative returns to acquirers and positive combined returns to acquirers and targets: B21

• Increase in M&A activity causes stock market collapses: C50

• To arbitrage between stock purchase price and asset replacement value, as roughly expressed by Tobin's q-ratio (market value of debt and equity ÷ asset replacement costs); high interest rates and inflation drive up asset replacement costs so cheaper to acquire assets through takeover rather than buy new ones: C83

• The level of merger activity (as well as GNP) is positively, **but not significantly**, related to changes in Tobin's q: D21

• The 1989/90 decline in takeovers and corporate share buyback programs reduced the long stock market advance the most since 1984. Corporations are becoming net sellers of stock, after seven years of being net buyers, in order to retire debt and reduce interest costs in a sluggish economy. Stocks which were selling for 50% of per share costs to replicating firm assets (q-ratio) are traded in 1990 at a premium to replacement value: B38

• In the 1960s and early 1970s in the UK, the valuation ratio (stock market value/reported book value) was low roughly 60% of the time for acquired companies, which increased probability of takeover: C46, I19, I20, I9, I3. However, both acquired and acquiring companies had higher industrial averages in manufacturing and distribution: I20

• Corporate restructurings led to an unprecedented retirement of outstanding equity shares, especially after 1982: B33

9.1.2.1 METHODS OF PAYMENT AND STOCK PRICES

• Returns on target firm stock prices are higher for cash offers than for stock offers: E9,E18,G12,I13,I38

• Corporate insiders who value control will finance by cash or debt rather than by issuing new stock, which **dilutes** their holdings and increases the risk of losing control: the larger the managerial ownership fraction of the acquiring firm, the more likely the use of cash financing: B2

• Likewise, negative bidders' abnormal returns in stock financings are mainly by acquirers with low managerial ownership: B2

• For bidding firms stock prices, the cumulative average residual (CAR) is slightly negative when stock is used: E18, G12. Thus studies argue that shareholder of bidding firms are penalized by takeovers: B39. Bidder stocks have low to negative returns (-2.2 to 3.5 %): B39

• Target firms returns are higher for cash offers than for all equity offers both in the US and UK, and stronger for the event month in the UK: E5

• After takeover speculation, target firm's stock prices rise even more after a firm's prohibition of greenmail payments, which are made to eliminate takeover bids, i.e., target firm managers offer to repurchase the shares of a single large blockholder seeking control

at a price above the market. Greenmail payments can cause
significant stock price declines: B11

• Share prices of targets in unsuccessful takeovers do not return to
pre-takeover levels: I1

• In the pre-announcement period, however, the target receives
more in a noncash tender than for a cash tender offer: C72

• If firms finance takeovers with equity, managers may judge stock
to be overvalued, and hardy enough for dilution: C35

• Announcement period returns to acquirers in mergers are
significantly more negative for acquisitions financed with stock
than those with cash: C10

• In 181 Canadian takeovers, the average announcement-month
abnormal stock return is significantly positive and larger for mixed
offers than for either all-stock or all-cash bids, i.e., there is a
positive relation between abnormal bidder return and the amount
of cash in a mixed offer: C30

• There is also a positive correlation between announcement
abnormal stock returns and post-merger increases in operating cash
flows: B19

9.1.2.2 MERGER PREMIUMS: STOCK PRICE
RETURNS TO BIDDERS AND TARGETS

• Target companies gain most in M&A:
B30,C24,C34,C37,D8,E20,F14

• Target returns are higher when multiple bids: B30 D8, and when
horizontal acquisitions: D19

• Acquired target stocks increase 15-20% on average: B39

• Bidders have 0 to slightly positive gains: C37, C47, C34

• Bidders' returns lower when buying high-growth target: B29

• Bidders' gains are negative, although overall gains are positive, suggesting value is created: B30

• Tough frequent bidders gain more than one-time softies: C56

• Returns to bidder are greater when takeovers are hostile; friendly takeovers are not arm's length and do not really represent transfer: B30

• Announcement period returns to bidders are lower when their firm diversifies, when it buys a rapidly growing target, and when its managers performed poorly before the acquisition: B29

• Acquirer returns and combined (acquirer and target) returns at acquisition announcement are lower for unsuccessful acquisitions than for successful divestitures, and for non-divesting acquisitions. This shows that the market evaluates managerial decisions in a sensible way and also correlates with event-study findings: B21

• The joint gain to shareholders in the late 1980s is 2.4% compared to 1981-84 figures of 8%, because target firm shareholders gains dropped from 35% to 16%: B30, D8

• Gains to both targets and bidders are highest in unrelated industries: B30

• Higher abnormal returns for cash (29-34%) than for stock offers (14-17%), or for mixed cash/stock offers (12-23%) (prolonged SEC regulation): C34

• M&A enhances shareholder value: C82

• Target shareholders benefit greatly from takeovers whether or not disclosure and other rules are in place (e.g., government antitakeover rules such as margin rules restricting use of debt; limits on number of entities under one ownership umbrella; mandatory information disclosure; prenotification rules; delayed execution of takeover bids; restrictions on foreign ownership participation): C30

• There is no evidence that M&A decreases firm risk, but if this is true it hurts shareholders: C57

• Event study evidence suggests that managers of bidders, but not targets, have valuable private information about the potential synergies from proposed mergers: B10

• Insiders on average do not outperform outsiders: E8

• M&A increases information for investors: D15

• The "excess demand" hypothesis that merger premiums are larger with increase in the number of potential bidders, is substantiated empirically:

> • Bank merger premiums are significantly larger in states that permit interstate banking.

> • Premiums appear to increase significantly in the year following the passage of enabling legislation.

> • Premiums are greater in states that allow unlimited intrastate holding company acquisitions: B1

• The "barriers to entry" hypothesis (premiums decrease as constraints on geographic expansion are relaxed) is also supported: B1

9.1.3 FIRM PROFITABILITY

• In the UK in the 1960s and early 1970s: 1) acquired companies experienced short-term deterioration in profits: 2) profits dropped below industrial norm in year before merger, but were higher 2 - 3 years before : I25, and 3) acquired firms were less profitable: I9, I19

• Acquired companies have short-term deterioration and are smaller, less dynamic and somewhat less highly valued than companies on average, and are systematically less profitable in the mid-term; acquirers are larger, and faster growing: C46

• Non-horizontal acquirers are more profitable than horizontal acquirers are less profitable than industrial average. Horizontal mergers are as likely to fail as to succeed. Non-horizontal mergers depend on post-acquisition monitoring: C46

• Merger waves bring huge windfall profits: C46

• Raiders make money; most others do not: F7

• Bondholders lose as higher levels of debt are assumed: I14

• Net operating cash flows to total assets at market are lower, although adjusted for industry, asset turnover improves, although operating income to sales does not: B19

• Operating margins do not decline: B19

• Operating margins decline: B32

• Taxes decline by 22 - 68 %, perhaps due to write-up of assets or cashflow declines: B32

• M&A moves resources to their highest and best uses, increasing efficiency and shareholder value: H1

• Asset turnover improves after merger: B19

• Asset turnover/productivity declines one year after merger, but rises 25.7 % four years out: B32

• The financial characteristics of the target firm do not change significantly (profitability, expense levels, and asset use): C33

• Acquired firms are already efficient: subsequent performance is not improved: D33, D42

• Kisses don't necessarily turn toads into princes, i.e., purchasing interests in princely turnarounds with toad-like, undervalued prices does not necessarily lead to prince-like performance: I4

• Mergers increase profitability in hospitals: C94

• Latest trend towards de-levering through restructuring due to banks tightening up on the availability of credit and difficulties for firms raising debt, and the relatively favorable costs of equity finance, (Alan Bond's Elders takeover and aftermath): B4

9.1.4 EFFECTS OF LBOS

• Most LBOs do not go public again: B30

• Buyouts make LBO-launching executives as well as investment bankers, lawyers, LBO firms and junk-bond dealers extremely rich: B24

• LBOs enrich a handful of executives at the expense of bondholders (e.g., pension and insurance funds), turning into junk the higher grade, pre-merger bonds of the target company: D40

• Junk bond financing permits fast tender offers so takeovers soar: B24 • LBOs can improve corporate efficiency by putting pressure on management and resources in servicing higher debt burdens: D5

• Larger gains to shareholders before LBOs weakly associated with tax liabilities and cash position of target firm: B30

9.1 WHAT DRIVES LBOs?

• LBOs started as "aid to the elderly", to allow founders of family-owned firms (that prospered during the postwar economic boom into the vast conglomerates of the 1960s) to keep control in the family, simultaneously avoiding estate taxes and exposure to stock market vagaries.

• Early buyout firms bought companies to work side-by-side with management, grow their businesses, and sell out in 5 - 7 years. Now buyout companies and banks strip assets for cash.

• The bootstrap deal, or leveraged buyout, is a standard solution for any company with drooping stock prices.

• The junk bond is not alone to blame for unduly burdensome debt burdens; there are also dangerous variants (e.g., PIKS, or securities paying interest only in other bonds; "cram down stocks" force fed to shareholders, and interest-rate escalating bonds). (B24)

RAIDERS:

• are attracted by the gap between the stock market price and the expected maximum stock price if the firm managed raider style

• maximize firm value by breaking it up and selling it piecemeal

• improve operations and boost profits

• recap tax benefits

• create more individual incentives to use leverage to improve short-term results

• focus most on current management weakness and use own management team to get results (C75)

• Employment, capital expenditure and research and development fall moderately after LBOs.

• Companies which go private experience strong improvements in operating performance: B30

• LBOS hurt bondholders whose holdings are devalued in the face of new, riskier debt: B24

• LBOs hurt Main Street employees, communities, companies and investors: A27a{mark}:check

• LBOs hurts employees: B24

• "LBO Symbiosis": raider seeks target; target seeks LBO, raider, target and LBO firm profit: B24

• As outstanding debt securities plummet, pre-LBO investors feel betrayed, losing confidence in corporate debt: C36

• LBOs create a greater potential for bankruptcy: C26

• "Lean and mean" LBOs lead to spartan cuts in research and other budgets to pay off debt: B24

• Pre-LBO investors feel betrayed as their securities plummet, and lose confidence in (US) corporate debt: C46

• LBOs can improve corporate efficiency: D5

• LBOs enrich a handful of executives at the expense of bondholders (e.g., pension and insurance funds), turning high-grade pre-merger target bonds into junk: D40

• LBOs amplify financial distress:

1. LBO prices have increased (relative to cash flows) but risks the same.
2. From subordinated private debt with strip financing (a safety valve in times of financial distress) to public debt.
3. More precarious financial structures:
   - debt to total capital ratios increase
   - lower cash flows to total cash debt
   - in late buyouts, low coverages necessitate asset sell-offs.
4. Management and deal promoters take out more money up front ∴ less assurance deal properly structured and strong long-term effects.
5. Underpayment led to abnormal positive returns in earlier LBOs.
6. Public subordinated debt holders (insurance companies, S&Ls) bear brunt of distress in later LBOs because of overpayment: A20

9.2 STRATEGIC

9.2.1 VALUE GAINS EFFECTING FIRM PERFORMANCE
[see Chapter 5]

9.2.2 SECTORAL SHIFTS
• Massive takeovers and rapid exponential growth of assets build world sectoral leaders, although high debt levels and market moves may deteriorate stock values: B7

• Mergers allows oligopolies to form: D15

• Mergers force other companies to merge: C45

• M&A's do not cause undue concentration of power: C53,C94

• Abnormal returns of competitors to nine US airlines announcing mergers supports the merger-for-market-power hypothesis, contradicting previous literature on horizontal mergers: B23

• Based on stock price data, mergers challenged by the US Government between 1963-78 were not, in general, anticompetitive, but would have promoted profitable collusion in the industry: I10

• New enforcement powers granted to agencies under the U.S. HSR Act of 1978 to delay mergers with anticompetitive effects have not improved the agencies' case selection record. Delays may reduce incentive to merge, as additional time allows rival firms to exploit valuable inside information: G4

• In general, government regulations which limit corporate control markets that promote efficient allocation of corporate resources - reduce efficient allocation without offsetting benefits: C30

• Capital outlays in acquired company increase after merger: B39

• Acquisitions in natural resource as well as flagging industries perform poorly, but well in nondurable goods industries: B32

• LBOs favor industries with low growth and stable technology: C60

9.2.3 EFFECTS ON ECONOMIC AND POLITICAL ENVIRONMENT
• Macroeconomic variables seem utterly unresponsive to any change in merger volume, with no systematic impact on interest rates or debt levels: F3

• National productivity decreases: C25, D15, G9

• LBOs adversely effect economic stability: C13

• M&A improves corporate efficiency and national competition: D26

• Mergers have had a significant role in post-war growth of business organizations: a concentration of power in private hands rather than democratically chosen governments, especially late 1960s in the UK: B 94

• The non-horizontal virtues of the stock market allocation process are being transplanted by the internal administrative market of conglomerate firms with loss of information in consolidated balance sheets: C46[122]

9.2.4 COMPETITION

9.2.4.1 GENERAL MARKET

• Firms may operate in unfamiliar territory after M&A: D25

• Creates market power: C79

• Small firms perform most poorly after M&A: B32

• Firms acquiring larger targets by 60% or more experience negative cash flow/sales growth; firms with smaller targets less likely to face operating declines: B32

• Hostile takeovers perform more poorly than friendly takeovers. Former may be bad performers with bad decisions, low levels of managerial shareholding, and agency problems, whereas friendly mergers may benefit from tax synergies, lower servicing costs, and no agency problems: D38

• Targets in friendly takeover tend to be in growth industry and above average industry performance; in hostile, mature industry and below average performance: B30

---

[122] Consequently, Hughes maintains that public interest criteria must be applied (eg., by the UK Mergers and Monopolies Commission) not only to competitive horizontal mergers, but also to "non-competitive" conglomerates.

9.2.5 DEFENSE AGAINST ACQUISITION
-•-

9.2.6 MANAGEMENT MOTIVES
• General upward shift in decision-making occurs towards new parent in capital spending, finance, insurance, legal services, data processing and clerical and management training, e.g., the managerial function of capital expenditure planning is relocated: I27 In the UK, this shift has occurred towards the Southeast, and from inner city to outer ring and suburban locations: C46

• The managerial function of capital expenditure planning is generally relocated to corporate headquarters: B39

• Managers work harder with high debt: F2

• M&A drains managements' time: C25, G14

• Corporate managers may be more likely to be fired after a "hostile" takeover: C30

• M&A eliminates (poor) managers: C64,D4,D15,D17,D35,F10

• Better management is brought in after takeover: C26,C70,C73

• Increases productivity and efficiency:
C62,C64,C67,C70,C93,D1,F12

• Ownership changes in takeovers reduce owners' commitment to the longterm interests of managers and employees: B13

9.2.7 EFFECTS ON STAFF
• Any gains to shareholders represent a redistribution away from labor and other stakeholders: D48

• Decrease in employee morale: D14

• Number of employees decreases: C42, C90

• Employees involved in horizontal/vertical/product extension M&A's receive higher wages: C33, C69
• It is *not* true that M&A's have negative employment effect: G9

9.3 LEGISLATION, TAXATION AND REGULATION
• US taxpayers subsidize multi-billion dollar buyouts: C13

• Taxes decline by 22-68 %, perhaps due to asset write-up or cash flow declines: B32

• MBOs cause negative conflicts of interest: D10

• "Lean and mean" LBOs lead to spartan cuts in research and other budgets to pay off debt: B24

• Need for more regulation, not less: 1980's style M&A effects the integrity of securities markets, and the safety of financial institutions due to general excessive risk-taking: F13

———— .***. ————

CHAPTER 10

A CHECKLIST OF SUCCESS AND FAILURE FACTORS

10.1 THE TRACK RECORD TO DATE

• Over one-third of M&A is later divested (particularly of diversifying companies): M&A may destroy value and challenge event-study outcomes asserting that the combined returns to acquirer and target stocks are positive: B21

• Little evidence that market power created by new vertical or horizontal concentration causes merger gains: B30

• In 400 cases, 25% were judged as outright failures and another 25% were deemed not worth repeating. Asked how to describe their company's acquisition experience over the last three years, 30% replied successful, 53% satisfactory, and 16 unsatisfactory: D37

• It does not seem that mergers raise relative profitability, but may have a negative impact, at least during the 1960s and early 1970s, e.g., unit operating costs do not drop: C46

• Takeover may inhibit long-term R&D and technological improvement because of pressure to keep up short-term profits and share prices up: C46

• Rather than spending enormous sums acquiring different kinds of service companies, an accounting firm reports that one UK firm would have done better with a savings account: (the firm retorts figures include costs but not profits): C46

• The growth and success of acquirers may come to depend on the capture of always bigger and more successful companies to maintain a given proportionate increase in size and performance. The shining captains of 1960s industry may be today's overambitious failures: D46

• But "none showed any disposition to stop acquiring": D37

10.2 MERGER SUCCESS

10.2.1 SUCCESSFUL ACQUIRERS:
1. buy targets that reinforce firm's position in its core business line/s: B37

2. seek strong local players and don't turn targets around: B37

3. focus on a few critical elements of target's business system, using bidder's competitive "tweak": B37

4. transfer a few key senior skills and systems rather than scale increases; (especially from slowing mature industries to fast-growing young industries: I7)

5. "patch" critical systems without heavy spending: B37

6. make many acquisitions and go up the M&A learning curve for international expansion: B21, B18

7. realize synergy gains in production and distribution as well as finance (reduce bankruptcy risks, diversification) I18, I2

. . . AND ESPECIALLY IN A
RECESSION:

8. make accurate valuations ("old valuation expectations"
of sellers must be modified to fit fundamental changes in
the world economy, i.e., less demand for properties and
more uncertainty regarding corporate performance): A9

9. do not overpay for target: A9

10. sustain an in-depth industry knowledge: A9

11. uphold a full global network of long-term corporate
relationships: A9

12. fit transactions to well-defined prior strategic and
financial goals: A9

13. monitor regulatory changes: A9

14. tailor earnouts to circumstances covering every
payment aspect including post-earnout motivation: A11

10.2.2 RULES FOR LBO SUCCESS
• Keep continuity of top management and key R&D personnel: D37

• Be thorough in pre-acquisition analysis; learn rituals and valued practices
as well as hardcore institutions: D37

• If you are going to act, do so quickly and decisively, simple and direct,
especially in coping with new winners and losers; stamp your mark in less
than a week: D37

• Maintain high visibility, emphasizing frank communications and organize
for feedback: D37

• Focus groups, quality-circle type initiatives and merger press offices are better than waiting for a "trickle-down effect" from top management: D37

• Make a 45-minute presentation explaining culture to new employees within hours or days, watching content and the manner which it is communicated: D37

• Act correctly - word about the company gets around: D37

• Partially integrate, or treat the acquisition as an autonomous or stand-alone unit: let management run the company; if they don't do well, change the management. A few key persons (high-added-value people) play a large role - pay special attention to them, especially with incentive pay arrangements: D37

• Treat people sensitively: recognize long service, and provide proper and generous separation arrangements, but refuse to promote mediocrity: D37

• Don't treat personnel benefits as a priority; arrange a trade-off between the firms that is seen to be fair. Protect inventors and innovators: D37

• Understand what you want upfront ; analyze pre-acquisition success: D37

• Repeat the message: maintain a clarity of purpose D37

• Carry out changes over time in a deliberate and unhurried way: D37

• Acquire basic industry with solid and reliable management, products and earnings: B24

• Keep up technological innovativeness: D37

• Use an aggressive, focused approach with strenuous goals: D37

• Larger companies can be acquired as easily - easier - than small ones, simply because dealing with larger cash flows: D37

• Build up experience: more experience, more success: D37

• Put a price tag on synergy and link it to manager performance: D37

• Keep overheads as low as feasible: D37

• Continue to explore synergy potential: D37

• Develop a fix on future earnings and cash flows: D37

• Be informed:

> • Know reasons for pre-acquisition success

> • Anticipate nasty surprises: e.g., closures in foreign countries arouse government and union opposition

> • Sell control system to new executives, seconding someone form the new parent

> • Adapt reporting system to smaller company, yet question and streamline parent's system: D37

• Build an acquisition integration plan three or more years forward with specific performance measurements and targets:

> o earnings per share
> o profits before tax
> o revenue growth
> o return on assets employed
> o criteria for management earn-out formula
> o management stock incentives
> o longer term shareholder value, or cash plus capital gains
> o contribution of target in next two years
> o price acquired company could obtain now compared to purchase price
> o how can acquisition be enhanced (added investments, restructuring, complementary acquisitions): D37

• Analyze and address cultural differences, especially regarding:

> o The basic corporate driving force
> o Key success factors
> o Executive reward system
> o The corporate climbing frame
> o The (high or low) margin environment
> o The operating environment, especially customary time frame
> o The personal attributes: D37

• Develop new loyalty focus: D37

• Identify some personnel irritant which has been dogging the acquired company for some time and fix it decisively: D37

• Identify most nostalgic elements or products of the old company and spruce them up or get rid of them: D37

• Articulate not only a strategy but a sunny vision ahead: D37

• Hammer on new goals, strategies and objectives: D37

• Meet and keep aware of external economic changes, e.g., allow for the business cycle, especially if entering unfamiliar areas: D37

• Pay attention to external relations of the acquire company, customers and supplier anticipating change: D37

• Keep unique marketing style: D37

• Be prepared for rapid external market changes and ability to compete.[123] Whole industries change dramatically: e.g., the petroleum equipment,

---

[123] Whole industries change dramatically: recall the petroleum equipment computer hardware, airlines, jewelry, watch, and business information industries. "It's not that companies don't see the traps - it's that they ignore them: C46.

computer hardware, airlines, jewelry, watch, and business information industries. "It's not that companies don't see the traps (such as tax questions and management succession). It's that they ignore them": D37

• Post-LBO acquirer must sell off enough assets and generate enough cash flow to service heavy debt burden: D5

10.3 MERGER FAILURE

10.3.1 WHY MERGERS FAIL

1. First and most importantly, corporate cultures clash (e.g., formal vs informal) : D37
2. Secondly, the acquisition price paid was too high: D37
3. Companies from outside the industry push up P/E ratios in buying sprees: D37
4. Firms tend to disregard longterm objectives: D14,G9,G14
5. The company bought at the wrong time in its corporate life cycle (e.g., success freezes into a strategy or niche: D37
6. The seller may know but the purchaser doesn't that acquisition target is obsolete in its sector: D37
7. More complicated organizations are created: B35, D37
8. Loss of flexibility and service: D37
9. Culture shock: Big company swamps little company with systems and people: D37
10. Longterm R&D slows down: C25, C79
11. Logistic strategies are disrupted: C35
12. People leave: acquired firm's top management and other key people quit (viz., in the "people businesses", e.g., financial services, pr/advertising, high tech): D37
13. Earnout problems: difficulty of integration; poor motivation; target earnings not sufficient to cover earnout payments; stock dilution; incompatibility of senior management; vendor's financial health is weak; full payment not forthcoming: A11

10.3.2 REASONS WHY 101 SELLING FIRMS "FAILED" OR DIVESTED

1. Change of focus; corporate business no longer synergizes with core business (43%)
2. To finance other acquisition or debt restructuring (29%)
3. Unit unprofitable or mistake (22 %)
4. Need cash (3%)
5. Good price (3%)
6. Antitrust (2%)
7. To defend against takeover(1%): B21

10.3.3 LOSS FACTORS

1. Expansion by non-value-maximizing managers (managerialism theory): B29
2. Hubris Hypothesis: mistakes are made by arrogant managers about "poorly managed, undervalued firms" for which they pay premia above what is a fair market price in an informationally efficient market: F14
3. Winner's Curse: at auction the buyer overbids due to competitive bidders: E20, F14
4. Takeover news, especially when acquirers don't complete: B30
5. (Majority of) takeovers are negative NPV investments: B30

——— .***. ———

CHAPTER 11
CONCLUSION

This presentation contributes the following:

1. A comprehensive review of the causes and effects of mergers and acquisitions in the twentieth century, with focus on the 1980s. While the checklists in Part Two offer an easy overview for practitioners and analysts, financial, strategic, and legal issues are explored in depth in Part One.

2. The reasons for success and failure in mergers and acquisitions.

3. A history of M&A explaining the functions of shifting capital costs, the rise of debt leveraging, LBOs, and new financing techniques.

4. A categorization of lead players on the M&A turf. The causal role of governments in mergers and acquisitions is also briefly evaluated.

5. Structural contributions include:

•A Merger Wave Model

•A Payoff Cycle

•An Organizational Cycle, or the evolution of the business structure as paralleled by developments in M&A

• A Financial Cycle: the "Debt-Equity Clock"

•The Maschmeier or Banker's Dilemma (when they want it you don't have it; when you have it they don't want it)

•The "M&A Barometer", or M&A as a leading indicator of economic change

•The Post Paradox, or growth specialization to doom

•The M-Curve

•Presentation of selected principles of inflationary behavior (the rules of acceleration)

•The Icarus Trap, or debt degradation.

6. A postulate on cyclical dynamics is applied to the M&A cycle and its financial, strategic, legal, economic and psychological factors. The model draws from previous M&A analysis and also from research on foreign direct investment and internalization, the product cycle, the technology cycle, and selected business cycle theories. The basic approach is a dynamic one that contrasts with the static Marshallian "scissor-snap" theorem. It is based on the intrinsic behavior of life cycle phase transitions with obvious relevance to the principles of evolutionary growth. One major conclusion that can be drawn is that a general evolution has occurred from organic market development to product or market manipulation in order to gain control. This trend is obvious in the rationalization and discretionary management of the product curve in the semiconductor markets in which competitive edges must be immediately and totally exploited to stay astride. However, markets, particularly today's M&A markets, absorb *all* information, *even product cycle manipulation.* Thus, no one can ever escape the ultimate organic nature of cyclical behavior. One may be clever in the short term, but cleverness gone public is discounted in the longterm.

• the advantages of a cyclical over a linear (and also a chaotic) paradigm: flexibility, gradualism, adaptation, deflection, continuity and repeatability

• seek and search

• coping with boundary conditions as triggers, dampeners, and accelerators

• consolidation, bifurcation and articulation at the limits of growth

• convolution and formation (lag effects)

• time demarcation (e.g., the vortical gnp clock)

• axial dynamics by category

• the drawbacks of linear growth and linear analysis

7. A categorization of merger phases and phase interactions through lagging phenomena: boom mergers and prosperity mergers as well as recession and trough mergers, the latter as subject to the rich man-poorer man syndrome.

—————— •***• ——————

LITERATURE SYNOPSIS

•SOURCES OF THE COMPREHENSIVE LITERATURE SURVEY IN PART TWO

1991

A1. Anand, Vilneeta, "Divesting Firms Learn a Good Buyer is Hard to Find", *Investor's Daily*, 19 Jun 1991.

A2. Anonymous, "Hanson and ICI", *Financial Times*, 17 May 1991, 27.

A3. Anonymous, "Japan: Shotgun Marriages", *Banker* 141/779, Jan 1991, 47-49.

A4. Anonymous, "Tender Offer Update: 1991", *Mergers and Acquisitions* 25/6, May/Jun 1991, 12-13.

A5. Anonymous, "The Deals That Fell Through", *Mergers and Acquisitions* 25/6, May/Jun 1991, 15-16.

A6. Blackman, A, "France: the new détente for dealmakers", *Acquisitions Monthly*, Jun 1991, 19-27.

A6a Blair, Margaret, Sarah J. Lane and Martha A. Schary, "Patterns of Corporate Restructuring, 1955-87", Brookings Discussion Papers in Economics No. 91-1, The Brookings Institution, 1991.

A7. Burckhardt, A, "The attractions of a united Germany", *Acquisitions Monthly*, Jul 1991, 44-45.

A8. Burckhardt, A, "Germany", *Acquisitions Monthly*, Feb 1991, 42-44.

A9. Crowley, W, L Lee and R Campbell-Breeden, "Cover story: Three Cross Border Case Studies. Only those transactions. . .", *Acquisitions Monthly*, Feb 1991, 33.

A10. Dijkum, K v, and P Horsten, "The Netherlands", *Acquisitions Monthly*, Feb 1991, 48-50.

A11. Harley, J, N Hughes, and J Peacock, "Learning the lessons of the late 1980s (Earnouts)", *Acquisitions Monthly*, Jun 1991, 50-51.

A12. Healey, S, G O'Dwyer, K Knudsen, and W Marlowe, "Special Report: The Nordic region", *Acquisitions Monthly*, Jun 1991, 37-47.

A12a. Lewis, Michael, *The Money Culture*, WW Norton, 1991.

A13. Lowenstein, Roger, "Goldman Study of Stocks' Rise in '80s Poses a Big Riddle", *Wall Street Journal*, 6 Jun 1991, C1-C2.

A14. Morelli, M, "Italy", *Acquisitions Monthly*, Feb 1991, 54-55.

A15. Muirhead, S, and I Beith, "Corporate Refinancings", *Acquisitions Monthly*, Jun 1991, 48-49.

A16. Ommeren, J v, and B Boreel, "Management Buyouts: The Netherlands", *Acquisitions Monthly*, Jun 1991, 52-54.

A17. Polo de Lara, E, "Spain", *Acquisitions Monthly*, Feb 1991, 51-53.

A18. Schmidkonz, R and B Press, "Sale of the Century", *Acquisitions Monthly*, Jul 1991, 48-50.

A19. Schwarz, A, and J Friedland, "Indonesia: Empire of the Sun", *Far Eastern Economic Review* (Hong Kong), 14 Mar 1991, 46-53.

A20. Stein, J C, and S N Kaplan, "The Evolution of Buyout Pricing and Financial Structure in the 1980s, Grad School of Business, U of Chicago, Draft, April 1991.

A21. Vineeta, *Investor's Daily*, 19 Jun 1991, 8.

1990

B1. Adkisson, J A, and D R Fraser, "The Effect of Geographical Deregulation on Bank Acquisition Premiums", *Journal of Financial Services Research* 4(2), Jul 1990, 145-55.

B2. Amihud, Y, B Lev and N G Travlos, "Corporate Control and the Choice of Investment Financing: The Case of Corporate Acquisitions" *Journal of Finance* 45/2, Jun 1990, 603-16.

B3. Anonymous, "Asian Venture Forum '90 explores venture growth", *Asian Venture Capital Journal*, Nov 1990.

B4. Anonymous, "Australian Corporate Finance", *Euromoney*, May 1990, 97-101.

B5. Anonymous, "How Pacific Rim Buyers are hitting the World M&A Scene", *Mergers and Acquisitions* 25/1 Jul/Aug 1990, 26 - 34.

B6. Buhner, R, "Der Jahresabschlusserfolg von Unternehmenszusammenschlussen (English summary), *Zeitschrift-fur-Betriebswirtschaft* 60/12, Dec 1990, 1275-94.

B7. Burrough, B and J Helyar, *Barbarians at the Gate. The Fall of RJR Nabisco*, Harper Collins, New York, 1990.

B8. Chowdhury, A, "M&A Mania: Tokyo Raiders Turn to New Europe", *Asian Finance* 16/5, 15 May 1990.

B9. Denis, D J (Virginia Polytechnic), "Corporate Investment Decisions and Corporate Control: Evidence from Going Private Transactions", Paper Presented at American Economic Conference, December 1990.

B10. Eckbo, B Espen, Maksimovic, Vojislav and Williams, Joseph, "Consistent Estimation of Cross-Sectional Models in Event Studies", *Review of Financial Studies* 3(3) 1990, 343-65.

B11. Eckbo, B Espen, "Valuation Effects of Greenmail Prohibitions", Feb 1990.

B12. Franks, Julian, and C Mayer, "European Capital Markets and Corporate Control", Paper at London Business School, 30 Sep 1990.

B13. Franks, Julian and C Mayer, "Takeovers", *Economic Policy*, Apr 1990.

B14. Gant, Joanna, "The changing pace of Europe", *Acquisitions Monthly*, Feb 1991.

B15. Garvey, G (University of N South Wales, Aust), "Do Concentrated Shareholdings mitigate the Agency Problem of 'Free Cash FLow'? Theory and Evidence", Paper presented at American Economic Conference, Dec 1990.

B16. Hall, B, "The Impact of Corporate Restructuring on Industrial Research and Development", Brookings MicroEconomics Annual, 1990.

B17. Hamilton, S, "Sons of Hanson", *Business* (UK), Jul 1990, 53-57.

B18. Healey, S, "Robust activity recorded", *Acquisitions Monthly*, Feb 1991.

B19. Healy, P, K Palepu, and R Ruback, "Does Corporate Performance improve after Mergers?" NBER Working Paper No. 3348, 1990.

B20. Kaplan, Steven and Jeremy Stein, "How Risky is Debt in Highly Leveraged Transactions? Evidence from Leveraged Recapitalizations", Manuscript, University of Chicago, Chicago, Ill., 1990.

B21. Kaplan, S and M S Weisbach, "The Success of Acquisitions: Evidence from Divestitures", National Bureau of Economic Research Working Paper No. 3484, Oct 1990.

B22. Klock, M (George Washington U) and C F Thies (U of Baltimore), "Tobin's q, Cash Flow and Investment", Paper presented at American Economic Conference, Dec 1990.

B23. Knapp, W, "Event Analysis of Air Carrier Mergers and Acquisitions", *Review of Economics and Statistics* 72(4), Nov 1990, 703-07.

B24. Lewis, Michael, *Liar's Poker: Rising Through the Wreckage on Wall Street*, New York: W W Norton &Co 1989.

B25. Matsuoko, Tokeo, "Taiyo Kobe-Mitsui Bank Merger Announced", *Business Japan* (Japan) 35/1, Jan 1990, 40-41.

B26. McCormick, J, "Connector Makers Buffeted by Shifting Market", *Electronic Business* 16/21, 12 Nov 1990.

B27. Meulbroek, L K , M L Mitchell, J H Mulherin, J M Netter, and A B Poulsen, "Shark Repellents and Managerial Myopia: An Empirical Test", *Journal of Political Economy* 98, 372-398.

B28. Mitchell, M L, and K Lehn, "Do Bad Bidders Become Good Targets?" *Journal of Political Economy* 98/2, Apr 1990, 372-98.

B29. Morck, Randall, Andrei Shleifer and Robert W Vishny, "Do Managerial Objectives Drive Bad Acquisitions?" *Journal of Finance*, 45, 1990, 31-48.

B30. Opler, T C, "Studies on Leveraged Buyout Finance and Corporate Mergers", Dissertation, 1990, University of California, Los Angeles.

B31. Opler, Tim C, and Sheridan Titman, "What Causes Leveraged Buy-outs?" Manuscript, Anderson Grad School of Mgt, UCLA, 1990.

B32. Opler, T C, and J F Weston (UCLA), "The Impact of Mergers on Operating Performance", Preliminary Paper Presented at American Economic Conference, Dec 1990.

B33. Pickering, M H, L E Crabbe and S D Prowse, "Recent Developments in Corporate Finance", *Federal Reserve Bulletin*, Aug 1990, 593-603.

B34. Riemer, B, and S Toy, "The French Hit Some Potholes on the Road to 1992", *Business Week (Industrial/Technology Edition)*, 5 Nov 1990, 65-66.

B35. Schlossberg, Howard, "Research Firms Feel Sting of Mergers", *Marketing News* 24/1, 8 Jan 1990, 10. cl.

B36. Titman, Sheridan, "Interest rate swaps and corporate financing choices", Jun 1990.

B37. Tom Angear, Director, M&A International, Speech before the Cornell University London Conference on Globalization, Mar 1991, in part assimilated from J Bleeke, J Isono, D Ernst, and D Weinberg, "Succeeding at cross-border M&A," *The McKinsey Quarterly* Nr 3, 1990, p 46-50.

B38. Wigmore, B, *Wall Street Journal*, 23 Jul 1990, C1.

B39. Weston, J Fred, Kwang S Chung, and Susan E Hoag, *Mergers, Restructuring, and Corporate Control*, Englewood Cliffs, NJ: Prentice Hall, 1990

1989

C1. Alster, N, "Sprechen Sie High Tech?" *Forbes* 143/8, 17 Apr 1989, 172-176.

C2. Anonymous, "A Court Ruling Unleashes Japan's Corporate Raiders", *Tokyo Business Today*, Sep 1989, 34-36.

C3. Anonymous, "Flying America's Way", *Economist* (U.K.) 312/7619, 9 Sep 1989, 77-78.

C4. Anonymous, "HCMR Review. Rodney Wolford." *Health Care Management Review* 14/3, Summer 1989, 89-94.

C5. Anonymous, "How Cash Became King", *Acquisitions Monthly*, Nov 1989, 33-34.

C6. Anonymous, "Restructuring 1990: Caution - Curves Ahead", *Directors and Boards* 14/1, Fall 1989, 20-25.

C7. Anonymous, "Roundtable: Global Positioning Through Cross-Border M & A", *Mergers and Acquisitions* 24/2, Sep/Oct 1989, 30-41.

C8. Anonymous, "The Bank Takeover Targets Sweepstakes", *Banks Monthly* 106/5, May 1989, 75-79.

C9. Anonymous, "Zenger-Miller Acquired by Times Mirror", *Training and Development Journal* 43/2, Feb 1989, 8-9.

C10. Asquith, P, D W Mullins Jr, and E D Wolff, "Original Issue High Yield Bonds: Aging Analyses of Defaults, Exchanges, and Calls", Harvard Business School, ms., Mar 1989 (cited in A6).

C11. Berkman, Barbara, "Spate of Mergers Challenges Europe's Top Companies", *Electronic Business* 15/22, 13 Nov 1989, 56-59.

C12. Bianchi, P, and G Gualtieri, "Mergers and Acquisitions in Italy and the Debate on Competition Policy", *Antitrust Bulletin* 34/3, Fall 1989, 601-624.

C13. Bina, Cyrus, and John A Texeira, "Leveraged Buyouts: Robber Barons of the Eighties", *Challenge* 32/5, Sep/Oct 1989, 53-57.

C14. Bittlingmayer, George, "Merger as a Form of Investment", School of Management, University of California at Davis, Manuscript, 1989.

C15. Borg, J Rody, Mary O Borg, and John D Leeth, "The Success of Mergers in the 1920's: A Stock Market Appraisal of the Second Merger Wave", *International Journal of Industrial Organization* (Netherlands) 7/1, 1989, 117-131.

C16. Britt, Bill, "Strategy for the 90's: Japan's Third wave", *Marketing* (UK), 21 Sep 1989, 21-22.

C17. Buccino, Gerald P, "Crisis Management: Are LBO's an Emerging Problem?" *Secured Lender* 45/6, Nov/Dec 1989, 26-29, 94.

C18. Clay, William L, "Congressional Committees Will Take a Hard Look at Pension Issues", *Pension World* 25/3, Mar 1989, 14-15.

C19. Conant, John L, and David L Kaserman, "Union Merger Incentives and Pecuniary Externalities", *Journal of Labor Research* 10/3, Summer 1989, 243-253.

C20. Coombes, Peter, "Partly Privatized & Eager for Growth, DSM Feels It's Oats", *Chemical Week* 144/12, 22 Mar 1989, 6-7.

C21. Cunningham, Timothy J, "M & A Activity to Continue for Agents & Brokers", *National Underwriter* 93/37, 11 Sep 1989, 9, 28-29.

C22. Davidson, Kenneth M, "Evolution of a New Industry", *Journal of Business Strategy* 10/1, Jan/Feb 1989, 54-56.

C23. Davidson, Kenneth M, "Fire Sale on America?" *Journal of Business Strategy* 10/5, Sep/Oct 1989, 9-14.

C24. Davidson, Wallace N III., Dipa Dufia, and Louis Cheng, "A Re-Examination of the Market Reaction to Failed Mergers", *Journal of Finance* 44/4, Sep 1989, 1077-1083.

C25. Davis, Nancy M, "Restructuring America's Trade Associations", *Association Management* 41/8, Aug 1989, 50-61.

C26. DiNapoli, Dominic, and Daniel Timm, "Seven LBO Issues; LBO's Issues for Today, Concerns for Tommorow", *Business Credit* 91/9, Oct 1989, 16-19.

C27. Dowding, Tony, "The Giants Add Up", *ReActions* (UK) Issue 12, Dec 1989, 60-61.

C28. Dubofsky, David A, and Donald R Fraser, "The Texas Probable Future Competition Cases and the Transformation of the Bank Expansion Movement: Evidence from the Equity Market", *Antitrust Bulletin* 34/2, Summer 1989, 395-410.

C29. Eckbo, B Espen, "Information Disclosure, Method of Payment, and Takeover Premiums: Public and Private Tender Offers in France", *Journal of Financial Economics* 24, 1989, 363-404.

C30. Eckbo, B Espen, "The Market for Corporate Control: Policy Issues and Capital Market Evidence" in Khemani, *Mergers, Corporate Concentration and Power in Canada*, 143-223.

C31. Eckbo, B Espen, Ronald M Giammarino, and Robert L Heinkel, "Asymmetric information and the medium of exchange in takeovers: Theory and tests", Paper. University of British Columiba Dept of Finance, Sep 1989.

C32. Evans, Richard, "East & West Battle for Austria's Banks", *Euromoney* (UK), Jan 1989, 85-91.

C33. Eyssell, Thomas H, "Partial Acquisitions and Firm Performance", *Journal of Economics and Business*, 41/1, Feb 1989, 69-88.

C34. Fortier, Diana L, "Hostile Takeovers and the Market for Corporate Control", *Economic Perspectives* 13/1, Jan/Feb 1989, 2-16.

C35. Foster, Thomas A, and E J Muller, "The Not-So-Nifty '90s", *Distribution* 88/1, Jan 1989, 30-35.

C36. Frank, "Pity the Poor Old Retail Bondholder", *Banker* (UK) 139/756, Feb 1989, 37-38.

C37. Franks, Julian R, and Robert S Harris, "Shareholder Wealth Effects of Corporate Takeovers: The U.K. Experience 1955-1985", *Journal of Financial Economics* 23/2, Aug 1989, 225-249.

C38. Fridson, Martin S, "Diversification Helps Find Gold Among Junk", *Pensions and Investment Age* 17/4, 20 Feb 1989, 31-32.

C39. Garland, Susan B, "Hospitals: Damned If They Merge, Damned If They Don't", *Business Week* Issue 3132, 6 Nov 1989, 48, 50.

C40. Geschuindt, Simon, "Benefits for Benelux?" *ReActions* (UK) Issue 3, Mar 1989, 57-69.

C41. Glazer, Alan S, "Acquisition Bridge Financing by Financing Banks", *Business Horizons* 32/5, Sep/Oct 1989, 49-53.

C42. Greenberg, Eric Rolfe, "The Latest AMA Survey on Downsizing", *Personnel* 66/10, Oct 1989, 38-44.

C43. Groshen, Erica L, and Barbara Grothe, "Mergers , Acquisitions and Evolution of the Region's Corporations", *Economic Commentary*, 1 Aug 1989, 1-6.

C44. Heller, Karen, "Will Sanity & Sense Return to M & As and Buyouts?" *Chemical Week* 145/19, 8 Nov 1989, 18-22.

C45. Holloway, Nigel, "Banking: Survival of the Fattest", *Far Eastern Economic Review* 145/37, 14 Sep 1989, 60-61.

C46. Hughes, A, "The Impact of Merger: A Survey of Empirical Evidence in the UK", in J A Fairburn and J A Kay, *Mergers and Merger Policy*, Oxford University Press, 1989.

C47. Jarrell, Gregg A, and Annette B Poulsen, "The Returns of Acquiring Firms in Tender Offers: Evidence from Three Decades", *Financial Management* 18/3, Autumn 1989, 12-19.

C48. Jennings, John, "Looking at Why Rather than Who in Mega Mergers", *National Underwriter* 93/5, 30 Jan 1989, 33-34.

C49. Kaplan, S, "The Effects of Leveraged Buyouts on Operating Performance", *Journal of Financial Economics*, 1989.a

C50. Kazemek, Edward A, "Why Mergers & Acquisitions Fail", *Healthcare Financial Management* 43/1, Jan 1989, 94, 97.

C51. King, Mervyn, "Economic Growth & the Life-Cycle of Firms", *European Economic Review* (Netherlands) 33/2,3, Mar 1989, 325-334.

C52. Kleppen, Anne, "Corporate Contributions in an Era of Restructuring", *Fund Raising Management* 20/2, Apr 1989, 50-54.

C53. Knight, Ray A, and Lee G Knight, "Have Recent Tax Acts Provided a Level Playing Field for Corporate Mergers and Acquisitions", *Accounting Horizons* 3/3, Sep 1989, 28-37.

C54. Kogut, Bruce, "The Stability of Joint Ventures: Reciprocity and Competitive Rivalry", *Journal of Industrial Economics* (UK) 38/2, Dec 1989, 183-198.

C55. Korostoff, Kathryn C, "Europe, 1992 & US Data Communications Suppliers", *Business Communications Review* 19/4, Apr 1989, 67-69.

C56. Leach, J C, "Credible 'take-it-or-leave-it' offers in sequential acquisition games", University of Pennsylvania, Philadelphia, PA., 1989.

C57. Lewellen, Wilbur, Claudio Loderer, and Ahron Rosenfeld, "Mergers, Executive Risk Reduction & Stockholder Wealth", *Journal of Financial and Quantitative Analysis* 24/4, Dec 1989, 459-472.

C58. Lindemann, Christoph, "Mergers & Acquisitions: Germany Comes Alive", *International Management* (UK) 44/4, Apr 1989, 46-47.

C59. Magee, John F, "1992: Moves Americans Must Make", *Harvard Business Review* 67/3, May/Jun 1989, 78-84.

C60. Malone, Stewart C, "Characteristics of Smaller Company Leveraged Buyouts", *Journal of Business Venturing* 4/5, Sep 1989, 349-359.

C61. Martin, John, "Why Managers are Starting to Think North American", *Business Month* 134/1, Jul 1989, 20-22.

C62. Mason, Todd, Robert Duffy, and Walecia Konrad, "The LBO Sails Down Madison Avenue", *Business Week* Issue 3124, 18 Sep 1989, 69-76.

C63. McDermott, James J Jr, "A Market View of Recent Merger Trends", *Issues in Bank Regulation* 12/3, Winter 1989, 15-19.

C64. McGee, Robert W, "The Economics of Mergers & Acquisitions", *Mid-Atlantic Journal of Business* 25/4, Feb 1989, 45-55.

C65. Moynihan, Jonathon, "Making Acquisitions Work for Shareholders", *Bank Administration* 65/9, Sep 1989, 14-19.

C66. Odagiri, Hiroyuki, and Tatsuo Hase, "Are Mergers & Acquisitions Going to be Popular in Japan Too?" *International Journal of Industrial Organization* 7/1, 1989, 49-72.

C67. Osterberg, William P, "LBO's and Conflicts of Interest", *Economic Commentary*, 15 Aug 1989, 1-5.

C68. Pallarito, Karen, "Healthcare Experts Predict Fewer LBO's in '90", *Modern Healthcare* 19/50, 15 Dec 1989, 48.

C69. Peoples, James Jr, "Merger Activity & Wage Levels in U.S. Manufacturing", *Journal of Labor Research* 10/2, Spring 1989, 183-196.

C70. Petronchak, Margaret M, "European Opportunities for U.S. Corporations", *Satellite Communications* 13/10, Sep 1989, 35-38.

C71. Phillips, Edward H, "Business Aircraft Utilization Moves Toward Early 1980's Level", *Aviation Week and Space Technology* 131/14, 2 Oct 1989, 46, 50.

C72. Queen, M, "Market Anticipation of Corporate Takeover and the Gain for the Bidders", Doc Dis, UCLA, 1989 (cited in A6).

C73. Rangan, Nanda, "The Takeover Mechanism as an Efficiency Enforcer: The Case of Bank Holding Companies", *Managerial Finance* (UK) 15/4, Dec 1989, 18-22.

C74. Reilly, Patrick, "Media's 'Big Bang'", *Advertising Age* 60/12, 20 Mar 1989, 1, 75.

C75. Rhodes, D W, "When Raiders Go Fishing", *Jrnl of Business Strategy*, Mar/Apr 1989, 48-50.

C76. Rivers, Richard R, and George S Vest, "Making Deals in Post-1992 Europe", *Europe* Issue 290, Oct 1989, 18-20, 46.

C77. Rizzi, Robert A, "Yoc Heating and Intercorporate Transfer of Assets: Still a Hot Issue", *Journal of Corporate Taxation* 16/2, Summer 1989, 168-174.

C78. Roth, Ellen Freeman, "Gearing Up -- Or Marking Time?" *World* 23/3, 1989, 12-15.

C79. Scott, John T, "Purposive Diversification as a Motive for Merger", *International Journal of Industrial Organization* 7/1, 1989, 35-47.

C80. Shandor, Donald B, "The Plant Closing Law: New Pressures on Acquirers", *Mergers and Acquisitions* 24/1, Jul/Aug 1989, 65-68.

C81. Spiegel, Daniel L, and Andrew G Berg, "The National Security Test for Foreign Acquisitions", *Mergers and Acquisitions* 24/3, Nov/Dec 1989, 32-37.

C82. Stapp, Andrew W, "Don't Let Dilution Wreck Your Mergers", *ABA Banking Journal* 81/10, Oct 1989, 132, 134.

C83. Stein, Benjamin J, "End of an Era? Why the Great Takeover Frenzy of the '80's May Have Peaked", *Barron's* 69/35, 28 Aug 1989, 14-15, 25-27.

C84. Sternberg, Ron, "Orix Leads a New Japanese wave", *Asian Business* (Hong Kong) 25/11, Nov 1989, 52-53.

C85. Tetenbaum, Robert M, "Scaling Back: Banks Weigh Lending Shift to Meet New Capital Rules", *Corporate Cashflow* 10/1, Jan 1989, 28-32.

C86. Thackray, John, "Britain's Bad Buys", *Management Today* (UK), Feb 1989, 74-78.

C87. Toy, Stewart, and Richard A Melcher, "The Race to Stock Europe's Common Supermarket", *Business Week (Industrial/Technology Edition)* Issue 3112, 26 Jun 1989, 80-82.

C88. Trieschmann, James S, and E J Leverett Jr, "Agency Valuations Under New Income Tax Rules", *CPCU Journal*, Sep 1989, 157-164.

C89. Tursman, Cindy, "LBO's: Lax standards or Good Management?" *Business Credit* 91/9, Oct 1989, 14-15.

C90. Weissman, Michael L, "The Plant Closing Laws: A New Threat for Secured Lenders", *Secured Lender* 45/3, May/Jun 1989, 16-21.

C91. Wells, G E, "The Revolution in Building Societies", *Long Range Planning* (UK) 22/5, Oct 1989, 30-37.

C92. Whitehead, Brian, "Planning for Systems Architecture at Regional Banks", *Bankers Magazine* 172/1, Jan/Feb 1989, 59-61.

C93. Wilder, Patricia S, "Productivity in the Retail Auto & Home Supply Store Industry", *Monthly Labor Review* 112/8, Aug 1989, 36-40.

C94. Wooley, J. Michael. "The Competitive Effects of Horizontal Mergers in the Hospital Industry." *Journal of Health Economics* 8/3, Dec 1989, 271-291.

C95. Wyderko, Leonard W Jr, "New Capital Guidelines: Will They Slow Merger Activity?" *Bank Administration* 65/2, Feb 1989, 34, 35.

C96. Yagil, Joseph, "Mergers & Bankruptcy Costs", *Journal of Economics and Business* (Temple University) 41/4, Nov 1989, 307-315.

C97. Zemedkun, Wold, "Bank Merger Bids, Managerial Control and Value Maximization", *Akron Business and Economic Review* 20/3, Fall 1989, 64-79.

1988

D1. "Characteristics of Merging Banks in the United States: Theory, Empirical Results, and Implications for Public Policy", *Review of Business and Economic Research* 24/1, Fall 1988, 1-19.

D2. Anonymous, "Grand Metropolitan: Brand Name Policy Boosts Assets", *Accountancy* (UK) 102/1142, Oct 1988, 38-39.

D3. Anonymous, "Le Buy-Out Invades Europe", *Economist* (UK) 307/7554, 11 Jun 1988, 75-77.

D4. Anonymous, "Mergers: Is a New Wave Coming?" *Electrical World* 202/7, Jul 1988, 13-14.

D5. Anonymous, "RJR-Nabisco: KKRackers", *Economist* (UK) 309/7579, 3 Dec 1988, 78-79.

D6. Auerbach, A J, and D Reishus, "The Impact of Taxation on Mergers and Acquistions", in A J Auerbach, Ed., "Mergers and Acquisitions", Chicago: The University of Chicago Press, 1988 (NBER Project Rpt) 25-48.

D7. Bickerstaffe, George, and Roy Hill, "Profile: Sir Adam Thomson -- New Carrer Take-Off", *Director* (UK) 42/4, Nov 1988, 56-59.

D8. Bradley, M, A Desai and E H Kim, "Synergistic gains from corporate acquisitions and their division between stockholders of target and acquiring firms", *Journal of Financial Economics*, 17, 1988, 3-40.

D9. Bruce, Leigh, "The Rise and Rise of European Takeovers", *International Management* (UK) 43/11, Nov 1988, 24-28.

D10. Bruner, Robert F, and Lynn Sharp Paine, "Management Buyouts and Managerial Ethics", *California Management Review* 30/2, Winter 1988, 89-106.

D11. Buescu, D G, "Brazil: First Rumblings of an Acquisitions Market", *Mergers and Acquisitions* 23/1, Jul/Aug 1988, 67-69.

D12. Byrne, J, and M Maremont, "The Dangers of Living by Takeover Alone", *Business Week (Industrial/Technology Edition)* 3065, 15 Aug 1988, 62-64.

D13. Celarler, Michelle, "The New Merger Landscape", *United States Banker* 99/1, Jan 1988, 12-19.

D14. Chakravarty, Subrata N, "When Everything's for Sale, You Lose Something", *Forbes* 142/13, 12 Dec 1988, 34-36.

D15. Connor, John M, and Frederick E. Geithman, "Mergers in the Food Industries: Trends, Motives & Policies", *Agribusiness* 4/4, Jul 1988, 331-346.

D16. Davidson, Kenneth M, "Tax-Distorted Mergers", *Journal of Business Strategy* 9/5, Sep/Oct 1988, 63-64.

D17. Dobrzynski, Judith H, "A New Strain of Merger Mania", *Business Week* Issue 3043, 21 Mar 1988, 122-126.

D18. English, Victoria, "Hambro's View Across the Channel", *International Manangement* 43/1, Jan 1988, 39-43.

D19. Gilbert, R J, and D M Newbery, "Entry, acquisition and the value of shark repellent", University of California, Berkeley, Ca, 1988.

D20. Golbe, D L, and L J White, "A Time-Series Analysis of Mergers and Acquisitions in the U.S. Economy", Chapter 9 in A J Auerbach, Ed., *Corporate Takeovers: Causes and Consequences*, Chicago: The University of Chicago Press, 1988, 265-309 (following mimeo of same title, presented at the NBER Conference on Mergers and Acquisitions, 1987).

D21. Golbe, D L, and L J White, "Mergers and Acquisitions in the U.S. Economy: An Aggregate and Historical Overview", in A J Auerbach, Ed., "Mergers and Acquisitions", Chicago: The University of Chicago Press, 1988 (NBER Project Rpt) 25-48.

D22. Golbe, D L, and L J White, "Theories of Merger Activity", in Alan J Auerbach, Ed, *Corporate Takeovers*, Chicago: The University of Chicago Press, 1988.

D23. Harper, Timothy, "M & A. Activity on Rise; Takeover Boom Now Under Way", *Pensions and Investment Age* 16/22, 17 Oct 1988, 13-14.

D24. Hawkins, Chuck, "Madison Avenue is Singing O Canada", *Business Week (Industrial/Technology Edition)* Issue 3069, 12 Sep 1988, 92.

D25. Hodes, Daniel A, Thomas Cook, and William M Rochfort, "The Importance of Regional Economic Analysis and Regional Strategies in an Age of Industrial Restructuring", *Business Economics* 23/2, Apr 1988, 46-51.

D26. Jarrell, G A, J A Brickley, and J M Netter, "The Market for Corporate Control: The Empirical Evidence Since 1980", *Journal of Economic Perspectives* 2, Winter 1988, 49-68.

D27. Kapstein, Jonathan, "The Acquisition Prelude to the Unification of Europe", *Mergers and Acquisitions* 23/1, Jul/Aug 1988, 62-66.

D28. Knobel, Lance, "The Pursuit of Privacy", *Management Today* (UK), Nov 1988, 70-71.

D29. Lester, T, "Brand Valuation: Big Money Talks Brands", *Marketing* (UK), 16 Jun 1988, 30-31.

D30. Lewis, Janet, "Bargain Hunting in France", *Institutional Investor* 22/7, Jul 1988, 163-165.

D31. Liscio, John, "The Buyout Bubble: When It Bursts, There'll be Fallout Aplenty", *Barron's* 68/44, 31 Oct 1988, 6-7, 32-33.

D32. Luse, Eric, "Making Sense Out of Supervisory Acquisitions (Part I)", *Bottomline* 5/5, May 1988, 49-56.

D33. Magenheim, E B, and D C Mueller, "Are acquiring-firm shareholders better off after an acquisition?" Chapter 11 in J C Coffee Jr, L Lowenstein and S Rose-Ackerman, Eds., *Knights, Raiders, and Targets*, New York: Oxford University Press, 1988, 171-193.

D34. McGoldrick, Beth, "Little Bang Brings Down Barriers", *Euromoney* (UK), Nov 1988, 159-162.

D35. McGurrin, Lisa, "A Different Game for Thrifts", *New England Business* 10/12, Aug 1988, 77-85.

D36. Mitchell, A, "The Balance Sheet: No Accounting for Brands Authors", *Marketing* (UK), 7 Jul 1988, 24-25.

D37. Mitchell, David, *Making Acquisitions Work*, London: Business International, 1988.

D38. Morck, Randall, Andrei Shleifer and Robert W Vishny, "Characteristics of Targets of Hostile and Friendly Takeovers", in Alan J Auerbach, Ed, *Corporate Takeovers*, Chicago: The University of Chicago Press, 1988.

D39. Petruzzi, Christopher R, "Mergers and the Double Taxation of Corporate Income", *Journal of Accounting and Public Policy* 7/2, Summer 1988, 97-111.

D40. Piontek, S, "Met Sues RJR to Protect Its Bond Holdings", *National Underwriter (Life/Health/Financial Services)* 92/48, 28 Nov 1988.

D41. Rauschenbach, Thomas M, "Competitiveness and Cooperation in a Global Industry", *International Journal of Technology Management* (Switzerland) 3/3, 1988, 345-349.

D42. Ravenscraft, D J, and F M Scherer, "Mergers and Managerial Performance", Chapter 12 in J C Coffee Jr, L Lowenstein and S Rose-Ackerman, Eds., *Knights, Raiders, and Targets*, New York: Oxford University Press, 1988, 194-210.

D43. Reed, Randal L, and Don E Waldman, "Mergers and Air Fares: 'Contestable Markets' in the Airline Industry", *Antitrust Law and Economics Review* 20/3, 1988, 15-20.

D44. Reilly, Patrick, "A Gold Rush for U.S. Titles", *Advertising Age* 59/17, 18 Apr 1988, 1, 90.

D45. Roby, Edward, "Germany: Miracle Workers Fall Out", *Euromoney* (UK), Sep 1988, 46, 48.

D46. Ruback, R S, "An Overview of Takeover Defenses", in A J Auerbach, Ed., *Mergers and Acquisitions*, Chicago: The University of Chicago Press, 1988 (NBER Project Rpt) 49-68.

D47. Scherer, F M, "Corporate Takeovers: The Efficiency Arguments", *Journal of Economic Perspectives 2*, 1988, 69-82.

D48. Shleifer, A, and L H Summers, "Breach of Trust in Hostile Takeovers", Chapter 2 in A J Auerbach, Ed., *Corporate Takeovers: Causes and Consequences*, Chicago: The University of Chicago Press, 1988.

D49. Shleifer, A, and R W Vishny, in A J Auerbach, Ed., *Mergers and Acquisitions*, Chicago: The University of Chicago Press, 1988 (NBER Project Rpt) 87-102.

D50. Shleifer, Andrei and Robert W Vishny, "Value Maximization and the Acquisition Process", *Journal of Economic Perspectives*, 1988, 2, 7-20.

D51. Spellman, James David, "1992 Prompts Unprecedented Wave of Mergers", *Europe* Issue 282, Dec 1988, 26-27.

D52. Stein, J, "Takeover Threats and Managerial Myopia", *Journal of Political Economy 96*, 61-80.

D53. Taggart, Robert A Jr, "The Growth of 'Junk'. Bond Market and Its Role in Financing Takeovers", in A J Auerbach, Ed., *Mergers and Acquisitions*, Chicago: The University of Chicago Press, 1988 (NBER Project Rpt) 5-24.

D54. Tweedie, D, "Brands on the Balance Sheet: Putting a Price on a Name", *Marketing* (UK), Oct 1988, 28-29.

D55. Williams, Fred, "Who Made a Difference: Pickens Takes Up New Battle", *Pensions and Investment Age* 16/23, 31 Oct 1988, 46, 49.

1987

E1. Austin, Douglas V, Kimberley A Nigem, and Craig D Bernard, "Tender Offer Update: 1987", *Mergers and Acquisitions* 22/1, Jul/Aug 1987, 49-52.

E2. Babcock, Charles, and Michael Sullivan-Trainor, "Mainframe Software: An Industry Restructures (Part I)", *Computerworld* 21/35, Aug 1987, 1, 12-13.

E3. Bittlingmayer, George, "Shareholder agreement and the gains from merger", Science Center for Berlin for Social Research, Berlin, Germany, 1987.

E4. Fisher, Franklin M, "Pan American to United: The Pacific Division Transfer Case", *Rand Journal of Economics* 18/4, Winter 1987, 492-508.

E5. Franks, J R, R S Harris, and C Mayer, "Means of Payment in Takeovers: Results for the U.K. and U.S.", ms., Jun 1987. Cited in A6.

E6. Fuhrman, Peter, "Here We Go Again", *Forbes* 140/1, 13 Jul 1987, 242-246.

E7. Golbe, Devra L, and Lawrence J White, "A Time Series Analysis of Mergers and Acquisitions in the U.S. Economy", mimeo., Presented at National Bureau of Economic Research Conference on Mergers and Acquisitions, Feb 1987.

E8. Heinkel, Robert, and Alan Kraus, "The effect of insider trading on average rates of return", *Canadian Journal of Economics* 3, Aug 1987, 588-611.

E9. Huang, Yen-Sheng, and Ralph A Walkling, "Target Abnormal Returns Associated with Acquisition Announcements", *Journal of Financial Economics* 19, 1987, 329-349.

E10. Hunter, David, Ellen Lask, and Rose Darby, "ENI and Montedison Talk About Getting Together", *Chemical Week* 141/1, 1 Jul 1987, 36.

E11. Jarrell, Greg A, and Annette B Poulsen, "Shark Repellents and Stock Prices: The Effects of Antitakeover", *Journal of Financial Economics* (Netherlands), Sep 1987, 127-168.

E12. Keough, Lee, "Software & Services: Strength in Unity", *Computer and Communications Decisions* 19/12, Sep 1987, 89-91.

E13. King, Mervyn A, "Freeing Trapped Equity: A Tax Spur to Friendly Deals", *Mergers and Acquisitions* 22/1, Jul/Aug 1987, 45-48, 52.

E14. Melcher, Richard A, Mark Maremont, and Rose Brady, "How Guinness Suddenly Fell From Grace", *Business Week* Issue 2984, 9 Feb 1987, 44-46.

E15. Mueller, D, "The Corporation: Growth Diversification and Mergers", Chur, Switzerland, Harwood Academic Publishers, 1987.

E16. Space, William E, "Merger Fever: Catch It!" *Buyouts and Acquisitions* 5/1, Mar/Apr 1987, 13-16, 54-56.

E17. Travers, Nicolas, "Reed International: Paper Tiger or New World Giant?" *Director* (UK) 41/3, Sep 1987, 67-70.

E18. Travlos, N G, "Corporate Takeover Bids, Methods of Payments, and Bidding Firms' Stock Returns", *Journal of Finance*, 42, Sep 1987, 943-963.

E19. Waldenstrom, Martin M, and Philippe G Gastone, "France In Play", *Across the Board* 24/7,8, Jul/Aug 1987, 29-34.

E20. Weidenbaum, Murray and Steven Vogt, "Takeovers and stockholders: Winners and losers", *California Management Review*, 1987/24, 157-168.

E21. Weiss, Gary, James Ellis, and Jonathon B Levine, "The Top 200 Deal: Merger Mania's New Accent", *Business Week* Issue 2994, 17 Apr 1987, 273-292.

1986

F1. Alper, Alan, "Merger Activity to Reconfigure European Telecom Market", *Computerworld* 20/34, 25 Aug 1986, 81

F2. Anonymous, "T. Boone Pickens: The Paragon of Takeover Entrepreneurs Talks About His Impact on Corporate Restructuring", *Journal of Buyouts and Acquisitions* 4/1, Jan/Feb 1986, 24-32.

F3. Becketti, S, "Corporate Mergers and the Business Cycle", *Economic Review*, Federal Reserve Bank of Kansas City, May 1986, 13-26.

F4. Cooke, Terence E, *Mergers and Acquisitions*, Basil Blackwell Ltd, 1986.

F5. Graham, Judith, "Less Entrepreneur Ownership Could Lead to More Acquisitions by Hospitals", *Modern Healthcare* 16/15, 18 Jul 1986, 66.

F6. Hawkins, Chuck, and Aaron Bernstein, "Airlines in Flux: And Then There Were Five?" *Business Week* Issue 2936, 10 Mar 1986, 107-112.

F7. Jacques, Bruce, "Australia: Minnows Swallowing Up The Whales." *Euromoney* (UK), Aug 1986, 132-141.

F8. Laing, Jonathon R, "Power Play: Will Takeover Lightning Strike the Electric Utilities?" *Barron's* 66/22, 2 Jun 1986, 8-9, 35-37.

F9. Ma, C K, and G M Weed, "Fact and Fancy of Takeover Junk Bonds", Journal of Portfolio Management 13/1, Fall 1986 33-37.

F10. Mottur, Allen, and William Crum, "Playing the Corporate Restructuring Game", *Journal of Buyouts and Acquisitions* 4/1, Jan/Feb 1986, 8-15.

F11. Paulus, J D, "Corporate Restructuring, '"Junk', and Leverage: Too Much or Too Little?'" *Economic Perspectives,* New York: Morgan Stanley & Co., 12 Mar 1986.

F12. Pugh, Olin S, "Can Small Banks Survive Bank Merger Wave?" *Business and Economic Review* 32/2, Jan-Mar 1986, 25-29.

F13. Rohatyn, F G, "Needed: Restraints on the Takeover Mania", *Challenge,* 29, May-Jun 1986, 3.

F14. Roll, Richard, "The Hubris Hypothesis of Corporate Takeovers", *Journal of Business,* Apr 1986, 197-216.

F15. Schiller, Zachary, "Appliances: Turning Up the Heat in the Kitchen", *Business Week,* 4 Aug 1986, 76, 78.

F16. Smith, Geoffrey, "The Return of the Mighty Multiple?" *Forbes* 137/8, 21 Apr 1986, 38, 42.

F17. Spragins, Ellyn E, "The Corporate Shopping Spree Roars On and On", *Business Week,* 21 Jul 1986, 110-111.

1985

G1. Bittlingmayer, George, "Did Antitrust Policy Cause the Great Merger Wave?" *Journal of Law and Economics* 28/1, Apr 1985, 77-118.

G2. Brown, Paul B, Zachary Schiller, Christine Dugas, and Scott Scredon, "New? Improved? The Brana-Name Mergers", *Business Week* Issue 2917, 21 Oct 1985, 108-110.

G3. Christopher, Maurine, "Videotech Update: Park Builds His Media Empire Carefully", *Advertising Age* 56/88, 11 Nov 1985, 62.

G4. Eckbo, B Espen, and Peggy Wier, "Antimerger Policy under the Hart-Scott-Rodino Act: A Reexamination of the Market Power Hypothesis", *Journal of Law and Economics* 28, Apr 1985, 119-149.

G5. Hunter, David, and Stephanie Cooke, "Western Europe Sizes Up Seeds", *Chemical Week* 137/21, 20 Nov 1985, 9-10.

G6. Jonas, Norman, Stan Crock, Elizabeth Ehrlich, and James Norman, "How the Tax Code is Feeding Merger Mania", *Business Week* Issue 2896, 27 May 1985, 62, 64.

G7. Lester, Tom, "The Corporate Buying Spree", *Management Today* (UK), Sep 1985, 50-57.

G8. Myers, Del, "More Fun, More Opportunities, More Rewards", *Telephony* 208/7, 18 Feb 1985, 36-44.

G9. Ott, Mack, and G J Santoni, "Mergers & Takeovers -- The Value of Predator's Information", *Federal Reserve Bank of St. Louis Review* 67/10, Dec 1985, 16-28.

G10. Pekar, Peter, "A Strategic Approach to Diversification", *Journal of Business Strategy* 5/4, Spring 1985, 99-104.

G11. Sherman, Stratford P, "Are Media Mergers Smart Business?" *Fortune* 111/13, 24 Jun 1985, 98-103.

G12. Travlos, N G, "Corporate Takeover Bids, Methods of Payment and Stockholders' Returns: Some New Insights", manuscript., Jul 1985 (cited in A6).

G13. VerMeulen, Michael, "Guide to Corporate Takeovers (Part I)", *Working Woman* 10/2, Feb 1985, 75-79.

G14. Williams, Harold M, "It's Time for a Takeover Maratorium", *Fortune* 112/2, 22 Jul 1985, 133, 136.

1984

H1. Jensen, M C, "Takeovers: Folklore and Science", *Harvard Business Review,* 62, Nov-Dec 1984, 109-120.

H2. McCartney, Laton, and Joe Kelly, "Getting Away with Merger", *Datamation* 30/20, 1 Dec 1984, 24-32.

1983 and earlier

I1. Bradley, M, "Interfirm Tender Offers and the Market for Corporate Control", *Journal of Business*, Oct 1980, 345-376.

I2. Bradley, M, A Desai, and Han E Kim, "The Rationale behind Interfirm Tender Offers: Information or Synergy?" *Journal of Financial Economics 11*, 1983, 183-206.

I3. Buckley, A, "A profile of industrial acquisition in 1971", *Accounting and Business Research 2*, 243-52.

I4. Buffett, W E, Berkshire Hathaway Inc., *1981 Annual Report*, 4-5.

I5. Capen, E C, R V Clapp, and W M Campbell, "Competitive Bidding in High-Risk Situations", *Journal of Petroleum Technology*, Jun 1971, 641-653.

I6. Caves, R E, *Multinational Enterprise and Economic Analysis*, Cambridge University Press, 1982.

I7. Chung, K S, "Investment Opportunities, Synergies and Conglomerate Mergers", doctoral dissertation, AGSM-UCLA, 1982 (cited in A6).

I8. Chung, K S, and J F Weston, "Diversification and Mergers in a Strategic Long-range Planning Framework", in M Keenan, and L I White, Eds., *Mergers and Acquisitions*, D.C. Heath, Lexington, Mass., 1982.

I9. Cosh, A D, A Hughes, and A Singh, "The causes and effects of takeovers in the UK: an empirical investigation for the late 1960's at the micro-economic level", in D C Mueller (ed), *The Determinants and Effects of Mergers*, Cambridge, Mass.: Oelschlager, Gunn and Hain, 1980.

I10. Eckbo, B Espen, "Horizontal Mergers, Collusion, and Stockholder Wealth", *Journal of Financial Economics* 11, 1983, 241-273.

I11. Ellert, J C, "Antitrust Enforcement and the Behavior of Stock Prices", doctoral dissertation, University of Chicago, Jun 1975.

I12. Galai, D, and R W Masulis, "The Option Pricing Model and the Risk Factor of Stock", *Journal of Financial Economics*, Jan/Mar 1976, 53-82.

I13. Gordon, M J, and J Yagil, "Financial Gain from Conglomerate Mergers", in *Research in Finance*, 3, 1981, 103-142

I14. Gort, M, "An economic disturbance theory of mergers", *Quarterly Journal of Economics*, 1969.

I15. Haugen, R A, and T C Langtieg, "An empirical test for synergism in merger", *Journal of Finance*, Sep 1975.

I16. Higgins, R C, and Lawrence D Schall, "Corporate Bankruptcy and Conglomerate Merger", *Journal of Finance*, Mar 1975, 93-113.

I17. Jensen, M C, and W Meckling, "Theory of the Firm: Managerial Behavior, Agency Costs and Ownership Structure", *Journal of Financial Economics*, Oct 1976, 305-360.

I18. Jensen, M C, and R S Ruback, "The Market for Corporate Control: The Scientific Evidence", *Journal of Financial Economics*, 1983, 5-50.

I19. Kuehn, D A, *Takeovers and the Theory of the Firm*, London: MacMillan, 1975.

I20. Levine, P, and S Aaronovitch, "The financial characteristics of firms and theories of merger activity", *Journal of Industrial Economics* 30, 149-72.

I21. Lewellen, W G, and B Huntsman, "Managerial Pay and Corporate Performance", *American Economic Review*, Sep 1970, 710-720.

I22. Manne, H G, "Mergers and the Market for Corporate Control", *Journal of Political Economy*, Apr 1965, 110-120.

I23. Markham, J W, *Conglomerate Enterprises and Public Policy*, Boston, Harvard Graduate School of Business Administration, 1973.

I24. Markham, J W, "Survey of the Evidence and Findings on Mergers", in *Business Concentration and Price Policy*, Princeton, NJ: Princeton University Press, 1955, 141-212.

I25. Meeks, G, *Disappointing Marriage: A Study of the Gains from Merger*, Cambridge: Cambridge University Press, 1977.

I26. Melicher, R W, J Ledolter, and L D'Antonio, "A Time Series Analysis of Aggregate Merger Activity", *The Review of Economics and Statistics*, 65, Aug 1983, 423-430.

I27. Millward, N, and J McQueeney, "Company takeovers, management organization and industrial relations", Department of Employment, Manpower Paper 16, London: HMSO, 1981.

I28. Mueller, D C, "A Theory of Conglomerate Mergers", *Quarterly Journal of Economics*, Nov 1969, 643-659.

129. Nelson, R L, "Business Cycle Factors in the Choice Between Internal and External Growth", *The Corporate Mergers*, W W Alberts, and J E Segall, Eds., Chicago: University Chicago Press, 1966.

130. Nelson, R L, *Merger Movements in American Industry, 1895-1956*, Princeton, NJ: Princeton University Press, 1959.

131. Pickering, J F, *Industrial Structure and Market Conduct*, London: Martin Robertson, 1974.

132. Salter, M S, and W A Weinhold, *Diversification Through Acquisition*, New York: The Free Press, 1979.

133. Salter, M S, and W A Weinhold, "Merger Trends and Prospects for the 1980s", U.S. Dept of Commerce, Harvard University, Dec 1980.

134. Singh, A, "Takeovers, economic 'natural selection' and the thoery of the firm: evidence from the post-war UK experience", *Economic Journal* 85, 497-515.

135. Steiner, P O, *Mergers: Motives, effects, policies*, Ann Arbor: University of Michigan Press, 1975.

136. Stocking, G W, "Commentary on Markham, 'Survey of Guidance and Findings on Mergers'", in *Business Concentration and Price Policy*, Princeton, NJ: Princeton University Press, 1955, 191-211.

137. Wansley, J W, W R Lane, and H C Yang, "Abnormal Returns to Acquired Firms by Type of Acquisitions and Method of Payment", *Financial Management*, 12, Autumn 1983, 11-22.

138. Weston, J F, *The Role of Mergers in the Growth of Large Firms*, Berkeley: University of California Press, 1953, Chapter 5.

139. Williamson, J E, "Economics as an antitrust defense revisited", University of Pennsylvania, July 1976; and "Economics as an antitrust defense: the welfare trade-offs", *American Economic Review*, Mar 1968.

——————— .***. ———————

GLOSSARY

Acceleration: The acceleration principle sates that the demand for capital goods is a derived demand and that growth (or decline) in the demand for output leads to growth (or decline) in the demand for capital stock and, hence lead to investment. Thus, an acceleration or speeding up in the rate of change in output produces a proportionally much larger change in the output of investment goods. In brief, investment rises to meet larger output; if spare capacity is not enough to meet demand, the firms may invest in more machinery. The accelerator shows how much investment changes as a response to changes in output. As used in the Harrod-Domar model and with the multiplier by Samuelson and Hicks, in the upswing of the business cycle the accelerator translates expanded output into even greater increases in investment, which is further boosted as income by the multiplier.

Arbitrager: See arbitrageur.

Arbitrageurs: Professionals who hope to profit by buying target stock above the market but below the tender price and selling it to the aggressor at the tender price, often adding a dealer fee of 1.5 to 2.5 percent of the offer price. They tend to prefer cash payment. Their economic function is to reduce the uncertainty in the early stages that the deal will go through by providing liquidity by their willingness to jar as much stock as possible out of the portfolios of more cautious stockholders. The bigger the risk of deal failure, the lower the price paid.

Asset replacement value: The costs of buying usually new assets to replace old ones.

Bear hug: A letter to the directors of the takeover target announcing an acquisition proposal and price offer (say a tax-free exchange of securities and a soothing 49 percent in cash) and requesting access to financial information and an early reply. If the forced reply is negative, the appeal can be made to shareholders to offer their shares, and the takeover is **hostile**. The target management will be replaced if the bid is successful. Opposing bids may lead to an extended auction, and thus this method is costly.

Bogies: Certain performance incentives on the basis of which is extra stock granted to management - completing a divestiture program, targeting operating profits, reaching certain rates of return.

Buy-back or **stock repurchase:** The company buys back some of its outstanding shares of common stock, for example, to support the stock price or to prevent a takeover.

---

[123] Definitions conform with Weston in Literature Synopsis B39; M. Wright, S. Thompson, B. Chiplin & K. Robbie, *Buy-Ins and Buy-Outs, New Strategies in Corporate Management*, Centre for Management Buy-Out Research, Graham & Trotman (Kluwer), London, 1991; and Charles A. Scharf, Edward E. Shea, and George C. Beck, *Acquisitions, Mergers, Sales, Buyouts and Takeovers: A Handbook with Forms*, 4th Ed, Prentice Hall, Englewood Cliffs, NJ.

Coverage ratio: The amount that interest payments are covered by assets or cash flows. The coverage ratio is often incorporated in loans by debt covenants to bankers and other lenders to ensure them that the loan/s will be repaid in a timely manner.

Debt covenants: Requirements placed on the debt to maintain specified targets such as cash flow and capital expenditure levels and balance sheet ratios in order for the borrower to retain financing facilities.

Debt-equity clock: The dynamic and continuous relationship described by the author in the amount of total debt to equity at any one time. A time string of debt/equity ratios.

EBITDA: Earnings before income tax, depreciation, and amortization.

Employment-protection guarantees in merger agreements: Post-takeover severance arrangements

Equity kicker: An incentive to lenders such as an option, right or warrant (an option given to certain shareholders to subscribe to certain future issues) which allows lenders to the company to participate in future firm growth by entitling their holders to purchase securities for a specifeid price for a specified time period. Often anti-dilution provisions are included.

ESOP or Employee Share Ownership Plan: Share purchase is sometimes funded by borrowing. An ESOP may provide part of the funding for a buy-out. A trust to acquire shares in a company for subsequent allocation. Tax relief may apply to company contributions to the trust and to funds borrowed.
Eurodollar

Externalization: Opposite of internalization, the sourcing out or divesting of firm functions to other companies, or the market in general. It is currently held by many that externalization of many functions is cost effective.

Fallen angels: Bonds of blue-chip corporations now in trouble (buy them)

Foreign direct investment: The act of acquiring ownership of the means of production such as factories and land of companies outside one's home country. Direct investment also takes place if the ownership of *equity* shares *provides* control over the operation of the foreign firm. Mere holding of financial assets of firms abroad such as bonds and equity is considered indirect investment. The basic motivation for FDI is to gain control, enhance stability and thus reduce risk by internalizing externalities (suppliers, technology, marketing) and market imperfections.

Gearing: See *leverage*.

Greenmail: Repurchase of a substantial stockholder's interest at a premium above market price, for example, in order to prevent that stockholder from taking over the company.

Gun-to-the-head strategy: Senior corporate executives secretly work with a financial services firm to assemble financing and agree upon an offering price. The chief executive then presents the bid as a take-it-or-leave-it proposition to his board. Sneaking up on a board with a fully financed offer ready to be launched, keeping the process secret until a deal has been cut. By placing a gun to the board's head, the bidding is ended before it can begin.

Initial Public Offering: A first offering of stocks to the public. One refers to the firm **going public,** or selling shares on the open stock market.

Internalization: Bringing the business into the firm through direct investment, mergers and acquisitions (see externalization and foreign direct investment).

IPOS, or initial public offerings: First listing of company shares on the stock market, which constitutes going public.

Jamming: Take advantage of the customer by selling over-valued bonds or shares

Juglar cycle: Nine-year nonseasonal productivity cycles explained by capital investment patterns.

Junk bonds: High yield, high risk bonds which are given lower quality ratings by the credit agencies.

Kitchin inventory adjustment cycle: A short rhythmic forty-month fluctuation in business activity in terms of prices, production, employment, and so on. They are explained largely by changes in inventory investment and by small innovation waves, especially in fast-to-market equipment. There are said to be roughly three Kitchin cycles to every Juglar cycle and eighteen Kitchin cycles in each Kondratieff cycle.

Kondratieff cycle: Long waves in prices, production and trade lasting fifty to sixty years due to processes inherent in the nature of capitalism, especially regarding capital accumulation.
Changes in production, wars, and so on, are not random events, but are part of long wave rhythms. For example, the upswing period triggers new market expansion. The high-tension upward phase provokes wars and revolutions.

Kuznets cycle: Economic swings of fifteen to twenty-two years, not in the absolute expansion/contraction of any economic activity, but in the *growth rate,* especially evident in the construction industry.

Leverage: The amount of debt in a company's finance structure. Leverage saturation is opposed to equity financing, or issuing shares. Recently, many financial instruments combine debt and equity features.

Leveraged buyouts (LBOs): Acquisition of a company by an investor group or partnership, with debt (perhaps 70% of the total capitalization) with plans to repay debt out of operational cash flows and asset sales.

LIBOR or London interbank offered rate: The interest rate in London at 8:00 am when one banks lends to another

Long waves: see *Kondratieff cycles.*

M-Lag (or M-curve): The backlash of previous high interest rates on current cash flows and asset values due to overindebtedness and shifts in government monetary policy. For example, recessionary cash flows may not be enough to sustain the high interest rate burden vestigial of monetary restraint in the previous period. The M Curve be fatal. A familiar outcome is restructuring or bankruptcy.

MBI or Management buy-in: Transfer of ownership, risk and control of the firm to an incoming management team and their backers.

MBO or Management buy-out: Transfer of corporate ownership to a new set of owners many of whom are current managers and employees. Management often retains a substantial portion of total shares.

Mehrwert: Surplus value or value added, such as a value-added tax.

Mezzanine finance: All forms of financing instruments which can be tiered or floored between ordinary shares and senior debt to which it is subordinated. "Mezzanine" can often be traded on a secondary market.

Monetization: The process of taking **instalment notes** to the bank and receving money for them.

Multinational enterprises: A company with substantial operations in more than one country. The list of truly international corporations, i.e., firms with shared headquarters located in two or more countries, is spreading from the frequently cited pacesetters Shell and Unilever, both with dual headquarters in the UK and the Netherlands.

Ordinary shares: Shares carrying full voting rights, but which rank after all other claims on assets in cases of insolvency.

Participating shares: Preferred ordinary or preference shares with rights that provide for payment of an extra dividend based on an agreed share of remaining profits after the preferred portion of dividends.

Payment-in-kind securities: Debt or equity which do not earn interest or dividend payments in the form of cash. Payment is in more debt or equity. If cash-flow generation is low, these non-cash instruments may bridge the gap.

Payoff cycles: An income or profit cycle that parallels the four-phased product cycle: negative income, debt write-off, profits, cash and a tendency towards the overassumption of debt, finally declining profit margins.

Phase shift: As opposed to a phase change which denotes evolution or movement *along* the life cycle curve, a phase shift constitutes a relocation—say further down the x-axis, of the entire cycle, best portrayed by a technology leap or jump constituting a long lasting shift of the whole technological paradigm. A technology shift, for example, may lead to a cyclical realignment or resynchronizing of the economy (sailing vessels → steamboats → railroads → cars)

PIK: A Pay in Kind Note is a promissory note which requires payment of principal in cash, but permits the issuer to pay interest by issuing further notes of the same kind. These notes issued in lieu of cash payments cause subsequent problems.

Poison pills: Flip-in, flip-over and voting rights devices that give shareholders extremely favorable bargain purchase or voting rights in the event of a hostile tender offer opposed by management. The typical poison pill is not triggered by a friendly transaction approved by the board. Some forms have been upheld in court as they counter two-step takeovers in which a tender offer is made at an attractive price to acquire sufficient shares to permit the offeror to "squeeze out" a merger at a lower price.

Preference shares: A class of shares bearing the right to a fixed dividend and claim on assets in case of insolvency before ordinary shareholders. They are usually redeemable at specific dates.

Pro-rated shares: Only a portion of the shares of all stockholders will be accepted by the takeover bidders.

Product cycle: The entire life of a product starting with its inception and development, market launch, market expansion, market consolidation and final decline. The shape of the product curve varies, depending on the nature of the product and its industrial sector as well as the discretionary manipulation of its market stance.

R-squared analysis: Prediction of the accuracy of the regression fit to the read input-output relationship of the data model

Ramp-up: See *start-up*.

Real interest rates: Interest rates (the price of money) net of the inflation rate.

Recapitalization/refinancing: Change in the financial structure to enable debts to be rescheduled or capitalized, perhaps as a result of difficulties in meeting debt service costs or a need for extra investment. Recapitalization also enables initial investors to exit from a well-performing firm when management does not desire a flotation or trade sale.

Refinancing package: There are several types, one of which allows the acquirer to buy back its junk bonds and substitute less onerous forms of debt. The buyer is further crippled and fee takers are usually benefitted.

Regression: Equation that mathematically describes the relation between a set of inputs and a given output.

Reset mechanism: Guarantees that a junk bond or other security will trade at a certain price over time, reducing market risk for investors, but potentially costing the issuers insupportable billions.

Restructuring: See *recapitalization*.

Reverse merger: If the seller has valuable assets, such as franchises, which are not transferable even by operation of law, a reverse merger procedure may be instituted in which the seller becomes the surviving corporation and continues to operate the business. Thus it is not necessary to transfer assets and liabilities and assign contracts. In effect, a reverse merger accomplishes a purchase of all the outstanding stock of the seller. Even if some shareholder do not approve they are bound if the merger is approved by the legally required percentage.

Running the books: After a takeover, an one of the underwriting investment banks supervises post- takeover bond offerings, often very profitably. The bank's name appears on the left of the tombstone and in subsequent advertisements. Being on the left means bond sale records reside physically at that bank which manages the offering. An buyout firm is liable for the entire amount of the payment, if the bond leader can't sell the bonds to refinance the loan. For every month the bonds remain unsold, the loan's interest rates rise. Thus, prides are determined by bidding fever, the impact of financial public relations and press management on the independent committee, the bargaining and press power of the key players, and the Dun and Bradstreet and S&P ratings of corporate creditworthiness coupled with the amount of takeover debt already in the market, the first which assesses the price of a firm based on its ability to carry debt load in the market, the second which influences the cost of capital and the ability to place corporate debt.

Securitization: A method of taking banking assets, such as residential mortgages and credit card loans, off-balance sheet by selling them to a special-purpose subsidiary which then issues bonds using the assets as collateral. Bankers argue over whether banks have to set aside capital against loans which have been securitized.

Serial aquirers: Companies that expand by regularly acquiring other firms, usually in the same sector (horizontal).

Spin-off: Divestment of a division or other part of the company. The vendor often maintains a significant equity stake in its former subsidiary in order to maintain priority access to products or services.

Start-up or ramp-up: That phase of the product cycle that starts with completion of R&D and design and constitutes product development and fabrication up to the market launch.

Strategy mix: The local, regional and global sourcing and balancing of factor costs by chief corporate officers.

Strip financing: Financial practice in MBOs of inviting institutions to participate in specified layers of the financial package. In vertical strip financing, institutions subscribe to a mixture of each layer so that all financiers have similar portions of each type of finance.

T-bill rate: The rate at which short-term government securities are offered at weekly public auctions, usually for three or six months, but up to one year. The rate is used as a relatively stable benchmark for other rates. The US Federal Reserve System and other central banks use buy and sell large quantities of treasury bills to affect the cost and availability of bank loans.

Technology cycle: The evolution of products as well as whole industrial sectors due to fundamental changes in technology (see Schumpeter).

TED spread: The difference between the LIBOR rate and the interest rate on 3-month U.S. treasury bills.

Tender offer: A solo blitzkrieg approach that seizes timing advantage and stalls other teams, but with no information, often weak financing, and hostile, even though can make conditional on board approval

Toehold investments: Secret accumulation of stocks for a negotiating advantage.

Turnaround: A company in financial or operational trouble which can be restored to health through takeover and restructuring of finance, ownership, management or products.

Warranty: A statement concerning assets being sold included in the sales agreements to give the purchaser a claim against the vendor if the targets assets and liabilities are not as agreed upon. In a buy-out, management may need warranties to satisfy financial backers of the company's worth.

White knight: An acquirer who purchases all or part of a company which is subject of a hostile takover bid. A buy-out may be attempted where a white knight defense is not feasible.

Winners curse: At auction a bidder often pays *more* than usual because of bidding fervor and competition. The bidding effect is known as Winner's Curse. It is intensified by the lack of longterm rules for the bidding process, especially with regard to ending the auction. Most auctions close when bidding is too high for all but one party.

——————— .✦✦✦. ———————

254

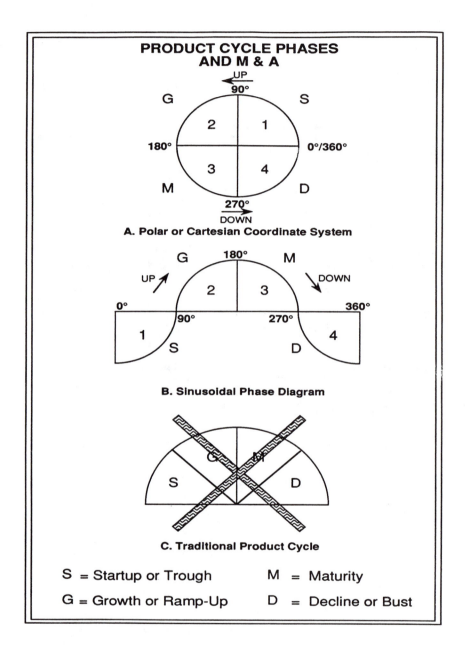

PRODUCT CYCLE PHASES AND M & A

A. Polar or Cartesian Coordinate System

B. Sinusoidal Phase Diagram

C. Traditional Product Cycle

S = Startup or Trough   M = Maturity

G = Growth or Ramp-Up   D = Decline or Bust

INDEX

A000016575981